ETHICS MANAGEMENT

Issues in Business Ethics

VOLUME 10

Ethics Management

Auditing and Developing the Ethical Content of Organizations

by

MUEL KAPTEIN

KPMG Integrity Consulting,
Amsterdam, The Netherlands,
Erasmus University,
Rotterdam, The Netherlands

KLUWER ACADEMIC PUBLISHERS
DORDRECHT / BOSTON / LONDON

A C.I.P. Catalogue record for this book is available from the Library of Congress.

ISBN 0-7923-5095-2

Published by Kluwer Academic Publishers,
P.O. Box 17, 3300 AA Dordrecht, The Netherlands.

Sold and distributed in the North, Central and South America
by Kluwer Academic Publishers,
101 Philip Drive, Norwell, MA 02061, U.S.A.

In all other countries, sold and distributed
by Kluwer Academic Publishers,
P.O. Box 322, 3300 AH Dordrecht, The Netherlands.

Printed on acid-free paper

Printed in the Netherlands.

"Where art thou?"
(Genesis 3:9)

Table of Contents

Introduction

*"Causes of unethical actions are not
simply the result of rotten apples
in the corporate barrel."
(Hoffman, 1990:630)*

Imagine that you are the general manager of an international trade organization. You are proud of the international quality award that you received last year and you are convinced that your company is in tip-top condition. However, during the past few months, you have been confronted with a number of unsettling matters. The US country manager appears to have been brushing up the annual figures systematically. He also has been entertaining certain business practices which have drawn the attention of the local officials of the Department of Justice. The media claim that you have been selling sport shoes which were produced with child labor in India. The trade inventory shows a number of unexplainable shortages. The criminal investigation staff paid you a visit in connection with a member of your sales department who they claim were overly generous towards several government officials during a transaction with their Ministry. To make matters worse, your secretary recently ran home in tears because she was tired of always being blamed for mistakes for which she did not bear any responsibility. During a personal meeting with her, she informs you that she is no longer interested in working for a sexist organization. Is there something that you missed? You begin to question the ethics within your corporation and start pondering the possible measures that should be taken to set matters straight. What are you going to do?

Imagine that you are the CEO of a large, profitable international oil company. One of your floating storage tanks, weighing 14,500 tons and moored in the UK's territorial waters in the North Sea, has outlived its economic life. Your company has to decide whether to dismantle the oil tank facility and loading station on land or to sink them into the ocean. Upon your request, a number of salvage companies, engineering firms and universities have been researching the safest and most environmentally friendly solution. The results are unanimous: you should sink the platform. By sinking it in the ocean, you can reduce the risk of an accident six-fold. Dismantling the platform on land would require its transportation in a horizontal position to accommodate its unique length, with the increased risk of leakage. If the platform were to break, the consequences for people and the environment would be disastrous. One consequence of such a disaster would be that approximately 100 tons of oil reserves would flow into shallow water where it would damage the food chain. If the platform were sunk into the 2000 meter deep trench in the north-east Atlantic Ocean, two hundred kilometers off the coast of Scotland, the low oxygen content of the sea water at the location would prevent the hull from rusting away for approximately 4000 years. If the hull were to rust through after so many years, the oil emission would then be highly diluted. Moreover, sinking the platform will be four times cheaper than dismantling it on land. On the grounds of these hard facts, you and the other members of the Board of Directors decide to let to sink off the platform. The government of the UK supports and approves this decision. The member states of the European Union are informed of this decision, which meets with no criticism. Two months later, however, the situation becomes intense as thirteen activists from Greenpeace occupy the platform. The action has little initial effect. Several weeks later, public opinion begins to turn against sinking the platform. Greenpeace announces to the media that the ocean is not a garbage can. Several national governments suddenly condemn the plans for sinking the platform. Several ministers in these countries appeal to their citizens to boycott your gas stations. The international boycott quickly spreads into a mania. Churches, trade organizations and municipalities join the boycott. Your passionate attempts to use advertisements and brochures to present the facts and the motivation behind your decision are of no avail. The pressure on you from both inside and outside the company to reverse your decision does nothing but increase. Some gas stations report a loss in income of as much as seventy percent. Nevertheless, the British government sees no reason for reversing its decision. You are put in a very difficult position. On the one hand, you are still convinced that sinking is the best solution. Submitting to the pressure would seems to indicate that you are merely the plaything of external forces. On the other hand, you should take account of public opinion for economic and moral reasons. At the same time, you begin to doubt yourself. Is there anything that you overlooked? Have you done anything wrong? Could this trust-shattering crisis have been diverted? And what measures will probably have to be taken by the organization to regain society's trust and to reduce the chance of similar crises in the future?

0.1 Confidence as key

A critical citizen will agree that it is quite common these days to encounter situations which erode one's confidence in institutions. In many countries, the media serve up frequent examples of government officials such as police officers, soldiers, mayors, politicians, and judges who overstep their bounds. Professions which have been traditionally held in high regard such as accountants, lawyers, notaries, brokers, doctors, and pharmacists are also confronted with members who let their own interests or that of their organization unjustly prevail over the interests of their clients. The corporate world is no exception here. There is a surfeit of examples of corporations involved in fraud and corruption, the sale of unsuitable products, the intentional release of misleading information, the reckless emission of pollutants, and the violation of human rights. In such cases, the trustworthiness of an organization and/or those who represent the organization is at stake.

A realistic citizen will, however, also recognize that trust is often rewarded and that it is usually ingrained in his relationship as, for example, a stockholder, employee, consumer, supplier, or neighbor of a company. There is also a plethora of examples of companies which do fulfill their agreements, sell reliable products, provide correct information to the public, care for the environment, and respect human rights. As long as these practices constitute the rule rather than the exception, they provide the grounds for trust and an argument against pessimism and fatalism.

Trust is the adhesive for social and cooperative structures (Fukuyama, 1995). Trust is, according to Zucker (1986), of crucial importance for the continuity of a society and is necessary for even the most routine, everyday manners. Trust stands for the notion of "to be sure of," "being able to count on", or "believing in" something. Without the glue of trust, societies collapse like a house of cards (Bok, 1978). It would be a misconception to think that business is an exception to other social forms, and that trust is superfluous. Corporations cannot continue to operate without the trust of those who have a stake in them. A company which is experiencing a decline in trust may be faced with departing clients and suppliers, lenders who withdraw 'en masse,' a high percentage of absence through illness, and blockades at the company gates instigated by activist groups. A trustworthy corporation, in contrast, attracts those who, for example, want to invest in, want to work for, want to buy products from, and want to supply products to the corporation. As Torabzadeh et al. (1989) and Shaw (1997) contend, the success of a company is directly related to the trustworthiness of the company concerned. Trust is the value on which business relationships are built (Brand, 1989). If business people could not trust one another, corporations would collapse tomorrow (Solomon and Hanson, 1985).

Because a lack of trust in corporations can impede their functioning, corporations need to protect and reinforce this trust where necessary. The trustworthiness of an organization can be divided into several areas, including economic and moral trustworthiness. A corporation's economic trustworthiness concerns the extent to which the corporation is able to realize the expectations with regards to, for example, the profit and revenues of the organization. A corporation's moral trustworthiness concerns the question of whose interests the corporation pursues and how the corporation balances conflicting interests. Moral trustworthiness refers to the correctness, sincerity, intactness, meticulousness, and fairness of a corporation. Like economic trustworthiness, the moral trustworthiness of a corporation can be developed. The objective of this study will be to make a contribution to how corporations can develop their moral trustworthiness. Business ethics, a discipline which concerns itself with reflecting on moral norms and values in the business world, will serve in this book as the perspective for the analysis and development of the moral trustworthiness of corporations and other types of organizations as well. In the next section, I shall briefly sketch the outlines of the field of business ethics.

0.2   The ABC of Business Ethics

Within the field of business ethics, three fundamental questions require our attention. These make up what I call the ABC of Business Ethics.

> A. Can a corporation bear moral responsibility as a whole?
> B. How far does a corporation's moral responsibility extend?
> C. Can a corporation's moral responsibility be managed?

The first question can be reformulated as: are we able to consider a corporation to be a moral entity? Can a corporation, as a whole or as a collective, be held responsible for the effects of its activities or is it only the individual employee who bear responsibility? And: who can be held responsible in specific situations? Two models have been developed to localize responsibilities within organizations: the association or reductionist model, supported by, for instance, Velasquez (1983), and the autonomy model, supported by, for instance, Goodpaster and Matthews (1982), French (1984), Werhane (1985), and Wempe (1998).[1] In the association model, the corporation is responsible to the extent to which the individuals within the organization are responsible. This model reduces corporate responsibility to a sum of individual actions: the corporation bears responsibilities only to the extent to which these can be traced back to individuals. The autonomy model considers the corporation as a moral subject that bears responsibility as a whole. A corporation is a moral actor and can, therefore, be judged in moral terms as there is a corporate culture and structure which can be distinguished from the individuals who work within the corporation. Following this model, it is possible to identify the actions, conscience, and intentions of a corporation.

The second question relates to the length to which the moral responsibility of corporations and/or of their representatives extends. The literature in this field of business ethics gives examples of many moral dilemmas in which it is not immediately evi-

---

[1]   For a detailed exposition of these types of moral responsibility, see Wempe (1998).

dent what is more or less ethical. A number of concepts have been developed in order to deal with these dilemmas. One of the perspectives that is used concerns the distinction into three types of responsibility: responsibility as contract, as reasonable care, and as subordination to social ideals (Velasquez, 1988, Wempe and Melis, 1991). A relationship can be seen as a contractual relationship: a corporation demonstrates moral responsibility when it fulfills the duties ensuing from the implicit and explicit contracts. Secondly, a relationship can be characterized as a relationship of care: the corporation in question demonstrates moral responsibility when it expresses reasonable care for the other party -- when it is obliging. This second type puts higher demands on the functioning of a corporation than the first. Thirdly, the responsibility relationship between a corporation and other parties can be seen as the pursuit of social ideals. A corporation demonstrates moral responsibility when it subordinates its interests to the interest of society. According to Wempe and Melis (1991), the situation determines which type of responsibility is desirable. Another distinction that is often made in the literature (see, for instance, Crisp and Slote, 1997) is between consequentialism, like the utilitarianism of Jeremy Bentham and John Stuart Mill, deontological ethics, like Immanuel Kant's theory of moral rights, and virtue ethics, like the approaches of Aristotle and Alasdair MacIntyre. In order to determine what is morally desirable in a given situation, consequentialism evaluates the results of behavior, deontological ethics evaluates the behavior itself, and virtue ethics evaluates the intentions behind someone's behavior.

If we can show that corporations bear moral responsibility as a whole, then the third question comes into view: how should the moral responsibility of corporations be organized or ingrained? Both the literature and practice have provided us with a number of tools, such as business codes of ethics, ethics committees, ombudsman, and ethics training (see, for instance, Ethics Resource Center, 1990). Despite the fact that these tools are often described one by one (see, for example, Ethics Resource Center, 1990), relatively little attention has been paid to how they can be applied collectively. Bringing them together, however, requires a vision of how moral responsibilities within an organization can be organized. In addition, the activities and measures that ought to be undertaken also depend upon the situation in which the company finds itself. In some situations the use of a business code or an ombudsman can even be counter-productive. The practice of organizing ethics requires tailor-made activities. It is, therefore, necessary to have access to methods and techniques which can be used to examine the actual and desired ethics of a corporation. As a result, organizations can work purposefully towards protecting and improving their ethics.

In the business literature, almost no attention is paid to the way in which a description and analysis of morally relevant aspects of an organization can be made. An ethics audit constitutes such a description and analysis. Laczniak and Murphy (1991), Hill et al., (1992), Ostapski and Pressley (1992), Cohen (1993), and Trevino and Nelson (1995) do pay some attention to ethics audits. However, there is not a single publication which makes the connection between an ethics audit, on the one hand, and the specific measures to be taken, on the other. This lack of systematic and intervention-oriented ethics audits and the absence of tested models for effective interventions to improve the ethics of organizations are reflected in practice as well.

Several organizations that I have advised initially attempted to develop a number of tools themselves. To this end, the Integrity Coordinating Committee of a large corporation, consisting of five high level managers, convened seven times. Despite the lively discussions on a wide range of ethical issues, they came to the conclusion that they were not able to develop a concrete policy. "For which situations should we draft a code, how can we style this into an issue which we may talk about, what other measures could we take, how can we prevent staff from seeing this project as a motion of no-confidence, and how do we know that our activities will have a long-term effect?" were part of the barrage of questions during the first, lengthy telephone conversation. In particular, the members of the committee lacked insight into the causes of the ethical issues under discussion and the knowledge and skills necessary to handle them.

This study examines how the ethics of an organization itself can be systematically reviewed and successfully developed (fundamental question C). In order to be able to develop the corporate ethics, I will characterize a corporation as a moral entity (fundamental question A) which can be described and reviewed on the grounds of moral virtues (fundamental question B).

0.3   Three research questions

This study sets out how the ethics of a corporation can be managed in an efficient and effective way. Prior to the managing process itself, the question arises as to what one is managing for? When speaking of an ethical corporation, what does that mean? When is a corporation ethical and what degrees can be identified in that description? I would like to define the ethical content as the extent to which a corporation can be considered ethical. The ethical content is, in other words, the ethical level or ethical nature of a corporation. The key issue of this study can be formulated as follows:

How can the ethical content of a corporation
be diagnosed and developed?

The following three central questions ensue from this formulation:

1. What is an adequate definition of the ethical content of a corporation?

2. How can the ethical content of a corporation be diagnosed or measured?

3. How should the ethical content of a corporation be developed?

Some authors, such as Coye (1986), Andrews (1989), Sims (1991), and Husted (1993), write about the ethical or moral corporation without defining it. Before the ethical content of a corporation can be developed (question 3), it is necessary to be clear about what we mean by the ethical content of a corporation (question 1). When we have found an answer to question 1, it will then be desirable and possible to develop methods for describing and evaluating the ethical content (question 2). I shall define the ethical content of a corporation in Chapter 3 as the corporation's efforts to meet the legitimate and fundamental expectations of the parties in and around the corporation. While the moral trustworthiness implies the effort or intention of a corporation as it is perceived by other parties, the ethical content relates to the actual effort or intention of the corporation.

0.4   Structure of the study

The three central questions in this study are treated in part I (defining the ethical content), part II (auditing the ethical content), and part III (developing the ethical content).

In the first chapter, the question of the rationale of corporations is put forth for examination: what is the mission of a corporation? We shall see that a corporation does not owe its existence solely to the pursuit of profit. In examining which missions can be considered morally worth pursuing, we shall gain insight into the moral responsibility of a corporation. The definition of the corporation's mission serves as the starting point for defining the ethical content. Trust on the part of stakeholders in a corporation's efforts to accomplish its mission is, as will become evident in Chapter 2, an important condition for the participation of individuals and groups in the corporation. I call the organization of this effort ethics management. In Chapter 3, the ethical content of a corporation is defined. In order to improve the ethical content of a corporation, the actual ethical content must first be identified. There are other moral aspects of a corporation besides its ethical content which could be examined as well. Chapter 3 gives an overview of six different parts of an ethics audit.

In Chapter 4, we will search for the criteria by which the ethical content of an organization can be described and evaluated. These criteria will be obtained by analyzing a large number of cases where the organization's efforts are inadequate. In Chapter 5, the criteria formulated will be transformed into an instrument which measures the ethical content of an organization. The examination methods presented offer starting points for the moral development of organizations. Chapter 5 concludes with a discussion about an organization that went through an ethics audit.

In developing the ethical content, many conflicting issues arise. Chapter 6 discusses a number of problems which may confront ethics management. Thinking these problems through before embarking upon a development path increases the chance of success of improving the ethical content of a corporation. In addition, we shall determine which perspectives apply to ethics management, how balancing and choosing in regards to the problems occurs, and how these perspectives can be converted into an ethics development process. In conclusion, Chapter 7 gives an overview of a large number of concrete measures which, depending on the outcome of the ethics audit, can be used in the ethical development of an organization. Custom work will then become possible.

The added theoretical value of this study is twofold. First, the ethical content of a corporation is defined. Second, based on empirical research, an exhaustive and cohesive set of concrete and normative criteria is developed for profiling the ethical content of an organization. The conceptual model of the ethical content of a corporation, provided in Chapter 4, differs significantly from the models developed by Kohlberg (1981, 1984), Victor and Cullen (1987, 1988, 1989), and Robin and Reidenbach (1991). Based on multiple measurements spread out over time, it will then become possible to describe the ethical development of a corporation. Furthermore, it becomes possible to make a proper comparison of the ethics of different organizations.

Stark (1993) and Weber (1993) feel that the current literature in business ethics offers managers an inadequate basis for analyzing and resolving the moral issues with which they are faced. The practical component of this study consists of offering methods and instruments which corporations can use to make concrete improvements to their ethics. This study aims at combining two extensive research methods which are applied in de field of business ethics. The empirical approach to business ethics entails practical research on the basis of which generalizations can be posited, for instance on the causes of unethical conduct (see, for example, Akaah and Riordan, 1989, and Trevinio and Youngblood, 1990). The philosophical approach develops theories of business ethics based on theories of general ethics and is highly deductive and normative (see for example Donaldson, 1982, Gauthier, 1986, Gilbert and Freeman, 1988, Velasquez, 1992, and Wempe, 1998). The combination of these two approaches in this study takes place in the following manner: first a more or less philosophical premise is given for the legitimacy of the moral component in the functioning of a corporation (chapters 1, 2 and 3), which makes it possible to develop a normative theory based on empirical research (Chapter 4), which can be applied in practice to describe and improve the ethics of corporations (the remaining chapters). This study entails a constant exchange between what is and what ought to be, but without falling prey to naturalistic fallacy.

Apart from studying the relevant literature, I have gained much information and insight from in-depth research of many profit and not-for-profit organizations (see Section 4.1 for a description of the empirical research). The ethics audit, the assumptions for ethics management, and the instruments that are developed, have all been applied in practice. Parts II and III of this book give examples of organizations which were audited from an ethics point of view. Due to the confidential nature of the investigations into the various organizations, it has been necessary to fictionalize most of the examples.

This study will attempt to provide more than a simple description of how corporations handle ethics (as, for example, Aguilar, 1994, does). At the same time, this study will try to be as accessible as possible to anyone who is faced with the problems formulated above. The trick, therefore, will be to avoid the fate of the mythical Icarus.[2]

Although this book is designed for ethics programs in the business world, the model of ethical content and the various examination and development methods can also be applied to not-for-profit organizations. The moral dimensions and criteria described in Chapter 4 can be applied to all kinds of organizations (a) where people operate on behalf of the organization with respect to other people or other organizations, (b) where the conduct of these representatives is seen in a collective sense, and (c) where these representatives have organizational assets at their disposal which they could misuse. A substantial amount of the empirical material consists of cases involving not-for-profit organizations. Chapter 5 and Appendix 3 give a few examples of applying an ethics audit to not-for-profit organizations.

An author is often faced with the dilemma when to wind up the research and writing process. Not solving the dilemma brings about a situation in which writing and rewriting threaten to go on forever. In order to prevent this, I am entrusting my findings definitively to paper. I prefer to close with a semicolon to show that my insight (and that of others) into this phenomenon will continue to develop. This study is merely a personal snapshot which will hopefully be a stimulus for other scholars in the field of business ethics. Appendix 1 provides a number of suggestions for further scientific research.

In conclusion, I would like to take this opportunity to thank the following persons who commented on the draft version of this book: professors Eduard Kimman and Cees Veerman, my university colleagues Hans van Oosterhout and Ben Wempe, and the critical backbenchers, Leon van den Dool and my father, Piet Kaptein. My greatest thanks goes out to my colleague Johan Wempe, who proved to be a worthy sparring partner during the quiet moments of the day, such as when we were in the elevator, the car, the hallway, and the cafeteria.[3]

---

[2] Icarus and his father Daedalus, the architect and builder of Athens, were imprisoned in Daedelus's own labyrinth. In order to escape, Daedalus devised wings of wood, held together with bee's wax. Before they took to the air, Daedalus said to his son, "Be careful not to fly too low. Your wings will become wet, and they will become too heavy and you will fall to your death. But do not fly too high either, or you'll come too close to the sun and the wax will melt, your feathers will come loose and you will fall." This having been said, they took to the air. For a while, everything went fine until Icarus become too bold. He flew higher and higher. The wax of his wings melted in the heat of the sun, his feathers came loose and he fell to his death.

[3] In line with the conventions of English grammar, masculine pronouns in this text refer to both male and female genders. Please note that words such as "he" and "his" should for all practical purposes be interpreted as "he or she" and "his or her."

PART I

DEFINING THE ETHICAL CONTENT

Chapter 1

The Corporate Mission

In his book *Alice in Wonderland*, Lewis Carroll describes the following conversation between Alice and the Cheshire Cat.

Alice asks the Cat: "Would you tell me, please, which way I ought to go from here?"

"That depends a good deal on where you want to get to," the Cat says.

"I do not much care where" says Alice "so long as I get somewhere."

At which point the Cat says, "Oh, you're sure to do that if you only walk long enough."

Applied to companies, the tenor of this conversation is clear. A company without a goal has no guide for conduct. Everything that is, or is not, attempted is not any better or worse than the alternatives. The development of a strategy, a plan setting out how to achieve the desired goals, then becomes completely misplaced. "We will see where we are when we get there" will be the corollary of this line of thought. After all, "we will get somewhere if we only walk far enough." That last sentence may be completely correct, but it does not mean very much. Running a business or organizing something becomes a pointless exercise, which is likely to produce results which are not appreciated retrospectively. In order to develop worthwhile and goal-oriented activities, it is important that everyone who contributes to the company's strategic process understands the ultimate goals of the organization. The question about ultimate goals can also be viewed from an ethical perspective: what are we, as a company, ultimately trying to achieve; for whom or what are we doing it, and can this attempt withstand critique? This chapter revolves around the question "which ultimate corporate goals are desirable from an ethical standpoint?" This first chapter attempts to make clear that moral choices intrinsically support a company's existence and, as such, are important in determining a company's effectiveness and efficiency. Furthermore, this chapter provides a foundation for the moral responsibility of corporations. On the basis of this responsibility, we will be able to investigate in chapters 2 and 3 where the ethical content of a company can be located. In the subsequent sections, the following questions will be raised: why is it possible and desirable to identify the corporate goals (Section 1.1), what is the function of a corporate mission (Section 1.2), and what are morally unacceptable corporate missions (Section 1.3), and what are morally acceptable corporate missions (Section 1.4)?[4]

1.1   The corporation as a responsible entity

Organizations have come to play an increasingly important role in contemporary society: over the years, the "organization quotient" of society has risen quickly (Edelman Bos, 1990). We live in a society of organizations. One way or another, every one of us is affected by organizations: from before birth until a point long after we have passed away. Organizations supply products and services people need for survival and comfort (i.e. food, security, education, care, electricity, transportation, and clothing). Just imagine how many organizations were needed simply to produce the paper upon which this text is printed: lumberjacks and a mill, several transport companies, a paper factory, an electric company, one or more governmental organizations, and a range of others. A modern society without organizations is unimaginable. The evolution of technology, which plays an important part in societal and cultural changes, finds its greatest expression in the corporation, due to its production function. In this regard, we can think of the social implications of the invention of the telephone, the automobile, the television, the airplane, and the computer, to name just a few. These changes have led to possibilities that were previously considered impossible. Modern society has become dependent to a large extent on the functioning of corporations.

The functioning of corporations has consequences for a large number of individuals and groups in society: employees, consumers, suppliers, stockholders, competitors,

---

[4]   This chapter was largely published earlier as "Ethische aspecten van ondernemerschap op de thuis-markt en wereldwijd: een zoektocht naar de missie van een onderneming," in *Besturen en Innovatie*, 4, Bohn, Stafleu and Van Loghum, 1994, C0600, pp. 1-30.

nearby residents, government, and the environment. So as to make a distinction between the concepts of stockholder and shareholder, these have been referred to in the business literature as stakeholders since the early fifties (see, for example, Freeman, 1984). Stakeholders are those individuals or groups who (can) influence or are affected by the operation of a company. Each of these stakeholders has a particular interest (stake) with regards to the company. Employees, for example, have an interest in employment, favorable working conditions, fair wages and acceptable career possibilities. Companies can contribute to the prosperity and well-being of most stakeholders in many ways. In offering employment, purchasing semi-manufactured goods, and paying dividends and taxes, the company provides income to its employees, suppliers, stockholders, and the government, respectively.

The activities of a company may have negative as well as positive effects. There are companies which cause great damage to the environment, lay off staff, sell products whose repercussions are insufficiently understood, employ damaging or wasteful advertising, do not pay creditors, cause disturbance and discomfort to those who live in the near vicinity, allow staff to work under hazardous conditions, and deviously spy on the competition. The question we should ask ourselves is who is responsible for preventing or lessening the negative repercussions of corporate operations? Should this task be reserved for the government which passes the laws, monitors compliance and punishes offenders, or for the market which minimizes such negative repercussions through the application of the mechanism of supply and demand? Or should the companies themselves be held responsible as well?

The marketplace and the government offer no guarantee for the elimination of negative effects (Stone, 1975). As mechanisms for regulating the conduct of companies, legislation and the market naturally have their own shortcomings and limitations. The government cannot be expected to anticipate every aspect of corporate conduct; legislation often lags behind social developments and often limits itself to prohibition (negative reinforcement) of certain conduct, instead of containing also prescriptions (positive reinforcements). Markets cannot regulate all desired conduct of corporations. It is sometimes quite the contrary. Precisely in those cases where immoral conduct results in savings in costs, this then leads to a reduction of the sales price and to an improvement in the competitive position, at least in the short term. Furthermore, the demand for a given product does not, by definition, make the product socially acceptable, as the demand for weapons and hard drugs illustrates.[5]

Two schools of thought attempted to formulate an answer that would serve to bridge the gap between legislation and the market, on the one hand, and responsible conduct, on the other hand. In the 1960's, the dominant model of appropriate business behavior was known as the social responsibility model. It was followed in the 1970's by the social responsiveness model. From these schools of thought, researchers tried

---

[5] For a more extensive analysis of the inadequate direction provided by legislation and the market, see Stone (1975), *Where the Law Ends: the social control of corporate behavior*, especially Chapter 10, "Why the market cannot do it," and Chapter 11, "Why the law cannot do it." See also Mulligan (1992).

to determine how a company can best react to or anticipate current or future stakeholder expectations (see Sethi and Falbe, 1987, and Mahoney, 1990).

Neither school of thought was able to provide a satisfactory answer. According to these schools, a company "only" has to react to or anticipate what the environment dictates. Both schools lack a measurement mechanism by which different and conflicting expectations can be weighed against one another. The social responsibility and responsiveness models do not provide an effective answer for questions such as "What must a company do if investment in less environmentally-damaging products comes at the cost of employment?" and "What is there to do when a company can win a huge order by paying a large bribe?" The mottoes "react" or "anticipate" provide no support in resolving these dilemmas. At the same time, expectations of the company might be misjudged or be found unacceptable. Expectations come to be misjudged because we cannot expect everything from a company. A company is, according to Wempe and Melis (1991), no "Florence Nightingale." With a view to making a contribution to society, it would naturally be unreasonable to expect a corporation to sell off its assets to benefit transients, for example. As noted above, expectations can also be unacceptable. By definition, it would therefore not be acceptable to accede to all the wants and needs of others. Mulligan (1992) cites the admittedly extreme example of a company in Nazi Germany that met all social expectations during the Second World War, but for which we must at the same time admit that every moral reason to meet these expectations was lacking. "The moral mission of a company is not fulfilled simply by doing what is required in order to survive in the social environment...." (Mulligan, 1992:70). If the majority of a country's citizens finds it unacceptable that companies give immigrant applicants favored treatment in order to help them fill a gap in the labor market, that still does not prove that such a practice is also morally irresponsible. It is nothing more than a description of what the majority finds worth striving for. What is generally accepted, is not necessarily moral. Ethics is not a question of "moral head counting" or "paying lip service to the prevailing morality." In ethics, as we shall see, it is arguments that persuade, not numbers.

In the stakeholder model (see, for example, Freeman, 1984), the company is seen in a web of relationships with all the stakeholders. The company is the central point of the web, where the interests of the stakeholders form a juncture and have to be weighed off against one another in the event they cannot all be realized. In such a situation, it is not enough to rely on direction from legislation, the market or social expectations. The stakeholders need to be able to trust the company as well: to trust that the company adequately balances the interests of the stakeholders, on the one hand, with those of the company itself, on the other hand. This trust is important because most stakeholders simply do not (whether for lack of time, information, knowledge and responsibilities) enter the boardroom in order to tell management what ought to happen. The company is itself primarily responsible for making moral choices. Companies have the freedom of action for making their own choices and in which they can express their preferences for one course of action or another. A company is not a heterogeneous player forced into choices by its environment, but an autonomous actor with the ability of making its own choices in its own unique and responsible way. Only autonomous actors can be held accountable. A heterogeneous actor will be able to shift responsibility by pointing out that he only does what others dictate via the market, legislation or social expectations.

Corporations, and their most important decision-making component, management, do have freedom in setting goals and choosing courses of actions. In the management literature, we find several instances where attempts are made to limit the role of managers to merely technical matters. Follet (1918) defines management as the art of getting things done through people. The question is rather where these "things" come from. According to Follet, these things are simply a given, an established fact. This way of thinking leads to a fairly mechanical and heterogeneous view of management. The management does not have the wherewithal to choose the company's goals. The consequence of this view is that the management is only responsible for achieving these goals in the most efficient manner possible. The result of this proposition is that the management cannot be asked to take the desirability of the goals into account. As a result, the management can take cover behind the fact that the objectives were dictated by someone else. Chandler (1962) defines management in this regard significantly better as "the determination of the basic long-term goals and objectives of an enterprise and the adoption of courses of action and allocation of resources necessary for carrying out these goals."

It would now make sense to discuss the ethical aspects of corporate goals. Ethical conduct, in fact, presumes freedom of action: it is only possible to ask someone to take responsibility in situations where the option of "can" and "cannot" exists. Because corporate conduct reflects implicitly or explicitly chosen goals, it is a point of departure for bringing corporate conduct into discussion and to call the corporation to account. Business ethics, as an applied form of general ethics, makes a contribution to this process. More than either the social responsibility or the social responsiveness schools do, business ethics offers concepts for determining which stakeholders have justified interests and expectations of the corporations and concepts for balancing conflicting stakeholders' interests.

1.2   The corporate mission as central principle

The mission is the "Leitmotiv," the "raison d'être," or "the intent" of the corporation. The mission is what the corporation is ultimately trying to achieve. It is the vision of the central and guiding concepts on which the company is based. A mission does not need to be committed in writing. The "real" mission encapsulates what is going on in the minds of those who make up the corporation. Neither is a mission identical to one or more goals (Pastin, 1986). A goal is closed. After it has been attained, it loses its value. A mission, in contrast, is open and, theoretically, never achieved. A goal is, therefore, less enduring than a mission. When a company wants to sell four thousand more products this year than last, that is what we call a goal. When results show that the company did, indeed, sell that many extra products, the goal has been reached. Striving to become and continue to be profitable, though, is a question of another order. Such an effort is permanent and inexhaustible. Year after year, it remains a challenge for the corporation to achieve its desired profitability. That is why we speak here of a mission. Only in exceptional cases is a mission accomplished. At that moment, the corporation's reason for existing ceases. This is most often seen in project organizations, which, as the term implies, are set up for a single project. The completion of the project may imply the end of the organization, unless the management finds a new project and defines a new goal.

No matter how global it may be, a company needs a mission. Pastin puts this as follows: "Having no purpose is exactly as feasible as having no strategy. To have no strategy is to have the strategy of letting the company drift at the whim of external forces, internal politics, and chance. To have no purpose is to have to stand the company for nothing. The zero option strategy or purpose is not attractive." (1986:153). Or, as McCoy writes: "Excellence performance requires that management and staff possess a common vision of what the company is about and how the company is contributing to the quality of life for themselves and for society." (1985:x). A mission supplies the core principle for corporate action. It only becomes possible to discuss a company's effectiveness and efficiency when we have an understanding of its mission. "Efficiency is doing things right: effectiveness is doing the right thing. And doing the wrong thing less expensively is not much help." (Kanter, 1983:22). The person trying to achieve a wrong goal is completely misguided. The person trying to achieve a worthwhile goal the wrong way can probably choose a different path. When someone becomes aware that he has chosen an inappropriate goal, he will have to change course completely or seriously ask himself what goal is indeed worthwhile. As Kanter says, effectiveness and efficiency are two separate things. Effectiveness is the degree to which a company follows its mission over a given period. It only makes sense to talk about effectiveness, and subsequently about efficiency, in the context of a worthwhile goal. Efficiency presumes effectiveness: without effectiveness, efficiency is worthless. A company could be extremely efficient, but if that does not bring the company one step closer to its goal, every effort is in vain.

A mission serves two fundamental functions: it provides the guiding principle and the yardstick for corporate action. A mission gives direction and purpose to the company's conduct. It, for example, justifies painful interventions over the short term which improve effectiveness over the long term. A mission supplies continuity and a long-term vision and leads to recognizable and predictable activities. Furthermore, a mission supplies a yardstick for the evaluation of conduct. If one or more activities clash with the mission, they should be canceled or the mission should be revised.

In business jargon, the term "helicopter view" is often used, which means that the management rises above the daily activities and asks itself "Where are we going?" or with the question posed by Drucker: "What business are we in?" The question of the mission is located even higher, at what we could call the satellite view level. That is when the viewer asks himself "What do we stand for?", "What is the mission of our company?" To answer this question, corporations have to ask themselves: "Why do we, as a corporation, behave as we do?" and "Why do we try to achieve certain goals?" By asking the "Why" question over and over, the so-called Socratic method, we come increasingly closer to the fundamental issues, the ultimate motivations for conduct. "What do we stand for?" is the question that goes to the heart of the company (Gilbert and Freeman, 1988). Following a similar path with one's personal life, one's life goals and philosophies can come into view in the same manner.

Just as there is a broad range of philosophies of life, there is also a large number of various mission concepts, defended by various schools of thought. All of these concepts presume their own moral perspectives and give their own answers to the question of what a company ultimately stands for. Each of these concepts gives rise to different strategies and to the manner in which the daily business is conducted. The choice of a mission, therefore, has great consequences for the way in which corporations relate to their stakeholders and conflicting stakeholder interests are weighed off against one another. This means that a mission is not ethically neutral.

When we ask ourselves which mission is ethically responsible or irresponsible, we arrive at the central issue of ethics and business. Business, as we have seen, is only sensible if it is effective. Discussing effectiveness is only possible when we know what the mission is. It is, therefore, of great importance that the mission will hold its own in a moral debate. In the following sections, I shall attempt to contribute to that debate.

1.3   What the corporate mission is not

In the search for a morally defensible corporate mission, we first encounter a number of missions which, on closer inspection, are unsatisfactory. In this section, I shall describe why missions as continuity, profit, growth, self-interest, production of goods and services, and promoting the interests of a single stakeholder group are inconclusive and incomplete from an ethical perspective.

* **Continuity**

Striving for continuity is sometimes seen as a company's mission. Ansoff (1981) sees the company's mission as to succeed and to survive in an industry. Drucker (1977) speaks of the corporation's welfare and survival as the reason for a company's existence. Is continuity really the ultimate goal of a corporation? I do not think so.

It is true that ensuring continuity can facilitate the realization of a number of future interests. For example, employees benefit by the fact that their jobs are guaranteed. Striving for continuity is generally desirable. And yet, two reservations lie hidden in holding continuity as the corporate mission.

First of all, continuity is not a gratuitous justification for violating the interests of any stakeholder. If it were, we certainly would not have to worry about whether the tobacco industry has a right to exist. In such a case, ensuring continuity would be valued, regardless of any potential negative consequences, and no matter what the price is. Issues such as whether companies should pay bribes to safeguard their continuity or whether companies, to ensure their continuity within Europe, should be able to sell unregistered medicine to Third World countries -- resulting in the illness or even death of dozens of people -- would then no longer constitute dilemmas. The concern for a company's continuity would then take precedence above everything else. However, these two examples show that we cannot always simply agree with the proposition that a company's continuity always comes first: something else is probably more important.

In the second place, continuity is an empty concept. Continuity for whom or for what? The reasoning "we are striving for continuity for continuity's sake" is not convincing. At the least, one would expect an argument on why continuity should stand as the mission rather than a repetitive statement such as in the example above. Continuity is, rather, only a precondition for achieving other goals. If continuity becomes the ultimate goal, that would mean that the company could never go bankrupt. An automobile's reason for existence is not to exist as an object, but to carry someone or something between two points with a certain degree of speed, comfort and safety. This purpose places a value on the automobile and that is why it is used (ignoring status considerations). A car that no longer can carry out its function should be stripped of its value and be ready for the junkyard. Its value would then equal its scrap value (the monetary value of its individual parts). Only a redefinition of its function could extend the life of the vehicle in question. As a collector's item, such an automobile could possibly have a purpose in a museum. For a company, the same rule applies. Corporations do not arise spontaneously and do not occur naturally. It was only in the 17th century that the predecessors of the modern corporation arose, with the United East India Company in 1602 as one of the pioneers. Where there is an organization, there is intent. The corporation is a deliberate initiative taken on the way to a chosen goal. The corporation's function determines its value. A corporation is not a goal in itself, but a tool or an instrument. When something has no value in itself (intrinsic value), or when it does not add value (instrumental or extrinsic value), it is impossible to assign it a reason for existence. If a business in general or one or more specific companies no longer provide any added value, they should be taken to the scrap heap -- preferably sooner than later. After all, no such thing exists as an open-air museum for businesses. What then is this extrinsic value?[6]

---

[6] An etymological search does not help much. The word "business," composed of "busy" and "ness," comes from the old English word "bisignis," meaning "activity," "being busy with," or "occupied with." Being busy for the sake of being busy offers no help.

- **Profit**

Is the pursuit of profit the extrinsic value of corporations? In conversations with entrepreneurs or in articles published on the business pages of newspapers, the suggestion is often made that profit-making is the ultimate goal of a corporation. At a multinational publishing concern, the reigning theme for business is known as the CEO's Iron Law: profit growth of 10 percent per year. Even at business schools, the implicit presumption is often made that trying to make a profit lies at the base of corporate activities: by applying models and theories like Porter's five forces model (1980) profitability can be increased or stabilized.

The idea of profit is a fully accepted concept in business. Trying to make a profit is generally considered as a legitimate activity: profit as a goal seems good, not dirty. But is the optimization of profit by definition good? Are we satisfied when a company says that its mission is to achieve optimal profit? The answer is no, as making a profit is only a goal and not a mission. As Sturdivant so pointedly says: "Making a profit is no more the purpose of a corporation than getting enough to eat is the purpose of life. Getting enough to eat is a requirement of life: life's purpose, one would hope, is somewhat broader and more challenging. Likewise with business and profit." (1985:13-14). We must, indeed, ask ourselves: why profit, and for whom? For whose benefit? Trying to make a profit simply for the sake of making a profit is not a convincing argument. If we put profit in a broader perspective, we see that it fulfills a number of fundamental tasks. Profit demands that corporations make careful calculations and shows whether a company is economically and socially engaged in a meaningful way. Careful calculation: if costs are not monitored, they can quickly lead to the waste and abuse of corporate assets. Economically engaged: whether companies efficiently meet the needs of customers. Socially engaged: whether companies meet the needs of the customers at all. The need for profitability demands the discovery of new opportunities, the competence to evaluate risks, and the courage to bear responsibilities. Furthermore, profit provides a necessary source for investments and creates the endurance needed for building longevity in the products and services. Finally, profit provides a number of stakeholders with financial assets, such as stockholders (dividends), government (taxes), and employees (profit-sharing). In its *Statement of General Business Principles*, Shell says that "profitability is essential to fulfill our responsibilities."

Trying to make a profit is, therefore, neither conclusive nor adequate as a mission. Although profits might be high, if they go hand in hand with irrevocable damage to the environment, abominable working conditions, shabby products, and dishonest supplier relations, the company in question will not deserve moral appreciation.

- **Growth and self-interest**

For the same reasons that apply to using profit as a mission, the proposition of business growth offers a similarly inadequate answer. Growth for what and for whom? Nor does falling back on self-interest offer solace. Whose interest is the self-interest of the corporation? As we have already seen in this section, the corporation's interest is a metaphysical concept. It cannot, by its very nature, be made into an end in itself. By itself, growth is also a nonsensical mission for a corporation.

- **The production of goods and services**

Is the corporate mission, therefore, the production of goods and services? Without a doubt, the production of goods and services is the basic activity of every company. In order to be able to produce, a number of stakeholders make a contribution (Section 1.4 describes this in more detail). The fact that something is being produced brings the stakeholders together. Yet, we can pose a similar question here as well: "Why is something being produced?", "Who is actually served by that production?", and "What is the motivation behind the production of goods and services?". Only when we have answered these questions, we will approach a company's mission.

- **Maximize the interest of a single stakeholder**

Is the corporate mission, then, the maximization of the interest of a single stake-holder? We can differentiate a number of so-called single-focus missions. These are the missions of maximizing the interest of the stockholders, the management, the employees, or the consumer. Below is a short description of why these different missions each have their own defenders.

Friedman writes: "Few trends would so thoroughly undermine the very foundations of our free society as the acceptance by corporate officials of a social responsibility other than to make as much money for their stockholders as they possibly can." (1962:134). Rappaport (1986) equally defends the stockholders' mission. According to Rappaport, business strategies should be judged by the economic returns they generate for stockholders, as measured by dividends plus the increase in the company's stock price. The stockholders are the owners of the corporation, and there-fore, the only group to which the corporation must direct its attention.

The management mission assumes that the management is the most important inter-est group. The managers are the ones who make the decisions. Considering that everyone acts in his or her own self-interest (descriptive) and should do so (prescriptive), that means that the management does not need to be excluded. In their book *The Modern Corporation and Private Property*, Berle and Means (1932) con-clude that that the division between property and control of the corporation has lead to the management mission. The stockholder mission differs from this mission. With regards to the stockholders, the concern is "How should the corporation try to maxi-mize profits for the stockholders?". The issue of the management mission is "How can the corporation satisfy the stockholders so that the management can extract the maximum benefit from the corporation?" (see also Gilbert and Freeman, 1988).

One reason to opt for the employee mission is that employees, both in a material and an immaterial sense, depend on the company to a great extent. Work is a significant source of income rendering a person's life meaningful. People spend a great deal of their time at work (Badaracco, 1992). Their interest should, therefore, be the guiding principle of corporate policy (Bowie, 1988).

A defender of the consumer mission would say that the fundamental task of the corporation is to provide consumers with products and services. This task is, after all, carried out to benefit consumers. According to Van Luijk and Schilder the following applies to businesses: "The reasons for existence lie in providing part of the world's population with products and services that the target groups deem to be of a higher quality and better price than the alternatives." (1997: 54-55).

The commonality of the missions noted above is that they identify the interests and expectations of a single stakeholder group as the guideline for the company's activities. Is this justified? In evaluating the effectiveness of the corporation, can the needs of only one stakeholder group be taken as mission? I do not think so.

When a single stakeholder group is used as the guideline for business activities, the consequence of this may be that all means are justified to meet that end. Everything seems justified as long as the interest of the selected stakeholder group is served. Other stakeholders, then, may become obstacles or insignificant factors in the decision-making process. An example of this way of thinking can be found in Freeman: "From the standpoint of strategic management, or the achievement of organizational purpose, we need an inclusive definition. We must not leave any group or individual who can affect or is affected by organizational purpose, because that group may prevent our accomplishments. [...] Theoretically, the term "stakeholder" must be able to capture a broad range of groups and individuals, even though when we put the concept to practical tests, we must be willing to ignore certain groups who will have little or no impact on the corporation at this point of time." (1984:52-53).[7] The stakeholders are seen primarily as either a means or an obstacle that can facilitate or obstruct the realization of the expectations of the chosen stakeholder group. Goodpaster presents another opinion: "Moral concern would avoid injury or unfairness to those affected by one's actions because it is wrong, regardless of the retaliatory potential of the aggrieved parties" (1991:60).

In order to keep the interests of more than one category of stakeholders in mind as a goal in and of itself, Kant's categorical imperative offers a starting point. This imperative dictates that: "Act in such a way that you always treat humanity, whether in your own person or in the person of any other, never simply as a means, but always at the same time as an end." (1971:96). Never treat people only as a means, but always also as an end. For Immanuel Kant, the human person represents an intrinsic value. The person as an end unto himself is the core of his scale of values. What it comes down to, briefly, is that Kant says that the person is more than just a means to something else, more than a tool that only has value when people assign value to it. What does it mean, after all, when we see ourselves simply as things? According to Kant, it means that we feel that our person has no value unless someone else ascribes

---

[7] However, Freeman reversed this statement in his later publications (e.g. Gilbert and Freeman, 1988).

24 Chapter One

value to us. That implies that the other person is a source of value, and is, therefore, more than just a thing. It is, however, unreasonable to assume that others are goals in themselves, while we ourselves are only tools. One must, therefore, assume that each person is a goal in and of himself. "Individuals are ends, and never mere means to someone else's ends" say Gilbert and Freeman (1988:82).[8] The extrinsic value of the corporation cannot be found in the maximization of the interests of a single stake-holder group. The maximization of the interests of one stakeholder implies that all other stakeholders are seen as instruments and are only important insofar as they make a positive or negative contribution to the interests of the stakeholder the corporation is concentrating on. We can see that this conflicts with Kant's postulate, and that the acceptance of a single-focus mission denies every moral responsibility towards other stakeholders. Every stakeholder has rights that deserve respect. Du Pont formulates it correctly in its *Guidelines*: "At the heart of the fundamental responsibilities lies the philosophy that we must protect the respect and the worth of the individual..." A defender of the single-focus mission could respond that the stakeholder group for which the corporation is acting has not only rights, but also responsibilities. These responsibilities could include looking out for the interests of others. The interest of the stockholder, indeed, includes ensuring profitability, but there is also the moral duty of stockholders to see that this does not take place at the expense of other stakeholders, the defender of the single-focus mission would say. So essentially, we are back at the beginning. What are the responsibilities of the owners or other stakeholder groups which the corporation focuses on? To answer this question requires a precise definition of the corporation's reasons for being. That is why we need to follow a different path if we are interested in defining the corporate mission.

1.4   What the corporate mission is

In order to answer the question of what a morally desirable mission is, we must first clearly define what a corporation is and how it comes into being.[9]

The founding of a corporation often arises from an idea or impulse from someone to fill a void in the market in an unique way. Often-heard motivations for incorporating a company are an increase in income, responsibility, involvement, and prestige of the founders. The social need for the product is often of minor interest. A hair stylist does not open a salon because he is concerned about the untidy hair style of local residents.[10]

---

[8] Donaldson (1996) defines this point of view as the core value for every company in the world.
[9] Like Rawls (1972) who develops principles for social institutions from the original position behind a veil of ignorance, I would like to try to develop fundamental moral principles for corporations from the point of view of the rise and continuation of corporations (the original position) as well as from a multiple stakeholder view (the veil of ignorance).
[10] In this connection, Adam Smith (1776) says: "It is not from the benevolence of the butcher, the baker, and the brewer that we expect our dinner, but from their regard for their own self-interest."

In order to meet his needs and to realize his desires, the founder seeks others with whom he can cooperate. From that moment, the number of stakeholders increases. A bank, family members, or acquaintances are called upon for the necessary capital. The municipality is approached for available room in facilities setup for beginning entrepreneurs. Possible government subsidies are applied for. Contacts are made with possible suppliers. A cofounder might be sought to help flesh out the ideas and who might be interested in contributing his capabilities and means to realize their ambitions. It is notable that in this initial phase, the stakeholders become voluntarily involved with the corporation. The parties want to participate in the undertaking insofar as that furthers their own self-interests. The supplier wins another customer, the consumer obtains better or less-expensive products, the financiers receive a good return, and for the government as the guardian of the public interest, prosperity and the common good flourish. The company has, therefore, the potential of satisfying a number of stakeholder interests.

The closer a company comes to its incorporation, the greater the chance that stakeholders will become involved who, uninvited and perhaps unwillingly, will experience the repercussions of the future company. The family situation of the founder may deteriorate because he is putting all his time into the business. The "starter's" employer sees one of his best workers preparing to leave. The competition fears its market share may decline with all the associated repercussions. The founder will also make greater demands on the environment. In the beginning, this might only entail a few sheets of paper, but once the business is running, electricity and fuel will be consumed and garbage will be produced. Nearby residents may have to deal with noise pollution, inconveniences of other kinds, unpleasant odors, and an obstructed view.

Nor will the company be able to keep its "hands" clean after the incorporation. To satisfy the needs of one stakeholder, the interests of others may be compromised. Choices sometimes have to be made among conflicting interests. Badaracco (1992) and others call this the "problem of dirty hands:" in order to satisfy one interest, another interest must be compromised.[11] As the company becomes larger, the "hands" could become dirtier. After all: you have to break an egg to make an omelet. The more omelets, the more broken eggs. The only way a company can keep its "hands" clean is by doing nothing!

Using a company to satisfy several interests implies that sooner or later other interests will be impinged. Even those who voluntarily chose to work with the company could discover after a time that the cooperation has not had the desired effect. It is not always possible to terminate such a relationship (depending on the exit barriers). An employee, for example, who feels himself abused often will not resign immediately, but will wait until he is certain he can gain employment elsewhere.

---

[11]   Chapter 4 discusses the problem of "dirty hands" at more length.

What a corporation is depends to a great extent on whom you ask. Each stakeholder has a different perspective from which to view the corporation's goals. For the consumer, the corporation's goal is providing products and services which meet his needs and which he can acquire for a reasonable price. For the employer, the corporation provides an income and opportunities for development. For the owners of the corporation, the goal is, for example, making a profit. But as was the case with the six blind Indians who each had taken hold of only one part of the elephant, none of these outlooks gives a view of the whole object.[12] When trying to ascertain the mission of the corporation, we must be careful that we do not look at it from only one point of view, thereby closing our eyes to other possibilities. It is precisely those other possibilities which allow us to provide an all-encompassing definition of a corporation.

Barnard (1938) identifies three prerequisites for the establishment of a company: (1) the individuals are able to communicate with one other, and (2) are prepared to contribute a share (3) in the achievement of the common goals. Cooperation for the achievement of common objectives is an essential characteristic of organizations. The corporation is comprised of diverse cooperative elements which are goal oriented. They try to accomplish together what they individually could not (sufficiently or efficiently) achieve on their own. That does not mean that we should limit the corporation to a cooperative venture of employees, but rather we should see it as a cooperative of stakeholders who participate in the corporation. The corporation is called into being as a association of stakeholders with the intention of increasing its value to which all are entitled a share. By organizing the mutual relationships, an attempt is made to achieve a synchronization leading to the achievement of the collective goals. This synchronization occurs because stakeholders are required to contribute a share in the cooperation. Employees make their physical and mental contribution in carrying out tasks that contribute to the collective goals. They accept a number of limitations as they do so. Employees are no longer able to behave simply as what they would like to do. By accepting these limitations, and carrying out their responsibilities, they make it possible for the cooperation to bear fruit. A constructive contribution of stakeholders results in a claim to a share of the proceeds. An exchange, as it were, of rights and obligations takes place in accordance with the dictum 'quid pro quo:' something for something.

Corporations are instruments to be used by the stakeholders (Gilbert and Freeman, 1988). Because the corporation must be seen as a cooperative venture in which each stakeholder has his own interests for participating, and because every interest must

---

[12] The first man feels a tusk and thinks that the elephant is a spear. The second man, who feels the side of the elephant, pronounces it a wall. The third Indian, on feeling the elephant's legs, describes it as a giant tree. Another Indian thinks he has a snake before him after feeling the trunk. The fifth man takes the elephant's ears in his hands and thinks of a fan, and the sixth man thinks, upon grabbing the tail, of a rope. When the elephant begins moving, the six men are even more confused. The man who held on to the leg experiences an elliptical movement. The man holding onto the tail is tossed from one side to the other. The movement of the elephant destroys all previously-formed opinions and makes reaching a consensus more difficult (Morgan, 1986).

be seen to be an objective by itself, a corporation should strive for the long-lasting creation of value for all stakeholders who participate voluntarily and enter into an interdependent relationship with the company. The mission statement of the American corporation NCR is a good example: "We believe in building mutually beneficial and enduring relationships with all of our stakeholders, based on conducting business activities with integrity and respect". The corporate mission is no longer only about achieving competitive advantage, but also about achieving mutual advantage. Most stakeholder are not competitors, a threat to the realization of the interests of the company. The stakeholders who enter into interdependent relationships with the company are partners together with whom the company strives towards common goals. Mutual advantage means that the positive and the negative outcomes are justly divided between the company and the stakeholders. The outcomes are the total sum of costs and benefits spread over the whole relationship. Mutual advantage does not mean that the company ignores, dominates or misuses stakeholders, but rather that the company respects and try to realize the legitimate interests and expectations of those stakeholders. Amsterdam Airport Schiphol (AAS) puts it as follows in its corporate code: "The AAS is concerned with the interests of our external partners. Because these interests do not always run parallel to each other, not all of these interests can be met at once. That is why it is important in the long term to find a fair balance." Striving for mutual advantage is the basis of a corporate mission.

With mutual advantage, I mean the advantage of the stakeholder (with whom the interdependent relationship is entered into) and the advantage of the corporation (as representative of the other stakeholders). Mutual advantage does not, of course, mean that all the interests of the stakeholders will be constantly met and the corporation, having sorted out all matters, will not have to get its "hands" dirty. On the contrary, more and more dilemmas will arise as increasingly more interests are recognized as justifiable claims. The corporation serves a constantly changing group of stakeholders. In one instance, the management will pay out a lower dividend in order to maintain employment. The next time, management will lay people off to keep the dividend high. In the first case, the corporation is serving the employees, and in the second case, the stockholders. It is clear that the management and the other employees bear a heavy responsibility in constantly striving to strike the right balance of interests.

Starting and carrying on relationships leads to a continuous exchange of benefits and costs. We noted above that a company and its stakeholders should strive for mutual advantage in cases where the partners have voluntarily come together. Stakeholders participate because of the advantages they hope to get out of the relationship with the corporation. In some situations, however, free consent does not come into play. The environment, for example, cannot be consulted over its role in the corporation, and we can hardly speak of the advantage for the environment. What could the environment have to gain? As we saw in the previous section, the environment is always short-changed: it is always impaired and never improved (except, perhaps, when a company starts to produce fewer environmentally detrimental goods than its competitors). A truly environmentally-friendly company, therefore, does not exist.

For a number of stakeholders, such as the environment and nearby residents, but also the media and people who do not buy the product but are affected by its use and sale, we can speak of one-sided dependence. One-sided dependence is present when one of the two parties can exist or even function better without the other. The environment and the residents may be quite able to "live" without the company, but the company cannot function without making a claim on the environment. From the stakeholders' point of view, they have a negative interest: their only interest is the minimization of the harmful effects of corporate conduct. Other stakeholders have a positive interest in the corporation, such as the media who serve the reading public by gathering information. These kinds of stakeholders try to benefit from the company. Corporations, though, generally do not employ an open-door policy towards the critical press. When there is a case of one-sided dependence -- following our conclusion that stakeholders are more than just a means to an end -- the corporation ought to respect the interest of the stakeholder in question. Respecting stakeholders means optimizing the positive interests and minimizing the negative interests. Amsterdam Airport Schiphol expresses its respect for the environment as "...the airport will conduct itself with care for the environment and concern for the interests of nearby residents." Striving for mutual advantage for stakeholders which are mutually dependent and respect for stakeholders which are one-sidedly dependent would be a morally desired mission.

The respect for one-sidedly dependent stakeholders is based on their intrinsic value and the role they play in society. If we define society such that it includes the stakeholders groups which depend unilaterally on the corporation, we can also define the relationship between the corporation and society as a relationship in which both parties should strive to achieve mutual advantage. By considering the corporation in this way as an "inhabitant" or "resident" of a country, we can expect a certain "civic virtue" from it, as Ophuls (1974) calls it. And where, for example, the "helping hand" of the corporation is necessary for solving social problems, we can expect a certain level of participation from the corporation (Van Luijk, 1993). From this perspective, society (usually by route of the government) may rightfully expect companies to put forth efforts for the good of society. One good turn deserves another. Examples of this could include a certain amount of openness (by means of a company's annual report, for example), refraining from building monopoly positions, engaging in positive discrimination of slighted segments of the working population, and restricting damage to the environment. The American department store Dayton Hudson limits its mission to three concrete stakeholder groups, but in its *Corporate Principles*, clearly states that it also has responsibilities to society: "We believe the business of business is serving society. [...] Our ultimate success depends on serving four major publics and none at the expense of the other: customers, employees, stockholders, and communities."

The benefits which the corporation derives from society include freedom of commerce, a more or less stable social structure (e.g. no war), a place of business, a claim on nature and the environment, and use of the social amenities and public works such as the infrastructure. The benefits for society are determined at three levels. Society determines the balance of social viability, the social sum of positive and negative effects, for business in general, for corporations by sector, and for individual corporations.

We can make the following general observations regarding the legitimacy of corporations from a social point of view. The basic activity that takes place within corporations is the effective and efficient production of goods and services. The corporation achieves efficiency through task and information specialization. The corporation's effectiveness is achieved through greater stability in delivering products, the speed by which that takes place, and the increased capacity for meeting consumer demands (Donaldson, 1982). The corporation's rationale is not only determined from its instrumental character, but also from the degree to which alternatives are available. But we know, says Wijffels (1991), that the alternatives for corporate-style production that have been tried so far are not necessarily palatable. And yet, says Brinckmann: "Because the possibility of an organization-free world is not imaginable, neither can a claim on the proceeds of many companies be proposed." (1991:16).

In many countries, the social acceptability of specific sectors such as the gambling sector, the tobacco industry, and prostitution has been subject to fierce debate. The central question concerning these sectors is whether they should be tolerated or prohibited.

The social discussion over individual companies' rights to exist has recently been targeting a number of companies charged with massive environmental pollution. The negative effects of these companies are being weighed against the positive effects, such as the extent to which these companies contribute to employment, gross national product, new technology, and government revenues. A number of people, such as Felix Rottenberg of the Dutch Labor Party in 1993, have become fervent proponents of instigating an environmental bankruptcy policy for companies whereby a company that causes too much environmental damage, relative to its sector counterparts, could be declared bankrupt, even if the corporation is doing very well financially.

One could counter the foregoing with the idea that the corporation that tries to achieve mutual advantage and respect is aiming for an unattainable ideal. People who represent and manage the corporation are not perfectly rational and moral creatures. In addition, heavy competitive pressures can lead to infringements on quite legitimate expectations. Those who say that the ideal of a responsible corporation is not only unattainable by definition, but that even attempting to reach such an ideal is a hopeless and frustrating endeavor, have, to this extent, nothing to contribute to this discussion.

Troublesome dilemmas and painful choices will continue to be unavoidable. Getting "dirty hands" is an inseparable part of running a corporation. But we should not submit to a doomsday mentality. Those who are less pessimistic will be heartened by

taking a realistic look at responsible corporations which seek to close the gap between their ideal and reality and to find a balance where neither the impossible is
expected (the moral image of the corporation is blown out of proportion) nor the
possible is despised (the moral image of the corporation is underexposed).

Chapter 2

Ethics Management

*"Confidence without support
is like a motherless foal
and support without confidence
is a riderless horse."
(Kuitert, 1992:22)*

Managing a corporation includes organizing the relationships with various stake-holders. Trust is an important element in initiating, maintaining and even winding down relationships between corporations and stakeholders. The willingness of stake-holders to bear uncertainty regarding the results to be expected from the relationship determines the degree to which stakeholders need something or someone to trust. If this trust cannot be established by various social mechanisms, stakeholders have to base their trust on the efforts and capacities of the corporation itself. The degree to which employees, as the corporation's representatives, are not able to realize the moral trust by themselves, determines the degree to which the corporation's moral trustworthiness needs to be organized. This chapter discusses the need to organize the moral trustworthiness of corporations as a base for living up to the corporate mission.

2.1   The moral trustworthiness of corporations

To achieve cooperation, the parties involved have to be favorably inclined. This co-operation depends on the degree to which the parties estimate that their expectations in regards to the cooperative relationship will be realized. They look for reasons and evidence on which to base their expectations. After all, the decision to cooperate never exactly reflects the costs and benefits of the cooperation. Internal and external stakeholders, therefore, run the risk that their contribution will not be in relation to the expected final results. In order to reduce this risk, stakeholders look for reasons, evidence, or points of reference which show that their interests in the corporation are being safeguarded as much as possible. These reasons increase the chance of the co-operation delivering the desired results. Stakeholders' trust in their relationship with a corporation can be defined as the extent to which they are convinced that the relationship will provide the desired results. Trust plays a role in both two-sided and one-sided dependence relationships. One-sided stakeholders also look for evidence that their interests are being respected. Knowing they run undesirable risks that are not complemented with sufficient confidence in the desirable effects of corporate functioning, one-sided stakeholders may take (corrective) actions.

Trust in this context comprises two crucial elements.[13] To be "faithful" implies, in the first place, predictability and consistency. With the word "faithful" we should think of constancy -- one can therefore speak of a particular trait over a given period of time. When we talk about a faithful person, we mean that he displays consistent behavior over a lengthy period of time: there is a fixed pattern in his conduct. The behavior of an unfaithful person, on the other hand, is difficult or impossible to pre-dict. Entering into a cooperative relationship with full trust in a person (the trustee) implies that the partner (the trustor) is sure that the key traits of the person will not significantly change.

A second element of trust is that it does not automatically imply what is expected. Trust is the belief that those on whom we depend will meet our expectations of them. Trustworthiness means being faithful to certain expectations. Trust only acquires meaning when it refers to expectations that relate to the object of that trust. Stake-holders evaluate the trustworthiness of a corporation in relation to what they expect from it. The only normative meaning for trust is that a trustworthy object is prefer-able to an untrustworthy one. A corporation's trustworthiness is determined by how much the stakeholders belief that the corporation was, is, or will be faithful to their positive expectations.

Trust is a remarkable concept. On the one hand, it implies dependence and, there-fore, uncertainty. On the other hand, it implies certainty. In a corporate setting, most stakeholders are dependent on the corporation. The realization of their interests depends on what the corporation in question does or does not do. This corporate

---

[13]   According to Hosmer (1995) there is little agreement on a workable definition of the term "trust" to be found in the literature.

conduct cannot usually be dominated by one stakeholder. This dependence, according to Rotter (1967), Zand (1972), Gambetta (1988), and Michalos (1990), increases
the vulnerability of the stakeholders. When entering into relationships, stakeholders
surrender a degree of authority and run the risk that the corporation will not meet
their expectations. According to Mayer et al., "trust is the willingness to be vulnerable." (1995:729). Corporate trust is the readiness of stakeholders to entrust the company with a certain degree of authority. When the risks are great, and the stakes are
high and stakeholders do not wish to take those risks, they will look for points of
reference to lessen the uncertainty. According to Deutsch (1960), trust is only necessary in risky situations. Without risks, there is no need for trust. Making oneself
vulnerable requires, at the same time, certainties. Seeking certainties does not mean
that one is interested in eliminating all risk and knowing exactly what the results of
the relationship will be. Risks are, however, inherent in life and are thus impossible
to avoid entirely. Sometimes, one needs only to have certainties regarding the level
of risk. In a casino, most players expect that everyone has the same odds of winning
or losing. People are sometimes willing to take huge risks in order to make huge
gains. On the financial markets, the rule of thumb is that the higher the risk, the
higher the expected return must be. Blind gambling, though -- not knowing what the
possible returns are nor having any insight into the possible division of profits and
losses -- is seldom or never an issue in a business setting. To greater or lesser degrees, stakeholders will always trust in their own knowledge and skills, in the
mechanisms which make certain results more likely, or in the abilities or efforts of
the corporation. Stakeholders search for anchoring points on which to base their
trust. This section is about how stakeholders will seek grounds on which to base their
trust.

To go into more detail, and obtain a better understanding of why it is necessary that a
corporation be trustworthy, the relevant factors are shown in the figure below.

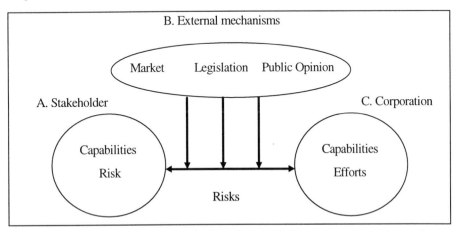

*Figure 2-1: Risk-reduction factors in the relationship between corporation and
stakeholder.*

The type of relationship that exists between the corporation and its stakeholder determines the level of risks the stakeholder faces. If that risk, in both one-sided and two-sided dependence relationships, is rather high for the stakeholder, the stakeholder can base his trust on three types of factors to reduce the risk. The stakeholder can (a) trust in his own knowledge and skills, (b) trust in the social mechanisms which stimulate the desired corporate conduct and effects, or (c) trust in the capabilities and efforts of the corporation.

- **Level of risk**

We can make a distinction among three types of relationships: transactions, contracts, and bonds.[14] In the simplest form of relationship, the transaction, an exchange is made by which a relatively direct counteroffer is made to what has been offered. The proceeds or benefits of the transaction constitute all positively-felt effects of the transactions. The costs are all the negatively-felt effects. Transactions imply relationships that have well-defined beginnings and ends, and which are relatively simple by nature. The distinction between advantage and disadvantage is relatively clear to both parties. On the other hand, bonds involve a complex relationship where the distinction between advantage and disadvantage is uncertain. Contractual relationships lie somewhere between these two. The more complicated the relationship is -- from transaction to bond -- the more uncertainty exists regarding the costs and proceeds. The greater the risk, all else being equal, the greater the need for trust.[15]

The degree of risk in a relationship, and the accompanying need for trust, can be reduced by focusing on the expected costs and benefits. The uncertainty about the costs of, for example, a product purchase, can be reduced by a guarantee or by offering a maintenance contract, a "no cure, no pay" construction or a time payment plan. A money-back-guarantee-on-defective-goods principle, a clear written contract in which the returns are assured, a trial period with employees, and put options on stocks reduce the risks on returns. Reducing the exit barriers for terminating the relationship will also lower the degree of risk.

- **Risk readiness**

The degree to which a stakeholder is prepared to take a risk depends on his risk attitude, which may be different for each stakeholder and every situation. Stakeholders' risk readiness can vary from risk-seeking to risk-avoiding (March and Shapira,

---

[14] This division in interdependent relationships applies to corporations. We are also familiar with the relationship of commitment (as in marriage, where the parties pledge fidelity until death does part them) and the relationship of covenant (such as we read in the Bible, when God makes a covenant with Abraham and He makes a promise that applies for many generations). It is possible to describe the merger of two corporations in terms of a relationship of commitment and to define thereby an appropriate level of trust. However, this study will not focus on such a relationship because the corporation itself is approached as an entity of responsibilities and in a merger both parties are fused into a single entity.

[15] According to Mayer et al.: "...assessing the risk in a situation involves considerations of the context such as weighing the likelihood of both positive and negative outcomes that might occur." (1995:725).

1987). Some graduates entering the labor market appreciate social security and seek employment with organizations offering life-time employment. On the other hand, job-seekers who require more variety could choose to work for temporary agencies where the work relationship can be terminated at any time. While the one share-holder plays it safe and invests his money in a fund with little risk, the other invests in shares with a high risk.

A risk gap in a relationship is the discrepancy between the risk of the relationship and the risk readiness of the stakeholder. Because risk gaps occur often, Butler and Cantrell (1984), among others, consider trust as a precondition for cooperative ventures. Trust can reduce the risk gap.

- **Stakeholder capabilities**

A stakeholder's trust in the benefits of a relationship can initially be based on his own knowledge, experience, and abilities (March and Shapira, 1987). When purchasing a new machine, for example, the buyer may purchase it on spec while checking the machine in depth to see if it satisfies his requirements. Similarly, stockholders will (partly) base their transactions on their estimate of the market developments.[16]

In many cases the stakeholder is unable to make a correct estimate of the risks he faces in a relationship. When purchasing a new car, the buyer does not begin checking to see if the impact specifications meet expectations. Nor do most airline passengers check to see what type of aircraft has the highest percentage of accidents. Stakeholders can base their trust in social mechanisms that promote the realization of their expectations and respect their rights.

- **Social mechanisms**

In Section 1.1, the social mechanisms which can ensure trust on the positive results of a relationship were identified. Among these are the market, legislation and public opinion. A consumer can base his trust of the quality of a new car partly on the thought that the auto maker also benefits from the sale of good quality automobiles. If the manufacturer were to introduce unsafe cars on the market, society at large would soon find out, which would subsequently lead to lower sales. Furthermore, automobiles are required to satisfy a number of official safety standards. A consumer can usually, therefore, count on the fact that a new car will meet his expectations.

In Chapter 1, mention was made that these social mechanisms do not always provide sufficient certainty for the realization of the interests and expectations of the stake-holders.

---

[16]   Gambetta does not mention the possibility of trusting in one's own abilities. He defines trust as "...the probability that a person with whom we are in contact will perform an action that is beneficial or at least not detrimental" (1988:217).

- **Capabilities and efforts of the corporation**

If social mechanisms cannot ensure the intended results, stakeholders can base their trust on the efforts of the corporation. The corporation's effort is the will to do what is within its ability to realize the expectations of the stakeholders. Cook and Wall (1980), Baier (1986), and Hosmer (1995) relate trust in relationships to the other party's effort, will or intent. Trust in the other party has, in addition, a relationship to the corporation's abilities. Good intentions alone, without the ability to carry them out, do not constitute a cooperative working relationship. Even if corporate motives are characterized by goodwill, stakeholders will not trust the corporation if the corporation is incompetent to fulfill the expectations stakeholders have. There is a distinction between the economic trustworthiness of a corporation, the degree to which the corporation is able to meet the stakeholders' expectations, and the moral trustworthiness, the degree to which a corporation is prepared or inclined to meet the stakeholders' expectations (see also Section 0.1).

Bromily and Cummings (1992) point out that a greater trust in the corporation reduces the costs of monitoring performance, and eliminates the need for control mechanisms. Hill (1990) is of the same opinion: a reputation of non-opportunistic conduct lessens such costs. Increasing moral trustworthiness reduces the need for social mechanisms and the efforts required from the stakeholder himself. To put it briefly, moral trustworthiness is not only important if the other risk-reducing factors appear insufficient (necessary minimum level), but also to reduce dependency and costs of the other risk-reducing factors (optimum level). Following what has been said above, the necessary and optimum level of the moral trustworthiness of a corporation depends upon the circumstances. It is beyond the scope of this book to determine what the optimum level of trust is in general and more specific from case-by-case. However, it is important to have established in this section that as external control mechanisms appear to be inadequate to realize and respect the interests of stakeholders, the moral trustworthiness of the company itself becomes more important when entering into and maintaining relationships with stakeholders. In view of the importance of the moral trustworthiness of corporations, we shall look, in the next section, at why the moral trustworthiness of a corporation should be organized.

2.2   The organizational context[17]

Corporations' moral trustworthiness does not spontaneously come into being and is not present by nature. "The level of trust will evolve as the parties interact" (Mayer et al., 1995:727). The moral trustworthiness of a corporation takes shape in the conduct of the personnel, who play a double role here. On the one hand, personnel are stakeholders who place their trust in de efforts of the corporation. On the other hand,

---

[17]   The original version of this section was published as: "De bedrijfscontext doorgelicht," in T. Geurts and J. de Leeuw (eds.), *Geef Bedrijfsethiek Een Plaats,* Damon, Tilburg, 1992, pp. 72-93.

employees shape the moral trustworthiness of the corporation by means of their daily conduct. Stakeholders "read" the conduct of the personnel to determine what the corporation really is trying to achieve and whose interests are being looked after.

For example, an employee of a placement agency maintains relationships with organizations seeking staff, and people looking for work. If an organization makes discriminatory demands in relation to staffing, the employee of such a placement agency has to decide whether he is going to comply with such demands. If this issue has never before cropped up within the agency, the employees are given free reign to make their own decisions in this respect. The chance of inconsistency among the personnel is therefore an issue. Employee A does not agree to the discriminatory demands of a company because he does not think people should be disadvantaged by race or color. Employee B, however, does agree to the client's demands because he thinks the customer is always right and because he happens to be a member of a racist political party. Employee C is an enthusiastic supporter of positive discrimination and purposefully sends an immigrant to the client. In this example, the conduct of these three employees can be seen as the conduct of the placement agency. Each employee deals on behalf of the corporation and represents the corporation he works for. Their conduct has consequences for how the corporation is judged. The disapproval or approval of their conduct is concurrently an indirect judgment of the corporation because, as Weiss (1994) says, employees embody the conscience of the corporation through their actions.[18] Each employee who comes into contact with stakeholders is either a trust builder or a trust destroyer. Dysfunctional conduct by one employee may damage the trustworthiness of the whole organization.[19]

Just as individual conduct can be ascribed to the group, so too can the conduct of the group be ascribed to the individual, although these individual employees do not, by definition, influence the conduct of the group. During the debate over expanding the Amsterdam Airport Schiphol with a new runway, employees were criticized by friends and neighbors over why they had to expand. Most employees, though, had no or quite a marginal role in setting policy at the airport. Some were even strong opponents to the expansion plans. Still, they were considered by outsiders as representatives of the airport and were considered as points of contact for the corporate policy.

---

[18]   A Shell spokesman said in this regard: "Shell is a very decentralised organisation. The subsidiaries have a great deal of responsibility of their own. But we are still all part of the one Shell." To illustrate, an environmental offence at one of the subsidiaries in a developing country is projected across the whole corporation. If a customer is dealt with discourteously by a staff member, such conduct can give the company a client-unfriendly image. The group receives blame or praise in accordance with the bad or commendable conduct of the individual.

[19]   This is undoubtedly what former Chief of Police Blaauw (1991) was referring to in his article, "A bad cop is a plague for the whole police corps." In the same article, Blaauw quotes the president of a Criminal Court, who said, during a case against police officials who had crossed the line, "If the police force wants to be able to carry out its true duties, the incorruptibility of police officials from the lowest to the highest level must be beyond doubt." (1991:48). The dysfunction of one or several workers influences the performance of the group as a whole.

Another example. During the debate over Shell's presence in an apartheid-dominated South Africa, some Shell workers stayed away from the company of their friends out of fear for the accusations they would be faced with. In 1995, Shell faced similar issues regarding its presence in Nigeria. The accusation that Shell had not tried hard enough to prevent the execution of writer Ken Saro-Wiwa (together with eight other activists who had carried out a campaign against pollution resulting from Shell's oil exploitation in south-eastern Nigeria) led to blockades of independent Shell fuel retailers in a number of countries. The demonstrators gave as reason for this that the individual station-owners were partially responsible for Shell's conduct. Yet, station-owners generally do not have any influence on defining Shell's strategic policy.

Because employee conduct could be attributed to the corporation as a whole, organizations have to take care that personnel properly carry out their responsibilities (i.e. carefully deal with the legitimate and fundamental expectations of stakeholders). Because personnel will not always deal in a responsible manner spontaneously, corporations must be organized to this end. If society expects a placement agency not to discriminate, the agency itself needs to ensure that its employees do not discriminate. The (management of the) agency cannot absolve itself of its responsibility by thinking that its own staff would never discriminate; after all, discrimination occurs at all levels of society. A placement agency can even indirectly encourage discrimination by its employees if, for example, employees are only rewarded by the number of vacancies they fill each period. The situation then arises in which employees are "punished" when they ignore discriminatory requests.

Moral trustworthiness within a corporation may be organized as one cannot rely exclusively on the intentions and intuitions of employees. In situations where intentions and intuitions do not lend themselves to responsible conduct, the organization should implement the necessary measures. Furthermore, an organization may take care that it itself does not directly or indirectly encourage irresponsible conduct. Processes are often created in organizations that put intentions and intuitions of employees under pressure.

In general, it is tempting to attribute a corporation's gross moral misconduct to one or several ill-disposed employees. When it became known in February 1995 that the British Barings Bank had gone bankrupt due to a loss in Singapore of one billion dollars attributed to derivatives trading, all blame initially fell on only one of the 4,000 bank employees, the 28-year-old Nick Leeson. The Chancellor of the Exchequer, making an announcement in British House of Commons, spoke of "...a specific incident unique to Barings centered on one rogue dealer in Singapore" (Daily Mail, 1995, 28 February). At first glance, it is quite attractive to choose one employee as scapegoat in cases of gross misconduct: everyone else is kept out of the range of fire. The victim can be put on display and used as a deterrent for the rest of the staff. Firing an offender today means a healthy organization tomorrow. "By getting rid of one rotten apple it will not be able to spoil the others and ruin the whole barrel" as the saying goes. It is, however, short-sighted and unjust to blame the consequences of improper practices on one or several ill-disposed employees. The organizational context can also contribute to these unethical practices if corporations take insufficient care to prevent such practices.

According to Ottoson (1989), most cases of unethical conduct in business are carried out by people who were not initially planning to deal unethically. According to Nash (1990), members of a group will behave immorally in a fashion that they would never have considered outside the group.[20] Niebuhr (1932) assumes that individuals display less morally responsible conduct in groups than they do in their private lives. In each group of people, there are, according to Niebuhr, fewer reasons to control one's impulses and to show understanding for the needs of others.

An important study in this area was carried out by Asch in 1952. He experimented with what happens when people are confronted with an opposing opinion, held by the majority of a group of which one is a member. A high percentage of test subjects appeared ready to conform with the majority opinion by making statements totally at odds with their own observations. These findings were relatively harmless because the conformity was limited to words.

A study by Milgram (1974), done at the beginning of the 1960's, shows that conformity can have quite shocking effects. Volunteers from all echelons of the US population were asked to participate in the study. A test subject who was actually a fellow-worker of the research leader was tied to a chair in the next room. The volunteers were to administer an electric shock to the test subject when he gave an incorrect answer. In reality, though, that did not happen and the subject only pretended to be shocked. Approximately 60 percent of the volunteers (who were really the test subjects) were quite obedient in the face of authority, in this case the research leader. Upon an incorrect answer by the test subject, the volunteers followed their instructions and delivered increasingly stronger electric shocks, up to 450 volts.

Apparently, the group one belongs to or the authority one has to deal with has a great influence on the conduct of the members. The group develops its own norms and values which are passed on to the other members and that serve as the standards for their conduct (Sims, 1991). The organizational context "...exerts enormous cumulative pressures on employees and managers" (Badaracco, 1992:71). Due to this influence of the organizational context, people are able to believe they are behaving responsibly when in fact they are behaving in quite unacceptable ways. Gellerman (1989) notes that most people are often not aware of the fact that they are exhibiting immoral conduct. People think that they are conducting themselves for the good of the group or, in the example above, are doing good work. According to Verstraeten and Van Gerven (1994), institutional factors contribute to the fact that the collective

---

[20]   This brings to mind the somber conclusions of Arendt (1948) and Levi (1986). According to them, the frightening thing about the Holocaust was not that it was carried out by evil or possessed people, but by people who in normal circumstances would fall under our definition of honorable, decent and charitable (Nash, 1990). Levi wrote of the average SS man: "They were made of the same cloth as we, they were average human beings, averagely intelligent: save the exceptions, they were not monsters, they had our faces, but they had been reared badly. They were, for the greater part, diligent followers..." (1986:xi).

results of well-intentioned individual conduct becomes quite negative from an ethical point of view. To achieve responsible conduct, it is necessary to find out how the group influences and guides its members. This has important implications for building a moral trustworthy corporation. It is, therefore, a misconception to think that immoral conduct is limited to bad people. The point is, according to Velasquez and others, that: "Unethical behavior in business is more often than not a systematic matter. To a large degree, it is the behavior of generally decent people who normally would not think of doing anything illegal or immoral. But they get backed into something unethical by the systems and practices of their own firms and industries. Unethical behavior in business generally arises when business firms fail to pay explicit attention to the ethical risks that are created by their own systems and practices." (1990:229). The systems and practices are partly to blame for urging employees towards unethical conduct. Steinman and Lohr (1992:26) even speak of system coercion, by which the personnel is forced to modify their conduct to conform to the desires of the system. Employees can be quite honorable and put their heart and soul into good work for any number of idealistic goals in their free time, whereas, during working hours, they continue to sell products that are of an inferior quality and quite damaging to the public health -- all because the corporate context encourages such conduct.

Trevino (1986) makes a distinction between the personal morality of personnel and other factors that are influential in corporate conduct. Frederick (1983) has analyzed ten scientific studies of reprehensible practices, and concludes that the main problem for unethical conduct lies in the corporate context. The study of Frederick shows that even "...the most upright people are apt to become dishonest and unmindful of their civic responsibilities when placed in a typical corporate environment." (Raiborn and Payne, 1990:3). "Individual actions are often a function of organizational imperatives. The core values of the business system ...drive all business firms to a social end that is perhaps not part of the intention of the individual business person caught in the system's toils," says Frederick (1983:147). In the words of Solomon and Hanson (1985), employees' immoral behavior may reflect structural deformities in the organization. Ferrel and Gresham's (1985) contingency model shows that as the pressure towards unethical behavior increases, the chance becomes greater that -- all else being equal -- employees will opt for the immoral choice.[21]

Recognizing organizational pressure, antecedent conditions (Knouse and Giacalone, 1992), the opportunity and exposure factors (Bologna et al., 1995),[22] pre-conditions, (Shrivastava, 1994), and institutional factors (Verstraeten and Van Gerwen, 1994)

---

[21]   Carmichael (1992) maintains as a rule of thumb that ten percent of people are honest in all circumstances, ten percent of people are always dishonest, and the remaining eighty percent react to the circumstances. Bologna et al. (1995) hold to a proportion of 20-20-60. Almost every employee has his price, says Gellerman (1989).

[22]   Bologna et al. (1995) present the GONE theory, which offers insights into an organization's vulnerability to fraud. The chance for fraud depends on the factors Greed, Opportunity, Need, and Exposure.

that lead to sacrificing or suspending one's individual morale, what Velasquez (1990) and others call the ethical risks, are, therefore, quite important.

Theft of company property by its own staff is by definition, therefore, not merely a matter of individual ethics. It becomes tempting for the personnel to take inventory home with them when, for example, store inventory is never checked, when management itself takes things home without paying for them, personnel are not respected and are significantly underpaid, and there are no clear agreements as to what is and is not permissible. This situation does not justify immoral conduct of employees, but it does make their moral slip understandable. "Opportunity makes the thief," does not take the blame off the thief. It is probably appropriate that in the case of Barings Bank, Nick Leeson was given a prison sentence. But when the circumstances contribute to the deed, they also deserve the blame. It is not only the employee who can be called to account in such a case. The organizational context should also be weighed. Rawnsley's study (1995) into the downfall of Barings Bank showed that trader Nick Leeson was granted a great deal of autonomy. He operated not only in the dealing room but also in the back office, whereas these two duties should be segregated in order to enhance control. The controls over Leeson were minimal: he had hardly been checked by his superiors. Leeson was the watchdog of his own deals. Barings as an organization failed at various levels and in a variety of ways to institute a proper system of internal control, to enforce accountability for all profits, risks and operations, and to follow up adequately on a number of warning signals over a prolonged period. Many of the staff had also been working under a great deal of pressure to perform and to score. There was a reward structure of attractive bonuses for large deals and a fierce culture of competition producing volatility and huge risk-taking. As the Governor of the Bank of England said: "It could have happened to anyone." Contextual ethics is concerned with the development of adequate structures and cultures in which employees can give expression to their responsibilities. In building up and developing responsible corporations, account should be taken of the influence the organizational context has on employee conduct. It makes sense to think through what the influence of the organizational context is and how this context can guide the intentions and intuitions of the employees correctly.

The desire for and awareness of responsible conduct from the employees is no guarantee for responsible conduct. Staff must also get the assets to give expression to their responsibilities. An employee who is responsible for dealing with stakeholder complaints, but is not given the time, information or support to do it, is not put in the position by the organization to give expression to the stakeholders' legitimate expectations. A corporation fails in a moral respect when certain responsibilities are not fulfilled because of a poor allocation of duties. In a cooperative relationship like a corporation, employees need to be given the authority, means, time, and information to be able to fulfill their responsibilities and to coordinate their actions among themselves.

I have stated that it is necessary to organize ethics when it is not enough to trust in the intentions and intuitions of the employees. Even if the employees are extremely honest and do their best to conduct themselves responsibly, a certain amount of responsibility could be lost. In other words, the way the corporation is organized, the organizational context, partially determines how employees voice the justified needs of stakeholders.

The need to organize ethics is partly a consequence of the increased decentralization within many companies. The organization of the corporation has long been based on a Taylorian hierarchical pyramid structure (Wijffels, 1991). Orders came from above, where knowledge was concentrated. The execution, partly due to a far reaching degree of division of labor, had a strongly mechanical character. Increasing turbulence of the corporate environment requires a greater degree of flexibility (Volberda, 1992). It becomes necessary that employees lower in the organizational hierarchy are given more decision-making responsibility. Only then a corporation will be able to respond adequately to the often quickly-changing environment. This decentralization leads to a shift in responsibilities. Employees in the lower echelons are given greater responsibilities. The corporation, thereby, has become more dependent on, and therefore vulnerable to, the intentions and intuitions of the employees. Management by command and control is often no longer enough. This leads to a situation where new management methods must be developed to protect and develop the ethics of the corporation.

2.3   Ethics management as discipline and practice

I would like to define ethics management as the systematic and coherent development of activities and the taking of measures in order to realize the fundamental and justified expectations of stakeholders and to balance conflicting expectations of stakeholders in an adequate way.

Ethics management is about the organization of ethics. The term management points to the activities and measures which are (a) more or less systematically or structurally thought through, (b) coherent, in that the different activities and measures are coordinated and not incompatible with each other, and (c) goal oriented, concerned with realizing the moral responsibilities of the corporation. Organizing ethics is about realizing the justified and fundamental expectations of stakeholders. In principle, all systematic and coherent activities and measures which contributed to the realization of one or more stakeholder interests could fall under ethics management. Considering that this includes many activities within a corporation (i.e. R&D can be in the interest of profit for stockholders, better products for consumers, or less waste for the environment), ethics management is involved when organizational issues are under discussion by which several fundamental stakeholder interests can be at odds. Organizing ethics is about stimulating a careful balance between conflicting interests. The issues are looked at from a normative-ethical perspective. Activities which are designed to increase client satisfaction (i.e. frequent-flyer miles or live music in a restaurant) cannot be called ethics management. Ethics management only comes into play if, for example, fundamental client interests could be in conflict with those of the corporation or other stakeholders and in which the steps to be taken are seen from the point of view of the corporation's moral responsibilities. Opening a telephone complaints line to substantiate the corporate responsibilities and to reduce any possible friction with customers could be viewed as ethics management.

Ethics management is about the reflection and development of the ethics of the whole corporation. Ethics management (or the management of ethics) is not the same as the ethics of management (Hosmer, 1991), ethics in management (Chakraborty, 1995) or management ethics (Evans, 1981). Management ethics describes and criticizes the norms and values held by the corporation's management. Management as an activity has its own moral questions, such as: what is a morally responsible way to spend time, how much use may management make of its position of power, what is a responsible way of gathering and distributing information, and what risks are acceptable with regard to policy and strategy? In ethics management, the emphasis is on ethics. In management ethics, the emphasis is on management.[ii]

Ethics management is not the same as culture management.[24] Ethics relates to situations where fundamental interests are at stake. Culture consists of norms and values which do not necessarily bring fundamental norms and values into risk. Corporate attire, etiquette, and parking spot assignments are frequently not morally relevant.[25] Furthermore, ethics management is not only concerned about the cultural aspects of a corporation, but also, for example, about the moral aspects of an organization's structure (i.e. sanction mechanisms and selection and recruitment procedures).

Ethics management is not the exclusive realm of the management.[26] In ethics management, the first consideration is not a position which is filled by someone (a so-called ethics manager), but the activities by which ethics are organized. As with many others activities in the corporation, though, management does play a central role and has a major moral duty in the organization of ethics (chapters 4 and 6 go into this in detail).

In the literature of business ethics, the organization of ethics is regularly discussed in terms of institutionalization (i.e. Weber, 1981, 1993, Tsalikis and Fritzsche, 1989, and Sims, 1991) and implementation (i.e. McCoy, 1985, and Murphy, 1988). These two terms are not the same. Institutionalization can be defined in two ways. According to the first definition, institutionalization refers to "an official agency" or "making something official." In this definition of institutionalization, the formaliza-

---

[23]   Ethics management is not the same as ethical management (see, for example, Blanchard and Peale, 1988, and Rion, 1990). Ethical management entails a positive judgment on the morality of the management itself.

[24]   Deal and Kennedy (1982) use the term "culture management."

[25]   In some cases, these aspects of culture are morally relevant. Corporate dress could be offensive or too sexy and the handicapped parking spaces can be at the far end of the parking lot.

[26]   This impression is implicitly created by, for example, titles such as *Die Moral der Manager* [The Morals of the Manager] (Fiedler, 1977) and *Deugden in de Directiekamer* [Virtues in the Boardroom] (Kimman, 1989).

tion or structuring of certain activities is what is at issue. An ethics committee is an example of the institutionalization of ethics within a corporation (see, for example, Weber, 1981). From this definition, Hummels (1996) proposes that institutionalization implies the risk of hindering, as opposed to facilitating, the reflection. The second definition reflects a sociological interpretation of the concept institutionalization. Institutionalization in this context means making something part of something else, incorporating something or setting a pattern (see, for example, Tsalikis and Fritzsche, 1989). "Implementing" means "introducing." Implementing ethics can take place either formally or informally. A manager can implement an ethics policy little by little by conducting a lot of discussions. The implementation affects both the "hard" (structure) and "soft" (culture) sides of the organizational context. Implementing is, therefore, broader than the first definition of institutionalization. Both concepts suggest a mechanical character, in the sense that what is being implemented or institutionalized is already recognized. Implementation implies a given set of measures. Ethics management is more. In organizing ethics, it is also about determining what should be institutionalized or implemented. Ethics management, as one of the management disciplines, is involved with developing instruments which contribute to the ethical development of a corporation, and methods that can be used to determine in what direction corporations should develop themselves. Ethics management involves making a description and analysis of the current situation, determining the desired situation, deciding which measures should be taken and activities implemented, and integrating these into the organizational context. Ethics management is about imbuing an organization with ethical responsibility as an indispensable element of the corporate existence.

In regards to the organization of ethics, we are faced with a paradox. On the one hand, the corporation seeks assurance of a communal awareness of responsibility. It is important that employees express the responsibility they bear on behalf of the corporation. On the other hand, the corporation needs to respect the intentions and intuitions of the employees. In striving towards a communal awareness of responsibility, the corporation has to respect the rights of employees as much as possible. The moral intuitions of the employees cannot be ignored. Indoctrination, manipulation or brainwashing can be very effective as extreme forms of socialization, but they are in conflict with the rights of individuals. A paradoxical demand is, then, made on the management of the corporation: respect for individual responsibility and at the same time ensuring a single communal awareness of responsibility. I would like to refer to this paradox as the ethics management paradox.

In this chapter, we have seen that the necessity of organizing corporate ethics depends, at least, on (a) the degree to which stakeholders are dependent on the efforts of the corporation for the realization of their expectations, and (b) the degree to which the intentions, intuitions and abilities of employees are insufficient to guarantee this effort from the corporation. I call the activities and measures which aim to organize ethics "ethics management." The management in particular bears responsibility for the management of ethics. Ethics management is a legitimate field of managerial practice because of the importance of ethics for the organization, the specific perspective from which organizations are seen (normative ethics), and because of the proper methods, skills and instruments for auditing, improving and safeguarding the ethics of organizations, which we will delve into in the next chapters.

Chapter 3

The Ethical Company

Those who want to go with us,
must understand it is so, and thus.

Organizing ethics in a systematic way, puts at least three questions to us: what is the current situation, what is the desired situation, and how can the desired situation be achieved? Brigley (1995) calls the discrepancy between the desired and the current moral situation the ethics gap. An ethics audit is a systematic approach for identifying the ethics gap. This chapter will consider the definition of an ethics audit and the elements of such an audit. One important element of the current and desired moral situation is the ethical content. The ethical content is the extent to which we can label a corporation ethical or moral. Section two of this chapter provides a definition of the ethical content of a corporation. This chapter closes with an overview of different examination methods, including the method which illuminates the ethical content.

3.1   An ethics audit as diagnostic tool[27]

The word "audit" is derived from the Latin "audire" meaning "to listen." Retired officers in the Roman army were taken on as auditors to listen to problems and complaints of the soldiers. Because they were so well regarded, and also had practical experience, they were particularly suited for catching developing problems at an early stage. They subsequently advised the army leadership as to how the problems could best be solved. "Audire" has come down to us in words like "audition." To do an audition means to show your expertise. The audience determine, on the basis of a relatively quick impression and on a number of criteria, which person is best qualified to carry out a certain task.

An audit of a company has the same purpose. Based on a number of measurements, the auditor makes a pronouncement on a certain aspect of the company being audited. Holding companies up to the light is a daily activity for consultants and financial auditors. A management consultant identifies the bottlenecks, analyses the causes, and, if asked, suggests ways to improve the functioning of the company. The most developed and applied corporate audit is the financial audit carried out annually by auditors. An auditor makes a declaration of whether a company's reported financial returns can be trusted. The income statements show how the company fared financially over the auditing period, while the balance sheet shows the financial position at the end of that period. But auditing a company is not limited to these two types. Others include the quality audit, environmental audit, legal audit, criminal audit, and security audit. Based on information gathered and analyzed by the auditor, and the conclusions arising from them, the client can then take appropriate action. In an internal used audit, the results are intended for internal purposes. External used audits focus on providing insight to third parties. External used audits reduce the risk that outsiders will make incorrect decisions based on incorrect information. The principal can be the corporation or, just as well, a stakeholder. An internally driven audit is initiated by the corporation itself, while an externally driven audit is initiated by an external stakeholder. Ex-post audits are mainly intended to provide an account of performed corporate activities or to call corporations to account, or both. Ex-ante audits are more prospective than retrospective by nature and are mainly intended to provide input for future policy.

One type of audit that deserves special attention here is the social audit.[28] In the United States, the idea developed in the mid-1960's that social performance could be

---

[27]   This section was largely published earlier as "Een morele audit voor bedrijven: een eerste aanzet," in *NOBO-Bundel, sixth research conference*, Nederlandse Organisatie voor Bedrijfskundig Onderzoek, 1993, pp. 123-130.

[28]   Some publications in this area are: C. Abt, *The Social Audit for Management*, Amacom, 1977; R. Bauer and D. Fenn, *The Corporate Social Audit*, Russel Sage Foundation, New York, 1972; R. Bauer and D. Fenn, "What is a corporate social audit?," *Harvard Business Review*, January-February 1973; D. Blake, W. Frederick and M. Myers, *Social Auditing: evaluating the impact of corporate programs*, Praeger Publishers, New York, 1976; J. Corson and G.E. Steiner, *Measuring Business's Social Performance: the corporate social audit*, Committee for Economic Development, New York, 1974; J. Humble, *Social Responsibility Audit: a management tool for survival*,

systematically assessed just as economic performance could (Blake et al., 1976). The first attempts were largely concerned with expanding conventional financial reporting to include information on corporate social expenditure. Several types of social audits have been developed over time. In some cases, the social audit was used to determine how much of the corporation's own social goals had been achieved over the auditing period. In other cases, the social consequences of the corporation's activities, such as the number of employees from minority groups, were brought numerically into view and compared among companies. The point of departure for this type of social audit is, according to Blake et al., (1976), often unconstructively critical and linked to a form of activism. In the United States, social reporting practices were a response to increasing criticism from stockholders and the general public. The information collected during the audit was used by stakeholders to call corporations to account and, if necessary, to take action to correct their wrongs. In very few cases, attempts were made to measure the contribution of the corporation to society using cost-benefit analyses (i.e. Linowes, 1972). The social costs and returns were summed up in financial terms in an income account using traditional accountancy procedures.[29]

A 1986 study in the United States by the Center for Business Ethics shows that 43 percent of the Fortune 500 companies audited their social performance in one way or another. The areas investigated included: equal opportunities at work (89%), compliance with laws and regulations (81%), involvement with the local community (67%), workplace safety (65%), product and service quality (57%), protection of the environment (55%), compliance with laws in foreign countries (50%), and safety of products and services (44%). The information obtained from these social audits is not limited to internal use. These social audits have an external function too: they give external stakeholders insight into the corporation's actions.[30] Companies may include a few pages in their annual financial reports to inform readers of their social performance. Yet, according to Paul (1987), most US corporations were in the 1980's not enthusiastic about the publication of the results, because they were afraid that providing information to the public would lead to increased activism from certain stakeholders whose capacity to articulate specific demands would be strengthened by increased information.

During the 1980's, another type of social auditing developed in the United States. Stakeholder groups such as consumers, employees, and investors audited various aspects of the social performance of corporations. The results of their investigations were released in publications such as *Rating America's Corporate Conscience,*

Foundation for Business Responsibilities, NIVE, 1973; and S. Zadek, P. Pruzan and R. Evans, *Building Corporate AccountAbility: emerging practices in social and ethical accounting, auditing, and reporting,* Earthscan Publication, 1997.

[29]   Solomon and Hanson (1985) propose a social balance sheet with all the activities that a corporation should and does do on the debit side, and all the activities that a corporation should but does not do, or should not but does, on the credit side.

[30]   In the literature, this external function is repeatedly stressed. See, for example, J. Humble, *The Organization of Social Responsibility: the social responsibility audit,* Foundation for Business Responsibilities, NIVE, 1973.

Shopping for a Better World, The 100 Best Companies to Work for in America, Ethical Investing: how to make profitable investments without sacrificing your principles, and the journals *Working Mother* and *Black Enterprise*.[31] Companies which do not wish to participate in the audits are dealt with critically by the researchers. These books and magazines do not only seek to influence the choices made by consumers, employees and investors, but are, according to Paul and Lydenberg (1992), especially intended to influence the corporations themselves. If stakeholders are more aware of the (mis)conduct of a corporation, they can decide to end their relationship with the corporation if it does not meet their expectations. Knowing this, corporations may take timely measures to consolidate trust.

According to Mahoney (1990), social audits, which identify the social consequences of corporate activities, have some serious shortcomings. In the first place, the problem with social audits is that they are quite labor intensive. To identify the social consequences of the corporate activities over a given period is an immense task. In the second place, a quantification of the social consequences is quite arbitrary. In the third place, voluntary external reporting has been done reluctantly by companies, because they do not want to air their dirty laundry in public. According to Weiss (1994), the problems with the use of the social audit have largely been in the measurement techniques used.

A social audit makes pronouncements on the social consequences of corporate activities. The social consequences are highly relevant for an ethics audit, but an ethics audit can, as further discussed in Section 3.3, cover more ethical aspects of an organization's functioning than its social consequences alone. The examination method by which the social consequences of an organization's activities are identified will be defined at the end of this chapter as a stakeholder audit or reflector. Here, it is important to point out that an ethics audit contains more elements of corporate functioning than a social audit. In the following chapters it will appear that organizations which seek to work on the protection and improvement of their ethics often require a different kind of information than that provided by a stakeholder audit.

I would like to define an ethics audit as a systematic approach which makes a description, analysis, and evaluation of the relevant aspects of the ethics of a corporation. The systematic and methodologically valid and reliable approach of the examination is characteristic of an audit. The method used should result in eliciting valid and reliable information which can serve as a basis for the evaluation by the principal. The choice of which aspects are included in an examination depends on what the audit is designed to achieve.

Besides social audits, little attention is given to ethics audits in the business literature. Madsen (1990) devotes a couple of sentences to an ethics audit. According to him, the examination of the internal organization is useful in order to trace the weak points which could lead to unethical conduct. According to Hill et al. (1992), an

---

[31]   These two journals regularly publish analyses of companies which offer positive work climates for women and blacks.

ethics audit should identify the situations where existing policy and control systems cause "ethical traps." Hill and others see the ethics audit as an instrument for an accountant to track down (possible) fraudulent dealings. The goal of an ethics audit is, according to Laczniak and Murphy (1991), to see if employees take their responsibilities seriously. Laczniak and Murphy consider an ethics audit to be a method of discovering where unethical conduct occurs. Madsen thinks more about the moral context of an organization than about the conduct itself. Ostapski and Pressley (1992) consider the goal of an ethics audit as the investigation of how much damage and return can be attributed to a corporation's activities. Ostapski and Pressley regard the object of an ethics audit not as the context or the conduct but as the consequences of corporate conduct for the stakeholders. De George (1990) follows the same line of reasoning. According to him, an ethics audit will identify the damage a corporation has caused. An ethics audit in his view can be quite useful if corporations are required to make the audit public. By publishing the audit in their annual reports, De George feels, corporations will be stimulated to adopt responsible conduct.

The aim of this study of ethics audits is the way in which the moral aspects can be revealed in order to improve the moral functioning of the organization and not to provide an account of performed activities to the stakeholders. The corporation itself takes the initiative to carry out the audit to use the results largely internally. In this study, therefore, I will not discuss the possibility of, for example, an ethics auditor who (a) periodically audits the company on behalf of an external stakeholder (i.e. the government, lenders or clients), and publishes a declaration of morally-responsible conduct, (b) verifies the accuracy of the ethics report prepared by the company itself, or (c) issues an ethics certificate. An ethics audit should, then, not remain limited to identifying the harm to stakeholders. Equally, the results of the audit should, by definition, not be released to the public. After all, the process of ethics development could require the organization and its staff to be put in such a sensitive position that the release of such information to the public could have counterproductive effects.

The crucial question arising from the definition of an ethics audit formulated here is: which relevant parts can be distinguished in an ethics audit? The next section takes up one of these aspects, the ethical content of the corporation. Section 3.3 will discuss the other parts of an ethics audit.

3.2   The ethical content defined[32]

I would now like to discuss nine misconceptions regarding the definition of the ethical content of a corporation. By setting out these misconceptions, it will become clear what can be understood by ethical content. Finally, I will define the ethical

---

[32]   This section was largely published earlier as "Een morele thermometer als instrument om het morele gehalte van een organisatie te meten," in H. Rijksen (ed.), *Onderwijs in Bedrijfsethiek*, Damon, Best, 1996, pp. 48-68.

content or degree of ethics of a corporation as the extent to which the actual organizational context stimulates and facilitates the personnel to realize the justified and fundamental expectations of the stakeholders and to balance conflicting expectations in an adequate way. The ethical content is the extent to which we could consider the organization moral or ethical. Therefore, the following question has to be answered: what has to be improved or decreased when we claim a corporation has become more or less ethical?

Misconception 1: The ethical content can be determined by what the corporation says it does.

Outsiders sometimes describe a corporation as moral or ethical based on what is said during a conversation with one or more employees. There can be, however, a substantial difference between what a corporation says it does and what it really does. Beautiful speeches about the interests of the stakeholders do not necessarily mean that a company is really stakeholder oriented. Such statements can be a form of window dressing, or ignorance about what is really going on within one's own organization. It is, therefore, a false assumption to think that the ethical content can be deduced from what the director says.

Misconception 2: The number of violations of law can be used as a yardstick for the ethical content.

The minimal level of morally responsible conduct is obeying the law (Robin and Reidenbach, 1991).[33] Moral responsibilities go further, however. Obeying the law does not imply that such a company is also functioning morally. Not everything that is considered morally (un)desirable is necessarily covered by legislation (see Stone, 1975, Mullighan, 1992, and Trevino and Nelson, 1995). If companies behave themselves as morally responsible through self-regulation, the government may have less incentives to legislate. In addition, it is simply impossible to cover all (im)moral conduct with regulations and legislation.

Misconception 3: The ethical content can be measured by the degree to which employees conduct themselves in the interest of the organization.

When a company is said to be immoral because the personnel systematically appropriate goods, money, information, and time belonging to the corporation, the ethical content is being equated with internal criminality, fraud, corruption, or internally reprehensible conduct. The morality of a corporation is not limited to the way in which employees deal with the interests of the organization, but also with the interests of the stakeholders, such as the personnel itself, stockholders, suppliers, buyers, consumers, and nearby residents. A company does not deserve an excellent moral reputation if, although employees are dealing carefully with the corporate assets, it knowingly ignores legitimate stakeholder expectations on a large scale. An ethical

---

[33] With the exception of some forms of civil disobedience in which the law is disobeyed in a morally responsible fashion.

corporation is, therefore, more than a corporation where the personnel do not misuse the company's assets.

Misconception 4: The ethical content can be determined by the degree of moral responsible conduct in one respect.

A company may be categorized as ethical or unethical based on a single incident. "This company is a morally responsible corporation because it withdraws its health-threatening product from the market," is an example of such reasoning. Many case study books in the field of business ethics, such as Velasquez (1992) and Jennings (1996), stimulate such isolated thinking because corporations are judged on a case-by-case basis. Of course, withdrawing the product is a morally praiseworthy action, but such an incident does not guarantee a similarly positive evaluation of all other conduct of the corporation. Furthermore, withdrawing a damaging product from the market can also constitute a public relations maneuver. A corporation that donates ten percent of profits to charity does not make it, thus, a perfectly morally praise-worthy organization. The profit could come at someone else's expense.

Misconception 5: The ethical content can be determined by the degree of morally responsible conduct in a limited number of activities.

The earlier-mentioned book, *Rating America's Corporate Conscience*, in which the 500 largest US corporations are ranked according to their conscience, presumes that the ethical content can be determined by the degree of responsible conduct in several activities. To determine the ethical conscience, the companies rated in the book are evaluated according to five criteria: (1) the amount of charitable donations, (2) the percentage of women and minorities as managers and supervisors, (3) the degree to which socially-relevant information is made known, (4) the degree of involvement during the apartheid era in South Africa, and (5) the degree of involvement with conventional and nuclear weapons. Although this is a relatively simple measurement to carry out (and, therefore, quite useful for some purposes), a positive evaluation on these five criteria does not mean a positive evaluation on the total ethics of a corporation. Should we not modify our evaluation if a company appears to positively fulfill these five criteria, but repeatedly and knowingly causes excessive and unnecessary damage to the environment, abuses employees, and ignores every justified criticism of corporate activities from outside the organization? A company that sells products with unnecessarily high risks to consumers does not deserve moral applause. For judging the ethics of a corporation, five criteria alone are not enough. Therefore, a broader spectrum of criteria ought to be included in the evaluation of the ethics of a corporation.

Misconception 6: The ethical content is the total sum of morally responsible conduct.

A product can have detrimental effects for users despite all the best efforts of a company. Nor can one blame a company when, due to the great social need for the product, it is forced to cause damage to the environment or, because of an economic recession and despite a thoroughly discussed policy, it has to lay off personnel. The evaluation of the ethical content is not about conduct or the results of the conduct (as, for example, Weiss, 1994, does), but about the intentions which lie behind it: the degree to which the company attempts to realize the interests of the stakeholders. We can consider the intentions as good or bad because they correspond with conduct that we label good or bad. When we know what good or bad conduct is, and what causes it, we can attribute a desirable characteristic to the cause. In an evaluation, it matters if conduct occurred by coincidence or conscious effort. When we say that "someone meant well," we acknowledge that despite the consequences of the conduct, the intentions of the person were praiseworthy. Similarly, when someone does something good by mistake, that is not viewed as evidence of a moral, honorable personality. A corporation can, therefore, be quite moral although the interests of several stake-holders are damaged, and a corporation can be seen as quite immoral without stake-holders' interests being damaged (if there is a favorable turn of events). A corporation which, for example, causes little damage to the environment, is not, necessarily, more moral than a corporation whose operations have disastrous reper-cussions for the environment. A moral evaluation of a corporation is about the effort, the intentions, of a corporation rather than the actual realization of stakeholders' expectations. Is the morality of the employees, then, the intention behind corporate conduct?

Misconception 7: The ethical content is equal to the average of individual morality of the personnel.

Recent years have seen an increased interest in applying Kohlberg's typology (1981, 1984)[34] to corporations.[35] In doing so, the moral level of reasoning used by personnel with regard to various dilemmas is analyzed and averaged so that the corporation can be placed on one of the levels of Kohlberg's model. This approach presumes apparently that corporate conduct results from the individual morality of the personnel. The implication is that the average of the individual morality equals the organization's morality. Employees act on behalf of the corporation and represent the corporation in their work. Their conduct, though, is not only determined by their own individual beliefs, but also by their surroundings, the situation they find themselves

---

[34]   Over 20 years, on the basis of insights from Sigmund Freud, Jean Piaget and others, Kohlberg developed a model for evaluating the moral development of individuals. His model proceeds from a cognitive development, the nature of the reasoning of employees, in which continually new interaction patterns with one's surroundings are constructed in consecutive stages. Kohlberg's arrangement consists of six stages: (1) punishment, (2) reward, (3) interpersonal agreement, (4) law, (5) social contract, and (6) universal principles. According to Kohlberg, this division is universal: independent of religion, culture, place, time, and social class. The arguments people use when faced with a dilemma depends on one's level at the time. For example, a person who does not do some-thing because he would be punished, falls into category one. At stage three, people look at what the small group around them considers to be morally desirable or undesirable.

[35]   Attempts in this regard have been undertaken by Trevino (1986), Wood et al. (1988), Weber (1990), and Pearson (1995). According to Pearson, companies do function according to Kohlberg's conventional level.

in. Part of the personnel's surroundings is the organizational context, the structure and culture of the organization. This organizational context exercises, as we saw in Chapter 2, a stimulating, limiting or correcting influence on the conduct of employees. A corporation is not a 'tabula rasa,' an empty entity, but, in the course of its existence it develops its own morality which influences the conduct of employees. It is the organizational context which separates the organization from the personal intentions and intuitions of the employees.[36] When we speak of the ethical content of a corporation, we are really talking about the corporation itself rather than the individual morality of the employees.[37] This is the crucial difference between the ethics of the corporation (corporate ethics) and the ethics of the people within the corporation (individual ethics).

Misconception 8: The ethical content is equal to the extent to which the formal organizational context stimulates the moral behavior of employees.[38]

The temptation is great to extrapolate the corporate context from what is formally or explicitly expected of employees. Many organizations have a large number of formal rules, guidelines and procedures. The fact of having adopted these measures does not of itself imply that they are followed in practice. The Herald of Free Enterprise disaster[39] in 1987, off the coast of the Belgian port town of Zeebrugge, was not attributable to the fact that no handbooks existed with rules and regulations regarding the safety of the boat and the passengers. One of the principal accusations directed at ferry company P&O Lines was that the crew ignored the handbooks and that, although management was aware of this, no measures were taken. A sloppiness virus was dominant.[40] Rules and guidelines can be simply a thin layer of varnish covering the immoral practices beneath. Evans says, correctly, that: "The fact that a company

---

[36] French (1984) posits that a corporation is a conglomerate instead of an aggregate because of the presence of cohesion, structure, and purposiveness. The characteristics of a conglomerate cannot be reduced to a sum of its individual characteristics.

[37] In the past few years, a number of moral typologies of managers have been developed. Steinmann and Lohr (1992) differentiate four types of managers: Eichmann, Richard III, Faust, and Organization Man. Hitt (1990) differentiates four moral leadership styles: leaders as manipulators (in which the ends justify the means), as bureaucratic administrator (in cases where strict attention is paid to rules), as professional manager (with a social contract ethic), and as transforming leader (in which individual ethics takes the lead). Weiss (1994) differentiates three types of managers: manager I sees rights and duties as the most important elements, manager II for whom fairness is the theme for conduct, and manager III who is led by exploitation and egoism.

[38] Pearson (1995) identifies the corporation's integrity by asking whether there is a written code of conduct, whether ethical performance is reported in the annual report, and whether attention is paid to ethics in training.

[39] The ferry-boat Herald of Free Enterprise capsized because the front loading-doors on this roll-on/roll-off ship were left open upon sailing, water rushed in, destabilized the ship, and in the ensuing calamity 197 people were killed.

[40] The official inquiry of 1987 laid the blame firmly on serious negligence within the company: "All concerned in management, from the members of the Board of Directors down to the junior superintendents, were guilty of fault in that all must be regarded as sharing responsibility for the failure of management. From top to bottom the corporate body was infected with the decease of sloppiness." (*Herald of Free Enterprise*, Report of Court No. 8074, Formal Investigation, HMSO, London, p. 14).

has a code of business ethics does not make the business itself ethical" (1991:871). No more than having an ethics hot line, a telephone line where employees can report their grievances, complaints, and problems anonymously, in and of itself makes ethical problems open for discussion. The ethical content cannot be deduced from the number of ethical instruments put in place. The opposite may just as well apply: ethical instruments may be implemented where the ethical content is not at its desired level. A corporation that in a jiffy decides to adopt ten new measures to reduce unethical conduct cannot be suddenly defined as more ethical. An organization that keeps adopting more and more measures to reduce unethical conduct does not necessarily become more ethical. Therefore, the ethical content cannot be located in the formal or explicit organizational context. In evaluating the ethical content, one must determine how the staff actually is stimulated: the actual organizational context. The actual organizational context of a corporation is the way employees are actually stimulated in their daily practice. In short, the ethical content cannot be read from an ethics policy on paper but has to be "read" from the actual coordination of employees.

Misconception 9: The ethical content is equal to the extent to which the actual organizational context possesses a number of non-prescriptive characteristics.

The ethical content of an organization is the degree to which employees' morally responsible conduct is stimulated or hindered by the actual organizational context. In the business ethics literature, the typology developed by Victor and Cullen (1987, 1988, 1989) is a frequently cited model for describing the ethical climate of organizations. This typology is not appropriate to describe and develop the ethical content of a corporation because (a) it does not give a complete overview of the possible relevant factors in the organizational context, (b) it provides no grounds for evaluating the current situation, and (c) it provides no direction for the organization's development. Based on Kohlberg's theory, Victor and Cullen have developed a two-dimensional matrix of nine theoretically possible ethical climates. The first dimension of the matrix refers to types of criteria, the second dimension to the level of analysis. Kohlberg (1981) specifies three major types of ethical standards: self-interest, caring, and principle. These three standards also reflect three major classes of ethical theory: egoism, utilitarianism, and deontology. These theories may be distinguished in terms of their basic motives, i.e., maximizing one's own interests, maximizing joint interests, or adherence to universal principles. According to Victor and Cullen, the climates of an organization also evolve along a dimension similar to Kohlberg's ethical standards and the three types of ethical theory. In addition to the types of criteria, the level of ethical analysis or concern may help distinguish the types of climates found in organizations. The level of analysis ranges from the individual (in which the basis for ethical decision-making comes from within the employee), local (whereby the source of ethical role definitions and expectations come from within the focal organization), and cosmopolitan (in which case the source or reference for ethical decision-making is external to the individual and focal organization). Based on factor analysis, five types of ethical climates emerge.

- Climate of Caring: the most important concern is the good of all people in the company;
- Climate of Laws and Codes: in this type of corporation, the first consideration is whether a decision violates the law;
- Climate of Rules: in this type of corporation, it is very important to follow strictly the corporation procedures;
- Instrumental Climate: employees are expected to do everything in the interests of the company with no regard for the consequences; and
- Climate of Independence: in this type of corporation, employees are expected to follow their personal moral convictions.

Victor and Cullen limit the influence of the organizational context to how employees are stimulated in making moral choices. They describe the ethical climate as the (perceived) divided individual decision-making theories present in the stimulation of employees. The ethical climate entails the shared perceptions of what constitutes ethically correct behavior and how ethical issues should be handled. Identifying the ethical content of an organization would mean, according to this typology, to determine the ethical criteria that are used to resolve moral dilemmas. For example, do employees primarily use principle-ethical considerations or utilitarian considerations in their conduct? However, one cannot formulate universally valid moral criteria for solving moral dilemmas. It is sometimes moral to accept a gift worth a hundred dollars, while in other cases, receiving a gift worth five dollars is immoral. In some situations, laying off personnel is morally permissible (from an utilitarian perspective), while in other situations it would be morally objectionable to fire a part of the workforce (from a deontological perspective). In determining whether something is morally responsible or not, the situation itself will have to be looked at. Therefore, no universal ethical conduct prescriptions for corporations can be formulated. The main reservation against Victor and Cullen's typology is that it can only be used descriptively. It does not indicate the direction in which the corporation should develop (unless, as Victor and Cullen say, there is an Instrumental Climate). There is, for example, no reason why a Climate of Caring should be worse or better than a Climate of Rules. As a result, the theory of Victor and Cullen offers no basis for the description and focused development of the ethical content of corporations. Another reservation against the typology of Victor and Cullen is that the ethical climate is not the only organizational stimulating or hindering factor. The structure of the organization also influences the conduct of employees. If employees do not possess the authority to realize their tasks or if employees do not get sufficient information for properly executing their duties, the organizational context fails to stimulate employees to realize the organizational responsibilities. The location of ethical content is therefore not limited to the climate, the culture, or the implicit or informal organization.

The comments above regarding what the ethical content is not, have brought us closer to what we can understand as a corporation's ethical content. When talking about the ethical content of a corporation, we are speaking about the moral evaluation of the corporation itself, the actual or factual moral stimulation of employees by the corporation. The context stimulates the employees' conduct in a positive or a negative way. The central question surrounding the description of the ethical content of an organization is "what does the organization add to the intentions, intuitions, and abilities of the personnel and where does the organization put pressure on the intentions, intuitions, and abilities of the personnel?" The ethical content of an organization concerns the moral quality of the coordination of the morale of employees collectively and not the individual or divided morality of the employees. An organization is based on what it actually expects from its personnel. In describing the ethical content, we must expose the institutional logic: identifying those organizational factors which create stimuli and impediments for ethical or unethical conduct. The ethical content of an organization can then be described as how the actual corporate context stimulates and facilitates employees to realize the justified and fundamental expectations of stakeholders and to balance conflicting expectations in a responsible way.

In determining the organization's ethical content, it is not necessary to identify what the justified expectations of the stakeholders are. The ethical content of an organization is about the evaluation of conditions within the organization that make a correct balancing of the conflicting interests of stakeholders possible. In that way, we avoid the necessity of, based on deontological or consequential ethical concepts, identifying which interest has priority over the other interests on a case-by-case basis. It is, after all, impossible to develop an adequate theory to indicate in minute detail what conduct is responsible and irresponsible in every situation. That would imply that there is only one solution for every moral dilemma. By making an analysis of which ethical context factors stimulate and which put pressure on the realization and respect of the interests of the stakeholders, morally desirable characteristics can be traced by which the organizational context can be evaluated from an ethical perspective. In doing so, it will become possible to develop a normative ethical theory that is applicable to every organization.

Evaluation of the ethical content has to be carried out on the basis of a relevant entirety of virtues or qualities.[41] Qualities are characteristics of the organizational context worth aiming for.[42] The degree to which a corporation achieves these qualities reflects the ethical content of the corporation. When a corporation achieves these qualities completely, one can label it as an ethical corporation. In the words of Aristotle, the necessary conditions, qualities or virtues have been achieved in order to

---

[41]   Solomon (1992b) formulates a great diversity of virtues for corporations, such as honesty, courage, benevolence, modesty, cheerfulness, toughness, sincerity, sensitivity, helpfulness, warmth, and hospitality. The qualities formulated by Solomon do not specifically apply to organisations, but apply to all human behaviour. His summary lacks cohesion and with equal ease one could add or remove one or more virtues.

[42]   In the original Greek or Latin, the term "virtue" does not contain the idea of a "must" but the idea of potential: developing to the best of one's ability.

realize the goal desired (read: the corporate mission).[43] The ethical content entails the moral virtuousness or excellence of a corporation. An ethical corporation is so constructed that maximum effort is made so as to realize the fundamental and legitimate expectations of the stakeholders. In developing an ethical corporation, it is, therefore, important to identify the degree to which the corporation possesses the relevant qualities. An audit of organizational moral qualities (the so-called Qualities Monitor) provides insight into the degree to which employees are empowered to realize the justified expectations of stakeholders.

Outside the corporation there are innumerable temptations and risks to which the personnel could be exposed. Staff who hold positions with a great deal of external contact have, according to Stead et al. (1990), a greater potential for moral conflicts than staff who hold positions with exclusively internal contacts. Significant competitive pressures increase the chance that only those stakeholders who can influence the competitive position will be included in decisions. For the ethical content, the important issue is what the corporation does to withstand these sorts of external factors and temptations which put moral conduct under pressure. An audit of the organizational qualities, in other words, identifies the defensible and vulnerable spots of an organization.

Vulnerable spots vary from relatively benign to very dangerous. The degree to which a vulnerable spot is dangerous depends on what is at stake and the chance of the conduct occurring. The vulnerability of an object is the degree to which something will not remain intact under certain conditions. A Qualities Monitor shows which context factors constitute the moral vulnerability of a corporation and the degree to which these factors are present, without making a prediction of the frequency at which unethical conduct will actually occur and what the consequences will be.[44] A Qualities Monitor identifies the actual moral risks of a corporation.

---

[43] For David Hume, every spiritual quality that results in love and pride is a virtue. Hume first determines the goal and sets the qualities in it afterwards. Plato follows a similar path in *Politeia*. In this instance, qualities are those characteristics that lead to ethical behavior: behavior geared towards fulfilling justified claims. The goal, therefore, leads to the qualities. Aristotle realized that one could not discuss the character of a morally good person without taking into account the social conditions required for the development of such a person. Personal morality requires institutional or organizational measures. The just city meets the necessary requirements for citizens to be morally good. The citizens in their turn create in this way a good society. The ethical content of a corporation is, to use a similar sort of definition, the degree to which a context is created in which the employees can give expression to their responsibilities. This study uses Plato's model of reasoning: we will seek the qualities the corporation ought to possess from a definition of the moral desired corporate mission.

[44] The analogy of a dike's vulnerability, the degree to which a dike resists a given water level, may offer some clarification. The weaker the dike, the sooner the dike will fail in the face of increasing pressure. In determining the likelihood that the dike will fail in the coming period, we need to look not only at its vulnerability, but also at the likely water level and other influences, such as the number of moles, the traffic, and the vegetation on the dike. Although the vulnerability is related to the water level, a prediction of a break in the dike is much more complex. There is a difference between the expression that with the spring tide, a north-west wind and a long-lasting water level of 4,5 meters above sea level, the dike will fail, and the expression that the chance that the dike will fail is equal to once in 150 years.

3.3   Six parts of an ethics audit: a brief outline

An ethics audit consists of the systematic examination of one or more morally relevant elements. An audit of the ethical content is identified by the term Qualities
Monitor. The parts that can be distinguished in an ethics audit for describing and
improving the actual moral position of a corporation, are as follows:
    1. Qualities Monitor
    2. Measures Scan
    3. Individual Characteristics and Circumstances Assessment
    4. Dilemmas Decoder
    5. Conduct Detector
    6. Stakeholders Reflector

The interrelationship of these parts can be illustrated as follows.

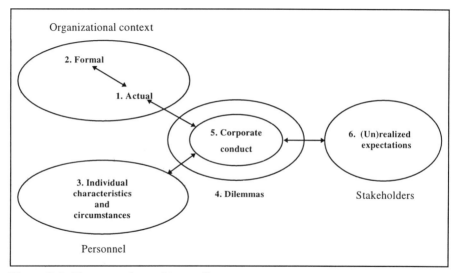

Figure 3-1: Elements of an ethics audit.

Individual and collective conduct is influenced by the organizational context, the
stakeholders' expectations and the characteristics and private circumstances of the
employees themselves. Corporate conduct leads to either the realization of or infringement upon the stakeholders' expectations. Personnel are confronted with moral
dilemmas when they perceive incompatible moral expectations among the stakeholders or between the stakeholders and the organization. The formal organizational
context attempts to guide the actual organizational context.

The different parts of an ethics audit are briefly set out below, following the num-
bering of Figure 3-1. Chapter 5 covers the audit types in detail.

1. Qualities Monitor

A monitor is usually an instrument which observes or checks how something operates or functions. A monitor of the organizational qualities determines the degree to which the corporation possesses certain relevant moral characteristics.

2. Measures Scan

A Measures Scan is a method for identifying and analyzing the formal organizational context insofar as it could impact the corporate ethics. The formal organizational context, the blueprint of the organization, consists, among other elements, of procedures, systems, rules, instruments, written codes, handbooks, organizational charts, duty and job descriptions, and mission statements. During this scanning process, the auditor analyses where and to what extent the formal context offers insufficient assurances against unethical conduct by employees.

3. Individual Characteristics and Circumstances Assessment

An Individual Characteristics and Circumstances Assessment identifies the morally relevant characteristics and circumstances of the personnel. The individual characteristics consist of the intentions, intuitions and abilities of the personnel. In addition, private circumstances can be examined to the degree that this can increase the chance of unethical conduct. High personal debt or a relatively expensive lifestyle in comparison with personal income, for example, can increase the likelihood of unethical conduct.

4. Dilemmas Decoder

A Dilemmas Decoder is a label for the method the auditor uses to establish an overview of the different conflicting expectations employees are confronted with. The actual dilemmas could be formulated by employees during special Dilemma Gathering Sessions. The analysis of the dilemmas provides insight into the moral expectations the employees consider important. Like a normal decoder, a device forming part of a stereo system which separates sounds into channels, the Dilemmas Decoder unravels conflicting expectations and converts these expectations into a clear and productive picture.

5. Conduct Detector

A detector is usually an apparatus which reveals the presence of something (a lie-detector is an example of such an apparatus). A Conduct Detector is the method which the auditor can use to reveal the actual (un)ethical conduct of the personnel and the corporation as a whole. For example, the auditor can examine whether bribes are offered or accepted, whether company property is used for private purposes, and whether confidential information is sold to competitors.

6. Stakeholders Reflector

A Stakeholders Reflector is an instrument for bringing the stakeholders' expectations into view and for revealing the degree to which the organization fulfills those expectations.

The selection of the audit parts to be deployed, depends also on the function of each part. Five functions an ethics audit can fulfill, are:
a.   descriptive: an ethics audit shows the current situation;
b.   normative: the desired situation is formulated on the grounds of a description of the current situation, or the current situation is described on the grounds of a pre-formulated, desired situation;
c.   discrepancy-identifying: an ethics audit shows the discrepancy between the current and the desired situation;
d.   sanctioning: an ethics audit provides information for sanctioning individuals and departments; and
e.   evaluative: by carrying out multiple ethics audits over time, improvements or deteriorations regarding the aspects under review can be determined.

In the table below, the functions that can be carried out are discussed for each audit type.

Function Parts	Descriptive	Normative	Discrepancy -identifying	Sanc- tioning	Evalu- ating
1. Qualities Monitor	+	+	+	+/-	+
2. Measures Scan	+	+	+	-	+
3. Ind. Char. & Circ. Assessment	+	+	+	-	+
4. Dilemmas Decoder	+	+	-	-	-
5. Conduct Detector	+	+	+	+/-	+
6. Stakeholders Reflector	+	+	+	+/-	+

Figure 3-2: Functions of audit parts (+ is for applicable, - for non-applicable, and +/- for partially applicable).

No single part of the ethics audit may fulfill all five of the functions completely. The Qualities Monitor, the Conduct Detector and the Stakeholders Reflector do have the most functions. Due to insufficient evidence of blame, no single part of an audit is suitable for giving legitimate grounds for sanctions. The Conduct Detector could be used to track down fraud, corruption and rule-breaking in order to sanction employees; but in order to pronounce proper judgment over the blame of the person(s) concerned, it is desirable to have some insight into the degree to which the actual organizational context makes such unethical conduct possible or even stimulates it. The description of the formal organization, by means of the Measures Scan, should generally be used in conjunction with other audits. Which measures have to be taken and which activities have to developed do not automatically ensue from the description of what is formally done in the present situation. The Measures Scan provides normative information if the auditor investigates where the formal organizational context leaves room for unethical conduct (for example, if the cash in hand is managed and checked by the same employee). The Individual Characteristics and Circumstances Assessment can be used normatively and analytically when the results of this audit are coupled with the desired personnel morals profile compiled by the company. The Dilemmas Decoder has a descriptive function insofar this method identifies which dilemmas occur in the organization and has a normative function insofar it clarifies which norms and values employees deem worthy of striving for.

The next chapter discusses how a Qualities Monitor can be constructed. Chapter 5 discusses the other parts of an ethics audit in more detail.

PART II

AUDITING THE ETHICAL CONTENT

Chapter 4

The Ethical Qualities Model

"It is sometimes less difficult
for a new police officer
to become corrupt than
to remain honest."
(Knapp Commission, 1973)

In Chapter 3, we saw that the ethical content of corporations concerns the degree to which the actual organizational context stimulates employees to ethical conduct. The question then arises: what qualities should an ethics audit contain in order to be able to describe and evaluate the ethical content? In Chapter 5, I would like to discuss the audit which examines the organizational qualities formulated in this chapter. This chapter describes twenty-one qualities which comprise the criteria for the ethical content of a corporation.[45]

---

[45] I have published parts of this chapter in "De bedrijfscontext doorgelicht," in T. Geurts and J. de Leeuw (eds.), *Geef Bedrijfsethiek een Plaats*, Damon, Tilburg, 1992, pp. 72-93, "Bedrijfscultuur in ethisch perspectief," in J. de Leeuw and J. Kannekens (eds.), *Bedrijfsethiek*, Damon, Best, 1994, pp. 94-115, and "Een morele thermometer als instrument om het morele gehalte van een organisatie te meten," in H. Rijksen (ed.), *Onderwijs in Bedrijfsethiek*, Damon, Best, 1996, pp. 48-68.

4.1   A conceptual model of evaluating the ethical content of organizations

An audit of organizational qualities must meet a number of requirements. Three of them are:

a.   validity: what is measured must be related to the ethical con-
                        tent;

b.   completeness: what is measured should consist of the various as-
                        pects of the entire ethical content: all the elements of
                        which the corporate ethics is composed must be
                        included in the audit; and

c.   reliability: the results of the first examination of a corporation
                        must be comparable with the results of a second
                        examination held at a later time.

Efficiency considerations (so the measurements do not constantly need to be modified for the corporation in question) and the possibility of bench-marking (to compare among organizations) make it desirable that the measurement be standardized. In order to obtain a conceptual model that meets the requirements of validity and completeness, I have taken the following steps.

From the morally preferable corporate mission described in Chapter 1, I looked at how the organizational context stimulates and hinders the personnel to give expression to the justified and fundamental expectations of the stakeholders. The ethical content shows the vulnerability or defensibility of the corporation: it relates to the possibility that inadequate encouragement can lead to the stakeholders' expectations not being realized. The vulnerability of an organization lies in those factors which work against and hinder the realization of these justified expectations. The defensibility is formed by those factors which stimulate and facilitate the realization of those expectations. The defensibility and the vulnerability complement one another:[46] increasing the defensibility leads to a decrease in the vulnerability and vice versa.[47] As defensibility and vulnerability complement each other, I have studied a great number of cases where the organizational context had contributed to infringements on the stakeholders' expectations. By approaching the subject in this way, I obtained an overview of the factors in the organizational context that determine the vulnerability and defensibility. The factors identified can be typified as moral qualities. The ethical content is, therefore, the degree to which the relevant moral qualities are embedded in the organization. Two practical examples illustrate this approach:

---

[46]   This will be shown in analyses later in this chapter.

[47]   For example: the presence of context factor X increases the moral defensibility (or decreases the vulnerability) and the absence of context factor X increases the moral vulnerability (or decreases the defensibility).

I   A child has been drowned in a swimming pool. The child was neither old nor experienced enough to swim in the deep end. It is the responsibility of the lifeguard to send such children back to the shallow end and to rescue drowning children from the water. None of the lifeguards had prevented that the inexperienced child had ventured into deep water. In hindsight, it appeared that there were no lifeguards present at the time to supervise the pool. Several weeks earlier, the lifeguards had been instructed by the managers to begin cleaning up a half hour before closing time. Despite the protests of the lifeguards, the management would not change its mind. "If we do this, you can go home half an hour earlier, which subsequently will save wage costs for the pool," was the management's point of view. At the time of the drowning, the "responsible" lifeguard was gathering cleaning supplies at the back of the pool area.

In this case, the organizational context failed because the personnel were not given the means to carry out their duties. The quality which is applicable to the context is called "achievability" of tasks.

II   In March 1989, a tanker of a major oil company lost eleven million gallons of crude oil off the coast of Alaska, causing great environmental damage. Seabird deaths climbed from 28,000 in 1989 to 580,000 in 1991. Local fisheries lost at least twelve million dollars in income. The oil company spent more than three billion dollars in cleaning up the oil and incurred one billion dollars in damage claims. The organizational context contributed to this disaster. The tanker's information system was antiquated so contact with the harbor and the coast guard was lost at the crucial moment; the captain was under the influence of alcohol; an unqualified and tired third mate was at the helm when the tanker left the harbor; the crew was undermanned (smaller boats had 40 crew on board, the tanker only 24); the crew consumed low-alcohol beer, and the management had taken virtually no action when they became aware that the captain had had drinking problems for years. And finally, the emergency procedures were inadequate.

Context-related factors in this case are therefore: stakeholders had insufficient information, untrained personnel, high workload for personnel, insufficient crew strength, and no correction on improper conduct. The qualities which can be distilled from this case include "achievability in regard to carrying out duties," "openness towards stakeholders," and "sanctionability of improper conduct."

By collecting and analyzing diverse cases in which justified stakeholders' interests are damaged, we may gain insight into how the organizational context influences the conduct of employees. By gathering as many different kinds of cases as possible, we can obtain as broad a spectrum as possible of the factors comprising the organizational context of a corporation. Determining the degree to which a case damages stakeholders' interests and the degree to which these interests are justified is always open to argumentation. That is why so much effort has gone into searching for cases in which the violation of the rights and expectations of stakeholders was clear and the stakeholders, therefore, had substantial reasons for complaint. While it is conceivable that there will be differences of opinion as to the degree to which an expectation is legitimate in some cases, the end result will be the same.

I have followed the following steps in this research:

1. gathering various actual cases in which the organizational context contributes to the damage of the fundamental interests of one or more stakeholders;

2. analyzing each case with respect to the role of the organizational context supplemented with a study of the literature on the contextual factors that influence employee conduct; and

3. categorizing the factors derived into a conceptual model of the ethical content of organizations.

The empirical information was gathered by:

-   research of newspapers and magazines for unethical practices, between 1 January 1992 through 1 January 1995;
-   a Stakeholders Reflector in 1993 at an international oil company into the unrealized expectations of stakeholders and an analysis of how the organizational context contributed to this. That research was repeated in 1994 at a Dutch university;
-   an undercover investigation of a company which was harming many interests (1994);
-   an investigation of an international company known for its harmonious relationship with stakeholders (1994);
-   forty in-depth interviews among personnel at a profit (1993) and not-for-profit organization (1994); and
-   ninety in-depth interviews among employees of small and medium-sized companies (1995).

To keep things orderly, I would like to present the results of the steps in reverse order. First, the final conceptual model of the ethical content will be described (step three). After that, the qualities will be individually described (step two) and illustrated with a number of the cases (step one). Due to the confidential nature of the cases, they will be fictionalized.

The conceptual model of the ethical content below will be explained further in this chapter.

Dimensions Qualities	I. Coordination of responsibilities *in regards to* the corporation: "Entangled hands"	II. Coordination of responsibilities *within* the corporation: "Many hands"	III. Coordination of responsibilities *on behalf of* the corporation: "Dirty hands"
a. Clarity	1.	8.	15.
b. Consistency	2.	9.	16.
c. Sanctionability	3.	10.	17.
d. Achievability	4.	11.	18.
e. Supportability	5.	12.	19.
f. Visibility	6.	13.	20.
g. Discussability	7.	14.	21.

Figure 4-1: The Ethical Qualities Model.

There are three types of relationships which are relevant from a moral point of view: the relationship between the employee and the corporation as such, the relationship among employees, and the relationship between the corporation and its stakeholders. An analysis of every case demonstrated that the organizational context inadequately encouraged the employees in one or more of these types of relationships. The co-ordination of the interests, expectations and responsibilities was lacking morally in these relationships. The ethical content can also be described in three dimensions. The following sections discuss these dimensions at length. A short description follows below.

• The "entangled hands" dimension relates to the degree to which employees are stimulated to deal carefully with the assets of the organization. Employees have their own personal interests and expectations which do not necessarily parallel the interest and responsibilities of the corporation. I will use the "entangled hands" as a metaphor for the potential conflicts between the interests of employees and the interests of the organization in which the corporate assets are at stake. This dimension would be irrelevant if employees had no other interest than the interests of the corporation: employees would then have no motive to misuse the corporation's assets.

- The "many hands" dimension relates to the degree to which employees are stimulated to give expression to the individual and collective functional responsibilities they are assigned to do. Within an organization, each employee has his own job-related duties. The distribution of these functional responsibilities may be, however, coordinated inadequately, with the result that certain corporate responsibilities slip through the employees' many "fingers" or get lost. Unclear responsibilities can result in employees being sent from one department to another while collective problems remain unresolved because nobody feels personally responsible for them. An inadequate coupling of duties and authorities can also lead to collective responsibilities not being met. The metaphor of "many hands" points to the moral risks ensuing from the need to employ more than one employee in an organization. This dimension will be irrelevant if a corporation consists of only one person.

- The "dirty hands" dimension relates to the degree to which employees are directly stimulated to balance the interests of the stakeholders against the interest of the corporation. The "dirty hands" dimension concerns the degree to which those qualities are anchored in the organizational context which ensure a proper coordination with the stakeholders. If an organization had no stakeholders, this dimension would be irrelevant. The metaphor of "dirty hands" points to the efforts of the organization to keeps its "hands clean" (i.e. to realize the expectations of stakeholders). Employees are representatives of the corporation as well as a stakeholder group. The "entangled hands" dimension involves the gearing of responsibilities of the employees as representatives with respect to the organization. The "dirty hands" dimension involves the gearing of corporate responsibilities with respect to, for example, the employees as stakeholders.

These three dimensions are three different ways of describing the ethical content of a corporation. Just as the size of an object can be measured along three dimensions (height, breadth, and depth), so too can the ethical content be described using three qualifications (entangled, many, and dirty). From the earlier chapters, we could initially expect that the ethical content is only concerned with the "dirty hands" dimension. The ethical content is about the relationship with stakeholders, after all. The analysis of the cases shows that the two other dimensions are separate dimensions which give us a better insight into the ethics of an organization. In this respect, realizing the employees' duties ("many hands" dimension) is, by definition, not fully related to realizing the expectations of the stakeholders ("dirty hands" dimension).

An employee can perform his duties well while still taking the stakeholders for a ride. The dimension of "many hands" refers to the degree the organization is task-oriented (i.e. the extent to which employees are coordinated to realize the implicit and explicit stated individual and collective functional responsibilities). The dimension of "dirty hands" refers to the extent this task-orientation is related to the realization of the expectations of stakeholders (i.e. the degree of stakeholder-orientation). The "entangled hands" dimension refers to the degree employees are stimulated to deal carefully with the assets of the organization (i.e. the degree of organizational asset-orientation). The three dimensions of the ethical content are related to one another. A corporation bears responsibility for a good coordination of the "entangled hands" dimension because if this is not done, employees may deal carelessly with corporate interests. In this case the external stakeholders could be the victims. When employees take bribes from a supplier, this is not only harmful to their company, but also to the supplier who would otherwise have received the order.

From the practical cases, I was able to distill seven distinct criteria which are applicable to each of the three dimensions. We can call these criteria "ethical qualities." Qualities are the organizational dispositions that stimulate the employees to give expression to the corporate responsibilities in the three dimensions. If these qualities are inadequately embedded in the organization, the chance of the corporation failing its moral mission increases. In total, the matrix is made up of twenty-one cells, which collectively constitute the ethical content of an organization. A short description of the seven qualities follows. In the next sections, detailed descriptions will be presented.

Clarity relates to the degree to which the organizational expectations towards the moral conduct of employees are accurate, concrete, and complete. As it relates to the "entangled hands" dimension, clarity is the degree to which the organization is clear about how employees should handle corporate assets. Lack of clarity regarding the acceptance of gifts, for instance, can lead to uncertainty among employees, to the idea that "anything goes," and to moral inflation whereby practice moves steadily away from the desired norm. "Where gray areas are permitted to exist, slippery-slope frauds and petty pilfering flourish." (Charmichael, 1992:181). The clarity of the expectations in regards to the conduct of employees is, then, also the first criterion by which the context can be described. Without clarity, employees do not, after all, know what the organization expects from them; they remain in uncertainty without any apparent guidance from the organization.

Consistency concerns the degree to which the organizational expectations towards the moral conduct of employees are coherent, univocal, unambiguous, and compatible. In their conduct, employees take into account the conduct of those they emulate (referents). The management is an important reference group. The organization may well pose clear expectations in regards to the behavior of employees, but if the behavior of referents undermines these expectations, the guidance of employees may become inconsistent. Adequate guidance requires that the desired norms and values be exhibited by the referents.

Sanctionability refers to the degree to which negative or positive sanctions can be applied in connection with irresponsible or responsible conduct. Sanctions constitute important behavioral stimuli and are, thus, a relevant aspect of the organizational context. A context in which the expectations are clear and are borne by the referents is still vulnerable if unacceptable behavior is not punished, but rather tolerated instead. Unacceptable behavior that goes unpunished sends a signal out that meeting expectations is not important. It reduces the necessity for employees to keep to the desired norms and values.

Achievability concerns the degree to which responsibilities can be carried out. It is not only important that moral expectations meet the requirements outlined above, but that expectations can be carried out in practice. Being able to carry out the expectations means that the expectations are achievable in practice. In regards to the co-ordination in the case of the "many hands" dimension, specific responsibilities may not be achievable due to insufficient authority, lack of time and means, insufficient knowledge and skill, and a lack of information on the part of the personnel. Achievability in the "dirty hands" dimension relates to the degree to which the corporation creates unrealistically high expectations among the stakeholders.

Supportability is concerned with the support of employees for the proper use of the corporate assets ("entangled hands"), for the close cooperation with the immediate co-workers and supervisors ("many hands"), and for the active realization of the interests of the stakeholders ("dirty hands"). The context can have a negative influence on this support from employees. If employees are of the opinion that they are not taken seriously, this may cost their loyalty and care with the organization's assets ("entangled hands"). If employees cannot trust their co-workers or immediate supervisors, this may deteriorate the coordination and cooperation within the organization ("many hands"). If employees are not able to present the policy of the corporation to the stakeholders, this may indicate an inadequate support for the activities of the corporation ("dirty hands"). A context in which the quality supportability is embedded comprises the conditions under which employees are prepared to be united with the interest of the corporation, co-workers, and external stakeholders respectively. This quality relates to the stimulus of the organization for the recognition by employees of the moral expectations concerning the three dimensions.

Visibility relates to the degree to which the conduct of employees and the effects for employees can be observed. Where clarity relates to the moral expectations in regards to the behavior of employees (input), visibility relates to the consequences of their actions (output). Visibility has two components, a horizontal and a vertical. Vertical visibility is, for example, the degree to which managers know when one of their employees has behaved unacceptably (top-down) and employees know when their manager has behaved unacceptably (bottom-up). Horizontal visibility concerns the degree to which employees know when one of their own has behaved unacceptably. If the context is characterized by a great deal of visibility, employees are able to modify or correct their own behavior or that of co-workers, supervisors, or subordinates.

Discussability is the degree to which meeting responsibilities is open for discussion. It is the degree to which (a) dilemmas, (b) problems, and (c) criticism can be talked about. A context with a high degree of discussability means, for example, that lack of clarity in regards to expectations can be discussed. In such a context, unethical behavior can also be brought up for discussion.

I would like to discuss each cell in the matrix by dimension. The discussion of the "entangled hands" requires the most attention as the qualities are defined there for the first time. During the discussion of the qualities, the mutual relationship and the logical distinction among the qualities and dimensions is further developed. The qualities (often) relate quite closely to one another. Visibility and clarity are necessary conditions to bring unacceptable behavior up for discussion and, subsequently, to sanction it. Furthermore, a supervisor will, in most cases, only talk to an employee about his unethical behavior if the supervisor himself behaves ethically (consistency). No attention will be focused here on the degree to which a certain quality is embedded implies that one or even several other qualities are also fully embedded. This question can only be answered with the help of statistical analyses of empirical information, which falls outside the scope of this book (see Appendix 1 for the agenda for follow-up research). In chapters 5 and 7, a start is made in calculating the correlation between the ethical qualities of an organization in order to trace so-called core qualities. For the moment, this chapter is concerned with illustrating that there are twenty-one separate qualities.

4.2   The "entangled hands" dimension

The "entangled hands" dimension relates to the coordination among the different roles employees can play. Inadequate coordination can lead to damage to the corporation and its stakeholders. The damage for the corporation can be both material or immaterial and direct or indirect, and can occur in both the short and long term. The advantage that employees derive from improper use of corporate assets consists, among other things, of financial gain, status, pleasure, convenience, and appreciation from family and friends.

Corporations can only act through employees. As such, there is frequently the matter of entangled roles. An employee is not only an employee but a "multiple being." Nash (1990) calls this the "fragmentation of the self." An employee fills multiple roles simultaneously and wears more than one "hat," which can conflict with one another. Those who act on behalf of the corporation play at least two roles and, as a result, represent at least two types of interests. These types of interests may be conflicting with each other. Velasquez speaks in this context of a "conflict of interests" which occurs when "...an employee or an officer of a company is engaged in carrying out a task on behalf of the company and the employee has a private interest in the outcome of the task (a) that is antagonistic to the best interest of the company and (b) that is substantial enough that it does or reasonably might effect the independent judgment the company expects the employee to exercise on its behalf." (1992:377). Nash devotes a chapter ("Wearing two hats") in her book to this issue. She describes the "conflict of interests" as the "...discrepancy between one's private self and the person you become as part of a larger organization" (1992:213). In addition to their responsibilities in and on behalf of the corporation, employees have responsibilities to others, to family and friends. Still further, employees occupy social roles as residents, citizens and taxpayers. Employees of airports which lie in densely population areas often live close to the airport. The interest of the airport, such as expansion of the runways, can be at odds with the interests of the nearby residents, who have an interest in the reduction of noise levels. In his capacity as a representative of the airport, such an employee can unjustly work in the interest of his own benefit above that of his employer. Employees have their own interests as individuals which do not necessarily coincide with the interests and responsibilities of the corporation. Employee interests may include career, personal development, power, influence, standing, pleasure, comfort, and a pleasant working environment. When the interests of the corporation and the employee are at odds, this can lead to unbalanced choices being made by employees. An example is the employee who, without permission, uses company resources to print the football club newsletter. The employee takes advantage, the corporation incurs the damage. The "entangled hands" dimension concerns those issues stemming from employees who misuse their authority as such, thereby damaging the interests of the company. This involves issues such as improper use of (a) information, (b) funds, (c) goods, (d) equipment, (e) decision-making authorities, (f) colleagues, and (g) time. Some examples of misconduct that could result from inadequate coordination within this dimension include the following:

1. Transport truck drivers run their own small, private transport business by (unbeknownst to their boss) transporting goods for a small charge during working hours. During some months their additional revenues are as high as their official salaries.

2. The personnel of the Soup department of a foods producer are up to their ears in a stew of hate and envy. Harassment is rampant and without limit. In addition to gossiping about one another, charring each other's reputation with the management, destroying personal mail (including invitations to meetings), locking colleagues in the restroom stalls, destruction of personal property, and even fights are not uncommon. The personnel manager claims that at least 25 percent of productivity is lost on such harassment.

3. A bank director raises a company's credit limit in exchange for a good entry-level position for his unqualified son in the company.

4. As a reward for providing important confidential information to an organization considering a hostile takeover, an employee is given a position in the post-takeover management team.

5. The director is having an affair with his secretary. As a result, she receives a bonus roughly twice as high as is customary.

6. Managers award contracts to family members representing companies that charge too much. Once these practices came to light, purchase prices dropped ten percent on average.

7. The wife of a company's accountant is ill. As a result, the accountant often fails to turn up for work on time. He does not want to explain this to his boss. A secretary comes to the accountant's assistance and they agree that she will clock in for him when she arrives in the morning. After a while, the secretary asks him to alter the books so she can receive a raise -- she has been a bit strapped for cash lately. The accountant does this as compensation for her assistance.

The "entangled hands" problem would be irrelevant if employees only had interests that ran parallel with or were extensions of the corporate interests. According to Hardin, it is often the case that employee's interests and corporate interests are in conflict. This tension leads, according to him, to unethical conduct because "...the chief problem in motivating people to act for good outcomes on the whole is that their own interests are better served by acting against the general interest" (1988:35). Situations where employees put their interest above the corporate (or related) interests are risky in that it is possible that stakeholder interests can be damaged also. Permitting a large gift from a supplier is harmful to the corporate interest if it leads to the best supplier not being chosen. It also harms the "best" supplier, who misses out on an order that he otherwise would have received. An organization which does not, or only barely, deal with the "entangled hands" issue can generally be characterized by a "...freedom-happiness-equality philosophy or, more precisely defined, nothing-required, anything-is-possible attitude" (Blaauw, 1991:41). In relation to the "entangled hands" dimension, the ethical company can be characterized by the empowerment of employees to handle corporate assets the right way. The next seven qualities are applicable to the organizational context.

1. Clarity

The clarity factor is the degree to which the organization makes clear how employees should handle the corporate assets. Do employees know what is expected of them when they are faced with an "entangled hands" issue, problem or dilemma?

If all employees were to act at their own discretion, with no reference to anything else, the likelihood of censurable conduct would increase. Unclear standards incite to unacceptable conduct (Grijpink, 1995). A corporation which makes no attempt to define what is acceptable or unacceptable, may give employees too much freedom. Accepting and giving gifts is a typical example of a gray area. What is the difference between a gift and a bribe? Accepting a ball-point pen is generally allowable, but can the same be said of a weekend away with the family at the supplier's expense? A corporation which does not draw clear lines could soon find itself on the fringe where personnel increasingly make broad interpretations of what is considered acceptable. For such corporations, what was initially an innocent incident can grow into a complex, bad practice.[48] At one company which I studied the lack of clarity with respect to rules and procedures regarding expense declarations led to salesmen going so far as to claim trips to the barber as office expenses. Clarity about the limits which show how far an employee may go are identified by Hoogstraten (1994) and Pijl and Muijen (1994) as an internal cause for unethical conduct. "It must be clear to employees in advance what is expected from them and what is absolutely unacceptable." (Pijl and Muijen, 1994:16). One employee described his company as "...soft, they are always trying to reach a consensus, with no one in management daring to say what is and is not allowed. This vagueness has led to a number of unethical practices." Vagueness or lack of clarity can lead, as Waters and Bird calls it, to moral stress. "We can say that the inherent abstractness of moral standards produces a condition of moral stress. It is often not sure how general moral standards should be acted out in a particular situation, and most importantly, there is frequently a double connection between fundamental standards of organizational responsibility and other competing moral standards. Also at the root of this moral stress is the ambiguity of the expectations indicated by these moral standards." (1989:18).[49]

The lack of clear guidelines and rules can lead to a situation in which once a practice has become corrupted, it will not be set right again. One of the employees of a medium-sized Dutch bank, which ran into difficulties because of the handling of illicit funds, said that "the view of the Board of Directors was that illicit money was not to be tolerated, but my urgent requests and recommendations to prevent such practices were, as far as I could see, not followed up by the Board." The result was that a discrepancy arose between values and practice on the shop floor. A corporation that has not developed a way for dealing with moral problems will see the problem increase rather than decrease or be resolved (Cooke, 1991). Trial and error tactics are, according to Cooke, sometimes necessary for unusual situations, but, as

---

[48]   A slow decline is often the result. With each subsequent immoral dealing, however, the crisis of conscience becomes less, increasing the chance of repetition of unacceptable behavior. Sherman (1985) shows through empirical research six stages in the process of the corrupting of a police officer. It begins with (1) small tips (free drinks, free meals) followed logically by (2) ignoring shop closing times and illegal parking near a restaurant. When small gifts of food and drink are accepted, it is only a small step to (3) accept money from traffic code violators who offer a small amount when they show their driver's license. (4) Regular payments from, for example, the gambling world, to guarantee a hands-off approach to this highly-profitable sector by the police and sometimes police protection, can be a next step down the hill. (5) Bribery by prostitutes and brothel owners is a heavier form, while the most difficult step is accepting money from drug dealers. After that, it is just a small step for the police officer to (6) cross the threshold to dealing drugs himself. In the police world, there is a distinction made between the passive herbivores and active carnivores. Once the offender realizes that he has conducted himself badly and there's no way back, the choice is made to take as much as possible while the stage is set for an actively corrupt attitude.

[49]   Seen from a principled, positivistic perspective, a high level of abstraction does have the power of concepts, but this power stands or falls by the degree to which employees are able to derive meaning from these concepts.

he writes further: "...if there are no existing guidelines to use as a reference, any actions taken may complicate the ethical problem. In other words, the anticipated solution may be worse than the initial dilemma." (1991:252).[50]

Following are a number of examples from real life which point out a shortfall in clarity in regards to the dimension of "entangled hands."

1. Within a company, no policy has been developed on accepting gifts outside the workplace. In the course of time, the only suppliers who are considered for an order are those who have made a generous gesture to the purchasing agent by loading the trunk of his car with consumer goods. According to the company's financial director, order costs are fifteen percent too high as a result of such practices.

2. Construction workers begin by retailing the bricks left over from projects they worked on. The contractors themselves had not decided what to do with left-over materials. In a very short time, a bustling retail trade develops after large-scale orders are made on behalf of the company.

3. The photocopier and fax of a company are used on a large scale by the staff for their own personal use, as if it is the most normal thing in the world. The rule "handle company property ethically" was too abstract for the personnel to translate into practice.

4. Police agents are asked by friends and family to check the police information system to see whether the people next door to the house they want to buy have a criminal record. Within the police force, it is unclear whether doing such favors for friends is acceptable.

5. Employees innocently use company letterhead when doing private business, giving the impression that the company stands behind them as guarantor while the company intends no such thing. No policy has been developed within the company to deal with this issue.

6. An employee often comes to work very tired because he has a job as a bartender during his off-hours. Colleagues accuse him of using the one job as an opportunity to rest up for his other job. Employees do not have a clear idea which jobs are allowed on the side.

---

[50] The so-called norm-blindness may affect personnel as a result of a gradual deterioration of the company's norms and values. A gradual shift may not be noticed and will, therefore, not be tackled, but newcomers or external parties, however, will be able to notice and condemn such practices. I would like to call this the boiling-frog phenomenon. A frog that is put in a pan of water that is brought to a slow boil will boil to death because it is not able to detect gradual changes in temperature. On the other hand, a frog that is tossed into a pan of boiling water will immediately jump out and will survive.

7.   The CEO of a company has a seat on the board of a consulting firm that com-
     petes for the company's business. Within the company, there is no policy on
     holding positions outside the firm. When the management awards a contract
     to the consulting firm, bystanders doubt the purity of the decision-making
     process.

8.   Off-duty police agents spend a good deal of time in a local bar while still in
     uniform. The trustworthiness of the police force is thereby decreased.
     Outsiders get the impression that police officers consume alcohol while on
     duty. There is no policy nor awareness within this police force with respect
     to the fact that these habits have a negative effect on the image of the police.

2. Consistency

The consistency of an organizational context is the degree to which managers and
co-workers apply the same standards in the same situation in handling the organization's assets. This quality relates to referent behavior within the organization.

Referent behavior is the conduct of those people (referents) on whom personnel
model their conduct. Management is an especially important referent group.[51] The
example which management gives is of crucial importance for the organizational
context. Setting the ethical tone begins at the top (Ford and Richardson, 1994).
Employees are quickly inclined to reflect the norms and values of employees higher
up on the corporate ladder. A manager who is careful in how he handles company
assets sets a positive ethical tone throughout the organization. Sincere leaders set the
tone for sincere followers. Likewise, ill-disposed leaders set the tone for ill-disposed
followers. An employee who sees that his boss pads his expense report (despite the
fact that this is prohibited in the code of conduct) will also be tempted to do so. A
manager who refuses to buy under-the-table confidential information on the most
important competitor sends a powerful message to the employees. "Why," asked an
interviewee, "should we remain conscientious when we have the impression that
things are much more 'flexible' at the top?" Employees can also incite or inspire one
another. An employee who regularly holds seminars during work time, and is paid
very well privately for doing it, will give his colleagues the idea that they should also
"enrich" themselves at the company's expense. This temptation increases all the
more as one's co-workers and superiors begin to display such reprehensible conduct
more frequently. In their findings, Zey-Ferrell et al. (1979), Izraeli (1988), and Ford
and Richardson (1994) conclude that the influential effect of the example of

---

[51]   The example provided by management is the most cited factor for stimulating unethical behavior.
       See, for example, Baumhart (1961), Brenner and Molander (1977), Carroll (1978), Hegarty and
       Sims (1978), Zey-Ferrell et al. (1979), Walker et al. (1979), Trevino (1986), Nielsen (1987), Posner
       and Schmidt (1987), Arlow and Ulrich (1988), Murphy (1988), Tsalikis and Fritzsche (1989),
       Gellerman (1989), Stead et al. (1990), Laczniak and Murphy (1991), and Wimbush and Shepard
       (1994).

management increases as the intensity and frequency of contact between management and employees increases.[52]

Sometimes, referent behavior works quite subtly, with the referent himself being unaware of it. For example, one company was just not able to stop employees from drinking alcohol on the job. Despite the memos sent to the personnel, no changes took place. Several years later, one manager found out that the habit of drinking on the job was still continuing, because the company journal included pictures of the management drinking at receptions. Although the receptions usually took place after working hours, the employees read the journal while at work. This indirectly created the impression that drinking alcohol on the job was permitted. Some of the workers had also noticed a small bar in the management's meeting room and had automatically assumed it contained alcohol. In fact, the bar only contained non-alcoholic beverages. The company's anti-alcohol campaign only had effect after the company journal no longer showed pictures of the management drinking beer and whisky and after the bar had been symbolically removed from the meeting room.

Another example concerns a grocery store whose owners set the wrong example by frequently taking things out of the warehouse during working hours to give to their family and friends. In reality, only small amounts were involved, and it was actually more a question of taking it from the one hand and putting it in the other. But because all the warehouse staff knew of these practices, they had an excuse to take things home themselves. Once begun, the practice progressed from bad to worse. By the time these practices finally came out into the open, the wife of one of the employees was even selling products from the store at the street market. According to Chewning et al. (1992), employees often have little reason to rise above the norms and values of their managers.[53] It is not only the direct conduct of management and co-workers that influences the attitudes of employees. Stories and anecdotes from the past also have an instructive effect. Because stories and anecdotes represent expectations regarding the conduct of the personnel, such stories contain reference points which can lead employees in both desirable and undesirable directions. An anecdote about how a company's marketing manager used his position to get two trainees into bed with him sends a different signal than a story that another manager was able to prevent an unsafe product from being brought out on the market.

The following are three examples of companies which lacked this quality partly:

---

[52] Zey-Ferrel et al. (1979) conclude that reference groups that are "closer" to the individual have a greater influence on his behavior than reference groups which are "farther" away.

[53] A study of Fortune 500 managers conducted by Lincoln et al. in 1982, found that managers sacrifice their own norms and values to a significant degree in order to increase their chances of success in the corporation. The degree to which people will sacrifice their own norms and values depends on the field-dependence of the manager, according to Witkin and Goodenough (1977). Field-dependent people use referents more in the making of decisions (Trevino, 1986). A manager who asks a subordinate to do something unethical can either redefine the conduct to make it less problematic or confirm to the subordinate that what he is asking is not unethical. Field-dependent employees will accept this sooner than field-independent employees will.

1. The managers of a quite successful business go on several deluxe business trips with their spouses. The added value of these trips for the company seems zero. These habits are picked up by the rest of the personnel and ultimately lead to great waste within the company. "Why should I keep to the rules when my boss only thinks of himself," is the feeling of one of the staff members.

2. An employee of the city development department of a large municipality relates his first experiences as an employee there. "My first impression was that people worked hard and that overtime was not uncommon. After a month, one of my co-workers asked me if I was interested in earning some extra cash on the side. I naively agreed after which he requested me to design several plans during working hours. I was instructed not to tell anyone outside the department about these practices. Later, I found out that most of my co-workers had their own architecture agencies and that they carried out many outside assignments for the municipality during working hours. The agencies were simply 'managed' by a straw man. With the added income I was able to double my monthly earnings. I thought to myself, why trying to be more Catholic than the Pope?"

3. A manager of a purchasing department receives a lot of gifts, which he takes home. His subordinates are not allowed to accept anything valued at more than 25 dollars. This double standard is not accepted by the personnel and they ask suppliers to deliver their gifts to their homes instead.

3. Sanctionability

The moral quality sanctionability indicates the degree that rewards (positive sanctions)[54] and punishments (negative sanctions)[55] could be applied, for both management and other employees. Sanctions can be either formal (i.e. an extra bonus) or informal (i.e. a pat on the shoulder, a wink or a compliment). Reward and punishment systems can influence the (im)moral functioning of employees. Hegarty and Sims (1978), using a computer simulation, evaluated a number of market decisions in different reinforcement circumstances for their morality. They concluded that extrinsic rewards for immoral behavior in the form of higher profit led to significantly more immoral behavior of the people rewarded. Another laboratory study in this area was carried out by Trevino and others (1985). The participants were more quickly inclined to choose immoral conduct when moral conduct was punished or immoral conduct was rewarded. Those participants whose conduct was stimulated in an ethical direction had a significantly greater likelihood of morally responsible conduct. The most ethical conduct was achieved when immoral conduct was clearly punished.

---

[54]   Weber (1981) identifies four possible positive rewards: recognition, appreciation, commendation, and monetary rewards.

[55]   Berenbeim (1988) identifies five possible negative sanctions: termination, suspension, demotion, probation, and appraisal comments.

The reinforcement theory (Trevino and Nelson, 1995) assumes that reward leads to repetition and punishment to avoidance. Reinforcement plays a large role: the consequences of a decision made in the past influence decision-making in the future.[56] Therefore, decisions display a certain coherence or pattern over time. Akaah and Riordan (1989) conclude that the failure of managers to take steps against unethical conduct acts as a formidable approval of censurable conduct.

---

1. One of the partners of a large accounting firm has been frequently harassing his female secretaries for several years. Such sexual harassment varies from questionable comments on the "tempting" clothing of the secretaries to physical advances and mandatory dates after work. Two secretaries claim to have been forced to kiss the partner. The victims of these advances assumed that they would be fired for their "blasphemy" against the partner. However, when word finally reaches the board of directors and the director of personnel, they refuse to take action against the accused partner. The reason behind their apathy is the director's contribution to the success of the firm. He is good for winning more than ten new major clients a year.

2. The upper management had been told a number of times that one of the company's drivers had a drinking problem and that he often was driving while intoxicated. Although the company rules prohibit consuming alcohol just before and while driving, management took no action out of fear for an uproar from the driver and his closest "buddies."

3. Every month, an employee who is editor of a sports club's newsletter makes at work photocopies of the newsletter for all club members. His boss does not take any action because he is chairman of the club.

4. A manager expresses his reluctance to punish his personnel as: "Out of fear of losing popularity, I do not act when an employee does not do what has been agreed to. To make myself look good, I gloss the employee's actions over with phrases such as 'it's not so bad' and 'there are worse things in the world.' That is how I justify my own conduct."

5. "Frequently, employees are punished neither directly nor indirectly. Those who are now in charge used to be co-workers of those they are supervising, and they also did things they were not supposed to. Therefore, they cannot say anything about censurable conduct." An employee thus describes the management style of this company as "management through avoidance."

6. A manager sees one of his employees misusing his business card. He does not say anything about it because he has done the same thing himself.

---

[56]   Studies which support this have been done by Fritzsche and Becker (1983), Hunt et al. (1984), Laczniak and Inderrieden (1987), and Ford and Richardson (1994).

4. Achievability

Achievability in the context of the "entangled hands" dimension means that employees are able to realize the stated expectations relating to the organization's assets in practice. This quality refers to the degree to which the desired norms and values can be applied in practice and the degree to which employees are directly instructed to adopt conduct that deviates from the organization's desired norms and values and their own conscience.

A study by Carroll (1978) in the United States shows that 61 percent of middle management and 85 percent of lower management will agree to carry out a request that they themselves believe to be immoral. Research by Posner and Schmidt (1987) demonstrates that nearly 40 percent of respondents indicate that their managers have occasionally asked them to do things they considered unethical. Wahn (1993) cites a study in which 30 percent of respondents indicated that their boss had asked them to do something immoral. Two-thirds of this groups felt that their job was at risk if they did not agree to the request. Managers who are lower in the organizational hierarchy are under greater pressure to sacrifice their norms and values than managers higher up in the organization (Carroll, 1978). Commenting on this, a manager said, "What is moral in the organization is what the man directly above you in the corporation wants from you and not what we collectively put in our code of conduct." Another reason to agree to an immoral request is the fear of failure. Bovens (1990) shows that obedience often promotes career opportunities. Employees play safe so that nothing can be blamed on them later. Cooke (1991) concurs: when there is a sharp division between personal values and values at work, unethical conduct will occur sooner rather than later. The private conscience is cleansed by the organization one functions in.[57]

An example. Due to the racist attitude of the management of a swimming pool, immigrant boys are regularly removed from the pool, put into a separate room and beaten up. Sometimes the immigrant boys file a complaint with the local police. The pool management forces the staff, against their better judgment, to testify that the boys had been harassing the female swimmers and that after they had been separated, they became aggressive and attacked the manager. The management has a lot of power, with no system of checks and balances. Once employees agree to such a request from the management, there is often no way back. The employees are also guilty of immoral practice from that moment on. This phenomenon is well known as the "foot in the door" technique. Those who first agree to a less serious request appear to be more prepared to agree to a more serious request than those who receive the more serious request immediately.

---

[57]   Arendt (1948) points to the dangers of the unraveling of the public and private domains. In public circumstances people will do things they would never support in private. Brons and Van der Lee (1989) argue for a segregation of roles. For them, it should be possible for an employee to help his company circumvent environmental laws during the day and to be an environmental activist in the evening.

Achievability also relates to how expectations can be realized in practice. This means that norms, rules and procedures constantly need to be checked for their practical value. A rigid application of rules can lead to undesired side effects. A punch-clock system was in place at a large company for all the staff. The system was not based on a shared awareness, because the system was not applicable to employees who, for example, had an appointment at the beginning or the end of the day. Because many employees, therefore, did not appreciate the use of such a system, often no one clocked in, or they clocked in for one another. Another example relates to the executability of a gifts policy. A norm such as "gifts valued up to 25 dollars may be accepted" is not always realistic. It is impossible to call down to the local wine merchant to ask the price of every bottle of wine that comes in as a gift. If the organization sets demands that are too high or rather unrealistic, employees may ignore other moral expectations as well. So some sort of moral inflation may start.

1. A manager asks one of this employees to falsify a report for a management meeting to hide the failure of the department to realize the annual departmental targets.

2. The chairman of the meeting frequently asks the secretary to rewrite the minutes of the meeting in his own interest.

3. The head of a department asks his subordinates not to report revenues from outside jobs to the management because, "They will only give me a hard time about it."

4. The mayor of a small community instructs employees of the Public Works department to work on his own yard during working hours. After several years, it appears the employees, too, have developed all manner of private activities which they carry out during working hours, using "the mayor's yard" as justification.

5. A crew foreman with a building contractor gives his crew orders to build a shed in his own yard during working hours, causing delays in the projects they should be working on.

6. Employees of an investment fund are not permitted to trade privately in a particular security within a period of 24 hours before or after a transaction by the fund in that security. It is by definition impossible for employees to observe this rule always as (a) they are often unable to assess what the fund is going to do within the next 24 hours, and (b) they are unable to reverse private transactions when it becomes clear that the fund has traded in the same securities. The result is a lack of support among personnel for both the letter and the spirit of the rule. It becomes common practice for employees to trade privately in securities of which it is internally known that the fund will be buying or selling a large package shortly.

7. A multinational company does not allow employees to accept any gifts and invitations, which is not practical because small presents are often given in gratitude for services rendered. This gives way to a great deal of apathy towards "those high and mighty company rules of ours" as some one employees puts it.

8. During the celebration of festive occasions during working hours, alcoholic beverages are served, although the organization carries a no alcohol policy.

9. Employees were not allowed to make personal calls from the office. When they have to work overtime without notice, the telephone is often the best way to let their families know. The strict adherence to the no-calls policy prohibited this. The staff considered the policy of strict prohibition ridiculous and flagrantly disregarded it. After the management changed the policy, the management concluded that more personal calls were being made with a policy of strict prohibition than in the actual situation where exceptions are possible.

5. Supportability

Supportability of the organizational context refers to how much support is stimulated among employees for carefully handling the assets of the organization. Blanchard and Peale (1988) are convinced that people's negative attitude towards the corporation is an important cause of unethical conduct towards the corporation. If people have the feeling that they are appreciated they can resist the temptation towards immoral conduct. If they are proud of their company and everything it stands for, employees will fight to keep the integrity of the corporation high, Blanchard and Peale say. In case of negative feelings, employees are out to cause harm to the corporation or to pay the corporation back for damage caused to the employee at an earlier time.[58] Tucker (1989) also concludes that employee dissatisfaction plays an important part in internal criminality. Negative feelings are often caused by unjust treatment, discrimination in regards to one's co-workers, abuse, exclusion and unfulfilled promises.[59] Solomon and Hanson feel that "...nothing corrupts an organization and

---

[58] A study by the University of Cardiff and consultants of Arthur Young supports this view (Carmichael, 1992). The report emphasizes that relations at work are very important. Not only fraud, but also damage to important equipment can result from dissatisfaction among employees. "People with a relatively low status and salary are often entrusted with crucial positions. When they develop resentment against what they consider to be their proper position, the results can be disastrous. 'Accidental' damage by unhappy employees is a daily occurrence," the report says. "A warehouse worker drove a forklift through a new bathroom. The management could not prove criminal intent, but the whole department knew it had been done with intent." (Carmichael, 1992:181).

[59] Cooke has made a list of fourteen factors to determine whether a corporation is at ethical risk. As an illustration of the negative employee feelings towards the corporation mentioned above, Cooke's eighth factor can be mentioned: "Any firm that treats its employees differently than its customers encourages unethical behavior. It reflects an arrogance that creates distrust and hostility within the

its employees faster than perceived inequalities within the organization" (1985:174). Weber (1990) suggests that employees in a large bureaucracy quickly feel themselves to be just cogs in the wheels of the machinery, which means that they not only reason with respect to a lower ethical level, but their loyalty is also lower. Because people do not feel involved in the corporation, there is no identification with the corporation. As a result, employees may not think and conduct themselves in terms of the corporate interest.

---

1.   Almost all of the 25 members of a complaints department of a multinational company have been given the short end of the stick by the organization. The department has been "temporarily" relocated to the basement of the building which lacks any kind of sanitary facilities. The motto "the smaller the complaints department the better" reigns within the company. "Moreover, the complaints department just costs money that will have to be earned back by the rest of the company anyway." As a result, the staff gets discarded furniture from the sales department, salaries have been frozen for four years (unlike in the rest of the company) and the department has no say in relevant matters of policy. Because of this, the staff does little work, staff members frequently call in sick, each staff member spends approximately an hour and fifteen minutes making personal telephone calls per day, and paper, pens and printer ribbons are frequently taken for private use.

2.   Differences in pay scales for doing the same work at a company lead to envy, causing the creation of a justification culture by which employees close the salary gap by making excessive expense claims.

3.   The employees of a large production company treat company vehicles recklessly and carelessly. During working hours staff regularly enter into rally-contests with the company vehicles on the company site. It is also common practice for employees to urinate in the company vehicles, to stick sandwiches into the radio fascias, and to disregard the traffic rules on the company site. If the oil-light comes on showing that the oil needs to be topped up, the general reaction is: "No need to do anything, the light will go out of its own accord." Among other things the staff blame their behavior on the lack of any sense of company pride. Staff feel little if any involvement with the company, as they consider the management has never displayed any appreciation of their efforts.

---

organization -- factors that often result in a series of ethical problems throughout the firm. Moreover, such distrust and hostility makes it difficult, if not impossible, to resolve justly those ethical dilemmas that may originate outside the firm." (1991:252). Charmichael writes in her article "Countering employee crime:" "There is evidence that employees who steal from their employees believe that they are in fact redressing a perceived unfairness..." (1992:181). On the basis of an analysis of fourteen alleged corrupt practices in police forces, Fijnaut (1993) concludes that the offender justifies his actions by considering himself underestimated, unappreciated, and unfairly treated.

4.   One interviewee says about himself: "I have had the experience that high
      work pressure combined with little appreciation from my boss led to me not
      doing my work with pleasure any more. I thought "Forget it. From now on, I
      am just going to mind my own matters."

6. Visibility

The quality of visibility refers to the degree to which the effects of one's conduct are
visible to the actor, to those who are affected by it, and to the co-workers and supervisor who are directly involved.

Carter (1990) investigated police corruption and concluded that "...after an officer's
initial corrupt act, there was a time when the officer feared being detected. After the
fear subsided and an opportunity for corruption occurred, the officer performed
another improper act. Again there was a period of fear of apprehension -- albeit
shorter -- followed by another incident. Failure of detection apparently reinforced the
"safety" of the practice. As time passed, the frequency of misconduct appeared to
increase cyclically until an undefined saturation point was reached." (1990:87). Fear
of being caught decreases and self-confidence in succeeding in a subsequent offense
increases. Visibility is a prerequisite for correcting or anticipating conduct, both for
the employee himself as for others. Feedback is, therefore, an essential quality.
Employees can only be held responsible if they know, or can know, the consequences of their actions. If one does not know what is going on, one cannot be called to
account.

A responsibility hearing, where one is called to account in front of a group, is one of
the oldest and most important ways of influencing peoples' conduct. Knowing that
you might have to explain your choice has an impact on the choice. Responsibility
hearings cast their shadows forward. Larger corporations are characterized by complexity and size, with less overview of people's conduct. Visibility can also be consciously avoided. Then a cover-up culture is created with the motto "you scratch my
back and I'll scratch yours." This mechanism ensures that unethical conduct is not
made public. In an interview, an employee said that every time he noted unethical
conduct by a co-worker, it gave him ammunition for later if he needed something
from that person. He kept a little black book of unethical conduct of several co-
workers. After a while, he had several co-workers completely in his power and he
could blackmail them to his heart's content.

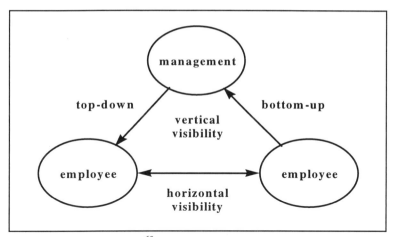

Figure 4-2: Aspects of visibility.[60]

1.	At a Dutch sales organization, it is impossible for management to verify whether travel expenses have actually been incurred. Employees have the room to claim far too much mileage. Some employees have made it a policy to calculate the distance between home and work 40 percent too high.
2.	The head of a purchasing department has a garage built onto his house by a contractor who receives a large contract from the purchaser's company in return. Because the purchaser lives far from work, he does not have to worry that the arrangement will be discovered.
3.	It is not obvious to the staff who receives an annual bonus. After five years it becomes clear that only "yes-men" and cronies have been getting bonuses, varying from one to four month's wages.
4.	"Employees who work late or come in early are in a perfect position of stealing goods. A good deal of internal crime happens out of office hours," a shopkeeper says.
5.	"We are all checked to a certain degree, but who checks the management? No one is looking over their shoulders, they are off by themselves and that is why things sometimes go wrong," an interviewee says. The things that have gone wrong were, for example, passing assignments to supplier acquaintances, many emoluments and excessive expense accounts. Even damage claims for defective semi-finished products (approaching 450,000 dollars) to suppliers were settled privately.

---

[60] In the case of vertical visibility, a difference can be made between downward visibility (the management's overview of the staff) and upward visibility (the staff's overview of the management).

6.   The manager of a security department is unaware that when he is away, the staff immediately stops working and starts playing cards.

7.   Employees siphon gas from company vehicles to their personal cars. Although this happens on a large scale, management is unaware of it.

8.   Employees stay in the same position for so long that their activities can no longer be overseen by their managers. Several buyers are able to manipulate the selection of suppliers to such an extent that the company's purchasing costs are approximately 15 to 20 percent too high.

9.   A transport truck driver is unaccompanied on the road. As a result, he is free to help people move to their distant cottages for a small fee.

10.   Funds transfers made by a bank's internal staff are checked by a staff member controlling whether the signatures are valid and whether the accounts can cover the requested transfers. The transfer slips which have been checked are placed in an internal mail-pouch which is not sealed until the end of the day. This gap in the processing process leads to several cases of fraud before the internal audit department becomes aware of this organizational failure.

11.   Dock workers who say that their tools have fallen into the forecastle or the water get new tools in replacement. The "missing" tools find their way to the homes of the employees.

7. Discussability

The quality of discussability refers to the degree to which employees can express criticism and may discuss moral problems and dilemmas. Just as with the quality of visibility, the possibility of discussing criticism, moral problems and dilemmas can be divided into a horizontal and a vertical component.

The lack of a negative response to censurable conduct from colleagues and supervisors creates the possibility of recrossing the line, with increasingly serious repercussions (Pijl, 1991). Bringing unethical conduct up for discussion can lead to the blunt reaction that "everybody should mind their own business." Other rationalizations for not bringing up unethical practices are for example: "It is not my business," and "I cannot bother with everything." Discussing unethical conduct gives the person in question the opportunity to tell his own story and creates the conditions for repentance. It also leads to better insight into what is and is not morally acceptable. "Ethics becomes a problem in most companies not because of ethical differences or ignorance but rather because it is just not part of the conversation," say Solomon and Hanson (1985:149).

Discussing a co-worker's censurable conduct with management can be difficult because people do not want to be seen as informants or as the boss's pal. At one company, several of the female staff were irritated by the fact that their male colleagues frequently watched pornographic films during the night shift. Despite several pointless requests to stop showing the videos, the women did not dare to take their problem to the shift supervisor who happened to be male. If there is a context where giving criticism is stimulated, management seems also open to criticism about their own conduct.

Discussing problems of conscience also falls under this quality. A manager asked an employee on Friday afternoon to do a job that would take up the whole weekend. Because of his religion, he would rather wish not to work on Sunday. The employee did not dare to make his reservations obviously out of fear of being labeled the "wimp" or "loser" of the department.

---

1. The nurses at a regional hospital have been given new uniforms. Because the uniforms are somewhat transparent, the nurses are frequently bothered and made the object of sexist comments by male co-workers, patients and visitors. The nurses do not dare to bring the matter to the director's attention because it is common knowledge that the director, himself, is something of a sexist.

2. An employee is aware of the outside activities of one of his co-workers. When he brings them up, he is roundly attacked. When he subsequently brings the matter up with the management, the incident is ignored. Before he can take his complaint to the CEO, the powerless employee is fired for dubious reasons.

3. The head of a department ignores criticism from employees about supposed fraud of a co-worker with the comment that "you have to work it out among yourselves and, furthermore, mind your own business. That will keep you busy enough."

4. A manager consistently ignores criticism regarding his sloppy style of leadership. The manager tolerates all unethical practices (like ganging up on co-workers, discrimination and intimidation) in his team. The executives do not seem to care either.

5. An interviewee on his organization: "Moral dilemmas are never discussed with co-workers. We laugh about it a bit. Everybody sets their own limits, depending on the situation, and thinks that everybody should decide for himself what to do."

4.3   The "many hands" dimension

The "many hands" dimension concerns the coordination of functional responsibilities which employees have in the corporation. Within every organization, employees have their own tasks, duties or jobs.[61] Internal specialization and division of labor make efficient functioning of organizations possible. To be able to speak of a virtuous organization, these functional responsibilities should be coordinated sufficiently in order to ensure that the sum of the total individual responsibilities is equal to the total of the corporate responsibilities. The "many hands" issue is about whether the duties or jobs within the organization are adequately distributed among the individual positions or whether collective responsibilities drift away or are lost within the organization.

Thompson defines the "many hands" issue for government organizations as follows: "Because many different officials contribute in many ways to the government's decisions and policies, it is difficult even in principle to identify who is morally responsible for political outcomes." (1987:105).[62] Ladd (1970), Stone (1975), Bovens (1990), Badaracco (1992), Cohen (1993), Trevino and Nelson (1995), and Wempe (1998) identify similar erosions of responsibilities in corporations.[63]

When it is not clear who is responsible for what, the situation can arise, for example, where stakeholders are sent from one department to another looking for assistance. The disaster of The Herald of Free Enterprise in 1987 was partly caused by the fact that at the moment of departure from the port of Zeebrugge, nobody took the direct responsibility for closing the bow doors. Passenger security was not sufficiently

---

[61]   This relates to one of the four meanings which Hart (1968) says the concept "responsibility" can have: responsibility as a function. The three other forms are: responsibility as cause, liability and as ability. Bovens (1990) distinguishes a fifth meaning: responsibility as a virtue. The concept of responsibility as a virtue enables us to make a distinction between passive and active responsibility, and between liability and after-the-fact accountability on the one hand, and virtuous conduct, in the sense of being responsible, on the other hand. As regards the ethical content of a corporation, I will use the fifth meaning.

[62]   With regard to the Second World War, we encounter an identical problem: "...who is to blame for the murder of six million European Jews...?" (Bar-on, 1985:255).

[63]   Baier (1972) and French (1984) use the example of the massacre in the Vietnamese village of My Lai, where the group caused great damage to others, but each individual member had a good excuse for what he did. In 1968, during the Vietnam War, at least 107 civilians (mostly unarmed old men, women, children and babies) of My Lai were killed by the platoon led by Lt. William Calley. Calley defended himself by falling back on the extreme stress the platoon was under. In addition, there had been an earlier message that the village was a base for the Viet Cong. The information could not be verified beforehand. Furthermore, he had received the direct order to destroy everything (a so-called search-and-destroy mission in a free-fire zone). Refusing such an order could have been taken by his superiors as insubordination. His superiors denied with all vigor that they had issued such an order. The entire incident rested on a misinterpretation by Calley. The commanders washed their hands off the affair even more by saying they could not be expected to know and to manage everything from such a great distance. Initially, only Calley was convicted, to life imprisonment. Under great pressure from the American public, Calley was released after serving four years of his sentence.

translated into individual responsibilities of the crew.[64] Collective problems that are identified may not be dealt with because no one feels responsible. "Responsibilities in organizations are often shared so no one feels personally and directly accountable" (Badaracco, 1992:71).[65] "Responsibility becomes diffused. No individual feels the need to take responsibility, so in the end no one does, and unethical conduct is more likely" (Trevino and Nelson, 1995:161). According to Paradice and Dejoice (1991), those problems are the result of an increasing complexity within large organizations leading to an increase in the inability to oversee everything. The complexity also means that no single person knows how everything works. Furthermore, in large organizations, policy goes through many "hands" before it is implemented. Therefore it becomes more difficult or even impossible to trace the degree to which each individual employee is personally responsible (Cohen, 1993). Based on the statement by Van Gunsteren (1974) that "The larger the organization, the fewer people can be held responsible," Bovens (1990) formulates a paradox: as the responsibilities for activities are distributed among more people, the individual responsibility of each individual declines more than proportionally. Downs' Third Law (1967) is echoed here: the larger any organization becomes, the poorer is the coordination of its actions. According to Bekke (1995), responsibility for conduct is especially difficult to localize because organizations consist of fluctuating and flexible relationships. Because responsibilities are difficult to localize, employees may shrug off their individual and collective responsibilities. The corporation exerts a downward pressure on employees' responsibility awareness when responsibilities for the effects cannot be traced back to individuals within the corporation.[66] In assigning concrete tasks, corporations run the risk that employees or departments no longer concern themselves with the duties of others. This natural inclination leads employees to focus on their own tasks and to try to fulfill those as best as possible, while at the same time they quickly lose the feeling that the corporation is a cooperative body. "Division of

---

64   The report of the Court of Investigation (No. 8074) stated that the Board of Directors must accept a "...heavy responsibility for their lamentable lack of directions. Individually and collectively they lacked a sense of responsibility. This left a vacuum at the center." (1987:15). There were frequent crew and officer rotations: there had been previous instances of ships sailing with bow doors opened but no management directives on this practice had followed: meetings between managers and masters were infrequent: and there were a whole series of technical matters related to passenger overloading, underestimation of vehicle weights, inability to read draughts, water ballast and instability. At the time of the fatal departure the assistant boatswain responsible for closing the doors was asleep in his bunk; the officer who was supposed to oversee the assistant boatswain was not at his post because operating instructions required him to be in two places at one time; and the captain had no mechanical means of knowing that the bow doors were shut despite several requests from masters for a warning device to be fitted on the bridge.

65   One can compare this "evaporation" of collective responsibilities with the situation when someone is drowning. The people on shore do nothing but wait for someone else to take the initiative to rescue the victim, who, in the mean time, will drown. Diffusion of responsibility in groups is used to explain the results of classic research on the likelihood that bystanders will help a seizure victim (Trevino and Nelson, 1995). Darley and Latane (1968) suggest, in their article "Bystanders' intervention in emergencies: diffusion of responsibility," that when others are present, responsibility is diffused among all of the bystanders and individuals are less likely to help.

66   Inadequate coordination of responsibilities can, in fact, also lead to the creation of doing twice as much as necessary because workers or departments work against one another. Instead of synergy, there is counter-productivity.

responsibility [...] means that organizational members essentially do their jobs with blinders on -- they see only what's directly ahead of them and no one sees (or takes responsibility) for the whole picture." (Trevino and Nelson, 1995:162).[67] Steinmann and Lohr highlight the selective nature of organizational structures: "....they prescribe what will be done, and thereby at the same time simply block out every-thing else that someone in a given position should not do." (1992:29). Vaughan (1983) points out that specialization creates units which compete with one another for corporate resources and where the interest of the unit is not necessarily the same as the interest of the total corporation.[68] The "many hands" issue has to do with pre-venting the moral problems which occur because corporate conduct come into being by "many hands." Some other examples of what can happen because of inadequate coordination in the context of the "many hands" issue are:

---

1.   The research and development department of a software company was "spending money like water" because the budget for that year had not yet been used up. Not using all of one's budget results in a budgetary cut-back for the coming year. "You have shown you can get the job done with less," is the reaction from the management. Afterwards, the R&D staff observe other departments laying people off because they are forced to manage it with similarly reduced budgets which are inadequate for their own departments' needs.

2.   Departments within an organization often provide one another with information that is incorrect, overdue or insufficient. The competition among departments encourages everyone to do as much as possible so as to look better than the other departments. There are all sorts of ways of allocating one's own mistakes to other departments and for claiming other departments' successes for oneself.

---

[67]   In a variation on the Milgram obedience to authority experiments, the diffusion of responsibility was simulated by dividing the teacher's role between two people, a "transmitter" and an "executant." The transmitter would inform the executant when a shock had to be administered and at what level. The experiment found that transmitters were significantly more likely to obey than executants. One can imagine that it was easier for the transmitter to rationalize his actions. "I didn't actually do the harm - someone else did" (Trevino and Nelson, 1995).

[68]   Individual conduct can also be amoral or at most, doubtful, while the sum of all the individual conduct does lead to immoral consequences. Parfit (1984) gives a hypothetical example of harmless torturers (1984). A prisoner is bound to an ingenious instrument of torture. Whenever the switch on the machine is turned on, the pain of the victim increases so slightly that he does not notice it. When multiple persons flip the switch in succession, severe torture is the result. On the individual level, there is hardly a causal relation, but collectively there is. The "tragedy of the commons" is another example where inadequate coordination among individuals leads to an undesirable situation collectively. A village has only one grazing meadow. All the residents have the right to graze their sheep on the meadow. But there are too many sheep for the natural balance. From the point of view of each resident, it is completely reasonable to let his sheep graze on the meadow. Where else can he go? The result is that the meadow is grazed bare and the common meadow is ruined and nobody can keep sheep any longer.

3. An employee, talking about his company, said: "First of all, our company can be described as a large number of fiefdoms. There is absolutely no sense of a 'we' feeling. The current reorganization is going to turn the fiefdoms into empires. In our company, the expression, 'Every man for himself and management for us all,' really applies."

4. A guest at an indoor swimming pool had fallen and hit his head, leaving behind a pool of blood on the floor near the snack bar. Removing the blood was the responsibility of the snack bar staff. Because the snack bar's bucket was missing at that moment, the employees of the snack bar asked one of the pool workers if they could borrow the latter's bucket. This request was refused with the comment that it was their responsibility and "they had to get their own bucket." The blood remained for hours, with all the associated health risks.

5. After the ethics review of a large bureaucratic organization, it appears that some departments are not willing to submit to the board's guidance. The interest of the departments is continually and wrongly placed above that of the organization. Every attempt made by the board to unify the organization is ignored by the departments. The board lacks the mechanisms to coerce the cooperation of the individual departments, resulting in a great deal of organizational problems. For example, the production department keeps churning out products which are of too high a quality for the sales department to market. At the same time, the sales department makes agreements with outside parties (concerning modifications, maintenance conditions and error margins) which are impossible for the production department to honor.

6. A company was trying to develop corporate solidarity. As employees were rewarded based on individual achievement, the collective responsibility left much to be desired. Job evaluations were based on how fast employees processed their daily assignments. Employees who had finished their assignments were then allowed to work on other things for themselves. Because the total number of assignments were processed by eight staff members, all sorts of work divisions had been introduced. For a while, everyone had to take an eighth of the assignments when they arrived at work. Within no time, the staff had developed a practice of snatching the easiest assignments for themselves. As soon as the disadvantages of this system had become evident, the management decided that everyone had to take one assignment at a time from the pile. As a result, the staff started hiding difficult and time-consuming assignments. After the management decided to divide the assignments among the staff itself, the management was accused of favoritism as some staff members would stop at nothing to get the management to give them the easier assignments.

In relation to the "many hands" dimension, the degree of coordination is equal to the degree to which the following seven qualities are embedded in the context.

8. Clarity

Ambiguity or a lack of clarity regarding the "many hands" issue means that the organization does not make clear to employees what are their own tasks and those of their immediate co-workers. This vagueness may result in a discrepancy between what the corporation expects from employees and what employees think the corporation expects from them. Vagueness can lead to a situation where everyone thinks that someone else is taking care of certain things while nothing, in fact, is done. Collective responsibilities may disappear between the cracks when employees and departments have vague task descriptions. Clear expectations relating to performing tasks are a condition for holding employees responsible. In the first place, it means that employees know what are their responsibilities. In the second place, it means that employees know what are the responsibilities of co-workers, subordinates and supervisors.

Vague task descriptions make it possible that responsibilities can be passed on to another level or another person either inside or outside the organization. "It is not my job, but my boss's or my co-worker's," is one of the rationales often heard. The risk of vague job descriptions is that employees hide themselves behind a lack of knowledge and consciously keep themselves ignorant. "Hiding one's head in the sand" or "washing one's hands in innocence" becomes just a matter of course: "I do not know anything," "I cannot know everything," and "What you do not know will not hurt you," are the excuses that may be heard. Stone (1975) refers to a kind of boomerang effect. In a number of areas, jurisprudence punishes knowledge of events and puts a premium on ignorance. It is precisely those people who have the opportunity to do something about the misconduct in an organization who can have an interest in knowing as little as possible. A Dutch police detective cited the example of his chief who tried to remain ignorant about the illegal methods used in patrolling in order to claim that he could not be held co-responsible for the practices. The expression "Success has many fathers, but failure is an orphan," (partially) refers to the failing organizational context in this regard.

---

1. At a marketing bureau the tasks and functions of each employee are largely unclear. There is also a lack of clear decision-making procedures on both major and minor matters. According to the staff there is a vacuum when it comes to decision-making powers. The staff believe that "decisions are not taken but arise" within the company. The lack of clear coordination stultifies the sense of responsibility among employees. Employees do not have the common interest of the marketing bureau sufficiently at heart. They set up their own projects without consent, and projects are stopped without any reason being given and without the knowledge of the management.

2. At a lawyer's office typing mistakes in important documents are common. The typist does not check her work because she thinks her boss goes through all the text a final time to catch errors. The manager thinks that the typist checks her work thoroughly.

3. Since it is not clear what can be expected of employees within a clothing company, the personnel just mess around and production is far below an achievable level. One of the employees of the company estimates that by establishing clear tasks and responsibilities, the productivity of his department could be increased by 40 percent.

9. Consistency

Consistency with respect to the "many hands" dimension refers to the extent to which referents set a good example in putting effort into the realization of the individual and collective responsibilities. Referents who (partly) ignore their task description give a negative impression to their subordinates and co-workers. Low work motivation could be the result of boring or tedious work, poor working conditions and the lack of any type of challenge. If low work effort does not result in sanctions, it can lead to a downward spiral in which workers' morals take on serious, undesirable forms.

1. The manager of a department claims all successes for himself while failure is blamed on one of the other members of the team. The effort and work satisfaction in the department decline sharply and risk-avoidance conduct is created: after all, only mistakes are meted out among the employees.

2. One of the managers of a firm of contractors consistently shifts difficult and thankless tasks onto one of his employees. At the same time he takes on those tasks with which he can easily make a good impression. In due course his employees get fed up. The result is disguised resistance towards the manager's projects. Time-consuming and thankless tasks in his department simply do not get done.

3. "My manager spends all of his time socializing, leaving us to take care of sales," said an unmotivated employee.

4. The manager tells his team that the art of being a good employee is to accomplish one's duties with the least possible effort so the rest of the time can be spent on nicer things (such as visiting the supplier's factories in exotic countries and attending professional conferences).

10. Sanctionability

In general, one is more inclined to evaluate measurable conduct than conduct which is difficult or impossible to measure. As Wheelen and Hunger (1995) say: quantifiable measures drive out non-quantifiable measures. It is precisely the morally relevant aspects of employee conduct that are often difficult or impossible to quantify. A difficult dilemma for those who must evaluate is the desire, on the one hand, to make an objective evaluation, and on the other hand, to incorporate qualitative factors into the evaluation. Qualitative factors, though, quickly threaten to become subjective. The disregard of qualitative performance can lead to goal displacement. Employees do what is evaluated and forget the rest.

An officer once said: "What you inspect is what you get. When the tops of cupboards are checked for dust, but no one ever looks under the beds, the cupboards will glisten while the dust gathers under the beds." What is measured becomes important and influences the object being measured. If a corporation undertakes no action in regard to those who do shoddy work, it is asking for problems. Based on clear responsibilities, employees and departments could be called to account for their irresponsible performance and be punished if necessary. The responsibilities of employees and departments will be undermined if they are never called to account for their irresponsible performance.

---

1. Within a public service office, an implicit promotion rule is in place that works against all logic: the less one achieved, the greater the chance that one would get a better position and an accompanying pay raise. Those who have been promoted during the past few years are the laziest employees in the office, but they have been quite successful in manipulating those who make decisions about promotions and pay increases.

2. A company's help desk is manned by four staff members responsible for assisting departments with software problems. Because two of the four never show enough effort, the departments become more reliant on the efforts of the two "loyal" staff members. During the course of time, the division of work fell out of balance. However, all four staff members receive the same wages, based on the number of years of service.

3. Within a computer company, it appears that vacant management positions are never filled with the best candidate. Investigations shows that other managers block the advance of candidates who are better qualified than they are. "A less skilled director is easier to manipulate than an outstanding director," according to the opinions of the actual managers.

---

11. Achievability

The degree to which tasks are not achievable, depends on five aspects: (1) insufficient authority, (2) lack of means, (3) too many responsibilities, (4) too little knowledge, and (5) lack of information.

11a. Sufficient authority

A police official described a recently completed reorganization as "the decentralization of a kilo of responsibilities and only a pound of authorities." Just as a fire brigade cannot function without a hose, assigning duties without authority is laughable. Position-related responsibilities have to be coupled to authority. If this is not the case, such responsibilities become empty concepts and hollow expectations.

<blockquote>

1. A process supervisor at a large chemicals concern has the function of ensuring that everything runs well. The arrangement is that if something goes wrong, it is to be reported to the relevant manager. Only the managers are authorized to intervene in the process. When the boss is absent, the process supervisor has no authority to intervene in the process. Only when there is danger of fire, he should intervene by sounding an alarm. Within a period of five years, this led to three situations in which a cooling system explosion only narrowly was avoided.

2. The security service at an indoor swimming pool is dismissed on account of cost considerations. The personnel is responsible, but do not have the power to ensure that the order in the swimming pool is maintained. Because the employees frequently have to deal with quite aggressive guests, they run the risk of physical injury. To enforce their authority the staff use unauthorized means, such as tear gas and laughing gas.

</blockquote>

11b. Sufficient means

Without the proper means, like budgets, instruments and equipment, employees may not able to give expression to their assigned responsibilities. Employees might see things go wrong but lack the means to intervene. Events can acquire their own dynamics and be considered as "acts of God." This can lead to a fatalistic mentality. In addition, having to watch powerlessly how things could have been done much better has a frustrating and discouraging effect.

<blockquote>

1. A disaster in a company producing hazardous chemicals was partially caused by the lack of control instruments. Bystanders could only watch helplessly as the disaster occurred before their eyes.

</blockquote>

2. The management of a dry dock has insufficient management options and an inadequate view of what was being done, which resulted in substantial sums of money disappearing into a bottomless pit. During the investigation, the director compared the inner workings of the corporation to a car being driven by the Board of Directors without the wheels -- the organization -- responding.

11c. Sufficient time

An employee can be saddled with so many tasks that he ignores or does not take seriously certain responsibilities or takes unacceptable risks in order to fulfill his responsibilities. Such tasks are sometimes identified as widow makers. Trevino (1986) says that people under great time pressure are less inclined to pay attention to the expectations and interests of others than those who have enough time at their disposal. Such individuals are so obsessed by fulfilling their assigned duties that they do not pay much attention to the needs of others. Neglecting certain tasks, employees can be tempted or forced by the system to camouflage any shortfalls in their performance. They can lie, mislead, or bluff to give a false impression of the state of affairs. In addition, they can develop devious ways and irresponsible practices (cutting corners) to fulfill their goals. Finally, too many responsibilities lead to apathy and fear of failure: "In short, neither men of weak responsibility nor those of limited capability can endure or carry the burden of many simultaneous obligations of different types. If they are overloaded, either ability, responsibility, or morality, or all three, will be destroyed." (Barnard, 1938:272). "Too many responsibilities can lead to reluctant performance, to shifting tasks and to other forms of risk-avoiding behavior. Many people will not longer have the courage to be able to make important decisions or to propose solutions that are creative but not without risks; individuals will try to cover themselves as much a possible against mistakes; and decision-making will be slow and strictly by the book." (Bovens, 1990:156).

1. The assistant boatswain of the Herald of Free Enterprise who was directly responsible for closing the bow doors was asleep when the boat embarked. He had worked so long without a break that he was overtired and no longer able to do his job properly.

2. At a small firm no quotes are requested from new suppliers due to a lack of time. The standard supplier is always chosen. Suppliers who have a better price-quality ratio do not get a chance.

3. In order to save time, there is no internal control in the choice of a supplier, resulting in the staff of a purchasing department setting up their own empires where no control is exercised. Undesirable practices, such as receiving huge gifts and favoritism, are the normal state of affairs.

---

4. A company disaster with more than 3,000 fatalities was partly caused when harsh cutbacks had reduced the number of supervisors by 50 percent and the number of process supervisors had shrunk by two-thirds. In cutting the departments which were responsible for safety, a deadly gas leak was not discovered in time.

11d. Sufficient knowledge and skills

Employees' tasks should be matched to their capabilities in order to enable them to realize their functional responsibilities. Some organizational practices may obstruct such a fit. According to the so-called Peter's principle, many people continue to be promoted until they reach a position that is too high a reach for them. Internal candidates for vacancies are evaluated on how well they perform in their present position but hardly or not at all with respect to how they would function in their new position. That is how people end up in functions or positions for which their skills and capabilities are unsuited. New job requirements that only apply to new recruits and not to those who are already settled is another phenomenon which has the same consequences. New appointees are therefore measured according to standards different from those which apply to the existing employees.

---

1. The explosion of a reaction chamber at a Dutch chemical plant, where three people died and eleven were wounded, was partly to blame on the insufficient knowledge and experience of the personnel. Employees were insufficiently trained to manage the process and to react adequately in case of calamity.

2. A high school is badly managed because the directors are selected on the basis of their teaching rather than management skills. Amongst the teachers, the directors have nicknames as "mediocrats," "stalagmites," and "waterheads."

3. The staff of a department store reproach the management for lacking personality. "They may bark, but they don't bite." The management dare not punish the staff when it becomes clear that they are neglecting to carry out their duties properly. The lack of resolute action means that responsibilities frequently go unheeded. "No-one here has ever been held to account for failing to meet working-agreements," says one member of staff.

11e. Sufficient information

Another factor that can cause unethical conduct is when the information flow (top-down and bottom-up) within the corporation functions badly. Without good information the chance of making good decisions decreases. Information can, due to the complexity of the organization, be out of date or changed by the time it gets to the right place. The information density can also be so great that people can no longer see the forest for the trees (Ermann and Lundaran, 1982). Cooke also says: "...any firm that lacks clear lines of communication within the organization encourages unethical behavior. Far too many cases of corporate impropriety have resulted from a basic failure to communicate." (1991:252).

---

1. A transport truck tipped over on the highway, spilling hazardous liquids onto the road. The driver did not know what he was carrying and what he should do in this sort of event. Therefore, the driver did not react adequately to the emergency which had arisen, and stood, according to eyewitnesses, with his hands in his pockets for minutes before doing anything.

2. A corporation's customer contact line was not given the information it needed from the departments. The departments consider the employees of the customer contact line as awkward and hard to please. As a result, often incorrect information was given to customers.

---

12. Supportability

Supportability regarding the "many hands" dimension is the degree to which employees can trust their co-workers: to what extent are employees and departments concerned with the interests of co-workers and other departments? Supportability is the feeling of belonging or affiliation among employees. Distrust among departments has a negative impact on working relationships and could lead to isolated departments within the corporation or transmission of incorrect information to other departments. Hyman et al. (1990) define the "good company" as an organization where employees are bound together by mutual trust and cooperation. Supportability, solidarity, or mutual loyalty is an important condition for internal cooperation and collegial assistance.

---

1. Within a government organization the relationship among departments had deteriorated such that it could not really be called one organization any more. There was great competition among the departments and departments took every opportunity to damage other departments or to put other departments in a bad light. The poor cooperation (and successful antagonism) was fed by a mutual lack of trust in one another.

2. Within a production company, a crisis of confidence developed between management and workers. The workers saw the management as slave drivers, while the management saw the workers as lazy and unmotivated. The co-operation between the two had deteriorated to such an extent that no new organizational project was implemented successfully.

3. In a municipality, the cooperation between and among the departments could not get off the ground because there were too many conflicts among the personnel to be dealt with. Heavy demarcations existed between staff with a university degree and those without, between staff that dealt with third parties and those who performed their work only internally, between staff with great career potential and those who had already reached the ceiling, between men and women, and between permanent and temporary or part-time staff. The fragmentation of the culture nurtured a context of mutual suspicion and hostility.

13. Visibility

Organizational invisibility as it relates to the "many hands" dimension means that the effects of the work are unclear to the employee himself, his co-workers and his manager. Employees who are not faced with the consequences of their actions are not able to change or adjust their conduct. Organizational invisibility can lead to a situation where the employees are only worried about the action itself without worrying about the consequences of the action. Limiting the function in the corporation stimulates employees to feel that they are merely a link in the whole or a cog in the wheels of the machinery.

Visibility of actions and consequences decreases with quicker job rotation and faster career tracks. For some corporations, employees may only occupy a position for two or three years. Such a policy does stimulate the employees to do their best for those few years. Employees in this position may try to reap many benefits of their activities within a short period while saving many problems for their successor. A similar story applies to corporations where employees are on a fast career track and will be in one place for only a short period of time. Such practices encourage the idea of "après moi, la deluge." It is also possible that the invisibility about what consequences can be attributed to whom gives employees "carte blanche" for irresponsible conduct because damaging effects can be attributed (read: shifted on) to one's predecessor. There is also a risk that people will hide behind collective decisions taken, for example, in meetings of project groups, teams and committees, because the contribution of every individual person in the decision-making process is not clear. Donaldson remarks that complex organizations: "...are less inclined than individual persons to display consistency over the long run. Members of committees change and often the changing of ideas of even existing members combine in surprising ways." (1982:115). Furthermore, a complex organization offers employees the chance to move out of the light or to throw up a smoke screen around them. So these employees do become invisible and also lose sight of others. It is easier to play hide-and-seek in a forest than on a lunar landscape. Social control is, then, impossible. The opaqueness is further increased if choices and decisions are not justified to team members. Without justification, there is no insight into the decision-making process, and thus no correction of decisions is possible. Explanation of motives and purposes is also important when assigning work. "Splitting work into small segments reduces the capacity of the worker to understand its purpose, while the concentration of large numbers of men and women in factories limits their exercise of personal responsibility." (Goyder, 1993:6). "I do not understand why I have to do it, just that I have to do it," demonstrates a lack of insight into the role of the individual in the whole. The larger the visibility of actions, the more opportunities there are for control, sanctions, and correction. As a common element of a number of cases, Bovens (1990) says that through the complex structure of the organizations concerned, internal bodies were not always able to become aware of possible derailings adequately or in time. Vaughan (1983) speaks of "authority leakage," a situation where management cannot manage the workers. Bovens concludes in noting that "the possibilities of management to influence the organization stand or fall with good information about the co-operation of the lower echelons" (1990:93-94).[69]

---

1. In a large bank, upper management has little insight into the situation on the floor. All the measures that are conceived and implemented by upper management perish because (a) many measures cannot be implemented and (b) there is no basis for a top-down approach. In this connection, after three cases of fraud had been uncovered, the number of passwords required of the staff increased from one to three. Moreover, the passwords had to be changed every two weeks and no one was allowed to write them down. The passwords were strictly personal. In the process of inventing a total of six new passwords per month, the staff used a great number of simple mnemonic devices to remember the passwords. The result was that the chance of fraud did not decrease because the extra passwords constituted only a false sense of security.

2. The staff at a not-for-profit organization does not have to make its schedules known to the boss or to the secretary of the department. As a result, there is no insight into what the staff is doing. Staff members can even "disappear" for a week (without having to use vacation days) without anyone noticing.

3. Instituting one-man police patrols in place of team patrols means that the management has virtually no overview any longer of the behavior of its employees. The coordination of the activities between employees and their managers and also among the employees themselves is, thereby, worsened.

---

14. Discussability

If there is a strong division between thinking and doing within a corporation, there is a risk that every non-routine decision that an employee has to make is passed to higher echelons and assignments that come from above are followed without criticism. Because of the feeling that employees must do as they are told by authority

---

[69] See also moral quality 11e: sufficient information.

figures, employees feel that they have no choice but to follow superiors' orders. In such organizations, it may be the rule that what is said is less important than who says it. Regardless of what the manager says, his instructions will be carried out even if they are wrong. In such organizations, employees are not involved in the development of policy. Thus, the information that the corporation possesses is not utilized fully. It seems to be reasonable to held a corporation accountable if the information spread throughout the corporation is not fully utilized. In contrast to an authoritarian structure, a democratic structure can help in developing the ethical development of employees (DeLeon, 1993). Trevino (1986) points out the importance of responsibility for consequences as an essential ingredient for a responsible corporation. When there is no responsibility for consequences, employees will be less inclined to reflect on their own conduct: "...employees are encouraged to do only what they are told, to be concerned only with localized outcomes of their work, and to take responsibility only for the most limited consequences of their actions." (1986:347). "Orders are to hand over responsibility for decision making and the individual feels that s/he has no choice but to give it up. If this sort of response become routine, individuals will come to believe that it isn't their responsibility to be on the lookout for ethical violations and they may stop bringing potential problems to the attention of superiors." (Trevino and Nelson, 1995:161).

A closed organizational context is characterized by the fact that giving criticism is not encouraged or accepted. People close their ears and eyes to what they do not want to hear or see. Bad news is not appreciated. Such a context can be characterized by "killing the messenger" (Kirrane, 1990), "screening bad news" (Bovens, 1990), "paying lip service" (Cooke, 1991), or "negative information blockage" (Bishop, 1991).[70] Bishop concludes "...it is clear that executives often do not know, and are not told even if others in the corporation have the information." (1991:379). According to Andeweg (1985), murmurs which rise upwards from below are most likely to be stronger than in the opposite direction.

When there is no opportunity within the corporation to exchange experiences, it does not promote learning from mistakes. According to Mulder (1993), a multitude of near accidents precedes most accidents. Learning from near accidents can prevent real accidents. The ability to discuss problems employees face in their work and the possibility to make criticism undoubtedly contribute to this learning process.

1.	"Decisions are not explained by our manager. What he assigns is thus often not understood by us. Changing circumstances are not reacted to properly: we have been taught not to think independently." a bank clerk said.
2.	An employee describes the dangers of not explaining things inside his organization: "...my director never tells us what goes on among the management, why should I tell him what goes on in the department?"

---

[70] Arrow (1974) says that important information can be re-worked or withheld in as it goes through hierarchical levels.

3. "Members of staff bearing major responsibility are never required to explain what they're up to. There's a big discrepancy here between being given and taking responsibility, on the one hand, and being held to and providing account, on the other. Due to negligence, no-one has ever been taken to task for any of the projects that have failed in recent years. This only results in even more failed projects. Nobody feels any responsibility," says one member of staff.

4. "The organization pretends to be open, but if people openly criticize things, they are shot down. This naturally works against discussability. Our organization cannot make mistakes, that is the dominant culture," one honest employee said.

5. Employees of a furniture factory do not discuss one another's failures out of fear of hearing criticism about themselves as well. As a result, the corporate "right hand" does not know what the "left hand" is doing.

4.4   The "dirty hands" dimension

The "dirty hands" dimension relates to the degree to which employees are directly stimulated to realize the legitimate expectations of stakeholders and to adequately balance conflicting expectations.[71]

An organizational context that encourages unethical conduct is often characterized by the great emphasis on corporate interest. According to Bovens (1990), complex organizations are not by their own prepared to take the interests of individuals into account. The basic idea behind this corporate strategy is that "what's good for the corporation is good." Chewning et al. (1992) conclude that a great deal of censurable conduct begins under the rationalization that the conduct in question will be appreciated by the corporation.[72] Orwell (1965) wrote that the roots of nationalism lie in the inclination to identify one's self with his country. The citizen has only one duty: to promote the national interest. The national interest is set outside every consideration of good and evil. People focus uncritically on this interest. They put blinders on and do not let themselves be distracted by anything or anyone. In his article "The parable of the Sadhu," McCoy (1983) describes an incident during a climb in the Himalayas where a feverish fixation on one goal leads to unethical conduct. During

---

[71]   In the Greek tragedy *Agamemnon* by Aeschylus, King Agamemnon is forced by the gods to choose between losing his war fleet and the death of his daughter Iphigeneia. Whatever the king chooses, he is doomed to evil. Jean-Paul Sartre gives the example of a young man, an only child, who cares for his needy mother during the war years, but finds himself in a dilemma when his friends urge him to help them in the resistance.

[72]   This kind of reasoning is also cited by Gellerman: "A belief that because the activity helps the company, the company will condone it and even protect the person who engages in it." (1986:88).

the climb the expedition meets an Indian man, a Sadhu, who is barely clothed and quite ill. If he does not get help soon, he will die. The expedition decides to leave the man behind and to continue with the climb. After all, a lot of effort went into setting up this unique expedition. McCoy notes that the circumstances during the climb has much in common with the business context: great stress, a lot of adrenaline, an over-powering goal and a feeling of getting an unique opportunity. Andrews (1989b) calls this fixation "teleopathy," a combination of the Greek words for goal and sickness. In teleopathy, a limited goal is pursued for which everything is sacrificed. One interest prevails and dominates all other interests. People shut themselves off to other justified expectations. Plato calls such tunnel vision "pleonexia," and Solomon, "sickness of purpose" (1992b).

Stakeholders can have a legitimate reason to complain when the company does not identify or recognize their interests or specific expectations towards the company, or both, or when the company inadequately distribute the costs and benefits between various stakeholders or between the stakeholder and the company itself. The "dirty hands" issue arises because a corporation is usually confronted with conflicting interests of stakeholders. Exactly because of the pressure of competition and the need to survive, corporations may become inclined to ignore those stakeholder expectations which are not necessary for realizing their competitive objectives. The necessity to produce goods and services and to make profits may be seen as a justification for neglecting legitimate moral expectations of stakeholders. It is sometimes inevitable for corporations and their representatives to make their "hands dirty" because a choice between conflicting norms, interests and expectations is unavoidable. The virtue approach concerns the degree to which those qualities are embedded in the organizational context which stimulate employees to realize the legitimate expectations of stakeholders and weighing off conflicting expectations in an adequate way.

Several cases where an inadequate coordination of the organization led to actual "dirty hands" include the following:

1. A car manufacturer launched a new kind of car. Great competitive pressures meant the car had to carry a low price and development time had to be as short as possible. As a result, a number of basic safety requirements were not met. For example, the chance was relatively high that the gas tank would explode in the case of a rear-end collision.

2. A dry dock company does nothing to compensate employees who develop lung cancer after years of exposure to asbestos at work. The management of the shipyard, however, has known about the danger of exposure for years, but has never informed the personnel. The management defends its silence with excuses such as "every occupation has its hazards," "if we knew about it, the personnel should have been able to figure it out as well" and "what are we supposed to do, stop building and repairing ships?"

3.   Sexual harassment and the assault of female guests at an indoor swimming pool take place frequently. The management is fully aware of it. Despite the fact that the means are available, no measures are taken. No manager feels responsible. "They should have been born male if they didn't want any problems," is the crude and cool reaction of each manager.

4.   The Public Works department of a municipality assigns a gardening company to de-weed the road surface. In doing so, the company uses a very stringent chemical. The desired results are achieved, but the condition of the soil worsens very quickly. The gardening company has the opinion that "these side effects are not our concern."

5.   A company hires students to acquire confidential information about competitors. The students are to present themselves to the companies as if they are doing confidential research for a thesis on successful businesses for the university. This company even goes as far as to force one employee to accept a job with a competitor so as to be able to obtain as much confidential information as possible while feeding the "new" employer false information about the strategic plans of his "former" employer.

The qualities below are the organizational factors which stimulate employees to realize stakeholders interests and to balance conflicting expectations.

15. Clarity

As it relates to the "dirty hands" dimension, clarity is the degree to which employees are able to determine who the stakeholders are, what their interests are, and what specific expectations they have in relation to the corporation. Without knowing what interests and specific expectations the stakeholders have, employees are not able to take the necessary steps to achieve them (either reactively or proactively). The chance decreases of a good relationship between the organization and its stakeholders.[73]

1.   At a software consulting firm, the director was the only one who had contact with clients. The programmers were expected to provide custom-work from behind their desks, without, however, ever having a good understanding of the desires and needs of the clients. As a consequence, customers paid a lot of money for poor programs. The quality of the products did rise significantly after the director took one of the programmers with him each time he visited a client.

---

[73]   According to Arendt, Eichmann was morally able to sink so low because "As Eichmann told it, the most potent factor in the soothing of his own conscience was the simple fact that he could see no one, no one at all, who actually was against the Final Solution." (1964:116).

2. Some advertising campaigns (such as those using illustrations of Jesus Christ and Adam and Eve in paradise) were prohibited by an advertising code commission because they seriously and unnecessarily offended a number of religious groups. The advertising agencies claimed that it was not their intention and that they were not aware that some religious groups would consider the advertising offensive.

3. The interests of the surrounding communities were not taken into account in a decision over the location for a new factory. Ultimately, a location in a densely populated part of the neighborhood was chosen. Due to the looming noise and odor pollution, the residents of the areas surrounding the new location rose in opposition. The CEO said during an interview that this came as a big surprise, because the board assumed that the residents would welcome a new factory. The interests of the residents were not properly documented.

4. A substantial number of employees of a teaching institution are inadequately aware of the material being taught at secondary schools and of the specific requirements of the organizations the students will subsequently go to. Within the teaching institution there is no communication from the top to the teachers with respect to the expectations of the job market nor do teachers have face-to-face contact with the future employers of the students.

16. Consistency

Consistency in the "dirty hands" dimension refers to the commitment of co-workers and managers to deal carefully with the interests and expectations of stakeholders, thus setting a good example.

1. Within a transshipment company it is widely known that the management has resorted to all sorts of subterfuges in its negotiations with a major client. The client has, for example, been deliberately misled with regard to delivery times and the quality of the products and services. On top of that, the management has procured confidential information concerning the client's negotiating strategy from one of the client's employees. This conduct on the part of the management is reflected in a lack of customer-orientation among the staff at shop-floor level. For example, staff strictly observe the scheduled starting time and length of breaks, even if they are engaged on loading and unloading customers' lorries and customers are in need of speedy service. Customers who comment on this find will meet resistance and may expect longer delays in the future.

2. A second-hand car salesman sees that his co-workers use unsavory sales tactics. After a few months, the salesman, too, changes his mind and uses them as well.

3.   Employees of a retail chain outlet witness their boss ignoring well-founded complaints from customers again and again. The employees interpret his conduct as a sign that client-friendliness is rather unimportant, so they adjust their own conduct accordingly. When a consumer survey is conducted, this outlet scores drastically lower than the other outlets where client-friendliness is considered of paramount importance.

17. Sanctionability

The extent to which the quality of sanctionability is imbedded in de organizational context refers to the degree to which the corporation rewards employee conduct that promotes the realization of stakeholder interests and punishes conduct that damages stakeholder interests. Evaluating employees on the basis of their sales or returns only can, according to Falkenberg and Herrenans (1995), lead to the neglect of one or more fundamental interests of stakeholders. "When performance goals are excessively demanding, the message conveyed to employees is that any means available may be used to achieve these goals, regardless of the legitimacy of those means, and anomie[74] ensues." (Cohen, 1993:347).

1.   Within a distribution company, employees are only rewarded on the basis of the profit margins they have achieved. Keeping the margins, though, makes such heavy demands on employees that they feel "forced" to achieve their margins in devious ways. Some employees extort the transport companies. Other employees do all they can to overcharge their clients.

2.   An university lecturer notes that his yearly performance is evaluated on the basis of how many articles he has written. "No one pays any attention to the quality of the articles, nor to the effort involved in my lectures. Therefore, I would be pretty stupid if I were to spend a lot of time preparing for my lectures or in researching for my articles." The consequence is that the quality of the publications and his teaching clearly suffers.

3.   A school librarian was very proud about the good condition of "her" books in the library. At the end of the year, she could report to the board that she almost never had to replace a book. Books did not get lost. In addition, she told them proudly that the expenses for repair of damaged books were very low that year. When asked how she accomplished this, she replied that she never let students take books home. The librarian had forgotten the actual purpose of the library in minimizing the budget for replacing and repairing books.

---

[74]   Following Merton, Cohen (1993) defines anomie as a condition of normlessness and social disequilibrium where the rules once governing conduct have lost their savor and force.

4. A transport truck driver causes a serious accident. Investigation shows that the man had only slept four out of the previous 48 hours. The man explains that his employer gives a bonus for every hour the shipment arrives at its destination ahead of schedule.

5. The planner of a painting company calculates per project the maximum number of hours employees may spend on the job in order to make the projects profitable. Because the contract price is often below the market level, the painters are given less time than they need to do their work well. Most projects are just knocked off and the painting work is sub-standard.

18. Achievability

The virtue of achievability reflects the degree to which the corporation is able to fulfill expectations it has raised. Raising too high expectations interfere with the autonomy of the stakeholders and can lead to disappointment. Raising too high expectations can also lead to the development of any number of destructive methods in order to realize these expectations at any cost. Because an official organization had to evaluate an unrealistically high number of permit applications, all applications that had not been reviewed within two weeks were automatically signed. As a result, a lot of citizens received permits they were not entitled to. Raising too high expectations creates doubts in the minds of employees regarding the credibility of the corporation. In addition, they could give employees justification for presenting their own work in a better light than it really deserves.

1. A software producer presents his revolutionary programs as 100 percent reliable. However, the software is far from perfect and contains countless errors. The producer uses the initial customers to learn from their complaints and to revise the software. He thereby strengthens his competitive position. Nearly all the programmers at the company are aware of these practices, in contrast with the customers who are totally unaware of these practices.

2. The police received a number of vacation notifications from citizens who wanted their houses watched a little more closely while they were away. Due to heavy workloads this was not done very often, contrary to what the citizens had been told. After the holidays, the police sometimes receive a thank-you present, like a cake, for looking after the houses. This is often, then, a reward for services not rendered.

3. A company has used the same kind of car for years. A dealer of a competing car manufacturer offers a test vehicle for a month completely free of charge and with full compensation of the fuel costs. The supplier says that his cars provide better quality at a lower cost. Changing manufacturers is out of the questions for the company, but the test vehicle is accepted anyway.

4.   A terribly upset older woman came to report a theft to the police. Her car had been broken into and a number of valuable papers were stolen. The complaint is taken and the women calmed. "We take this serious, we'll do everything we can to solve this case. Do not worry." the police official said. Reassured, the woman leaves the station. The complaint is lost under a large pile of other complaints and nothing further is done with it.

5.   A computer manufacturer has two conflicting norms which cannot always both be realized. First, the "client is king" and second, "maximize profit." Solving the conflict between these two points of view is completely left to the discretion of the employees. A municipal council asks an employee of the manufacturer for advice on the most appropriate computer system. After an investigation, the employee discovers that a competitor can fulfill the needs of the customer better than his own company. Eventually, the employee recommends his company as the most appropriate after all.[75]

19. Supportability

With regard to the "dirty hands" dimension, supportability concerns the way employees are stimulated to acknowledge the interests and expectations of the stakeholders. A corporation that damages the interests of the stakeholders without the support of the personnel is running a risk. The support among employees to achieve or respect the interests of stakeholders on behalf of the organization is placed under pressure. The degree to which this quality is embedded within the organization is characteristic of how employees deal with external criticism of the corporation. Do they feel themselves personally attacked, do they agree with the criticism, do they add to the criticism or do they say nothing because they do not have enough information to explain the corporation's standpoint? Employees at an European airport were constantly asked by outsiders why the airport continued to expand. Not all the employees were fully acquainted with the background of the policy and could not give the outsiders a satisfactory answer. The employees of a railroad company avoided going to recreational activities because they did not want to be bombarded with heavy criticism of the many delays and the bad customer relations at their company. The credibility of the corporation is at stake in such situations. If the quality of supportability in relation to the "dirty hands" dimension scores low, it shows that employees cannot understand or cannot support the corporate policy. In both cases, the corporation fails in communicating its policy convincingly to employees. Such a low level of supportability creates the risk of employees distancing themselves from the corporation or the stakeholders.

---

[75]   According to Shrivastava, "...opposing forces that create tensions within a system [...] make failures within the system more likely. [...] There may be conflicting organizational objectives. The organization may be divided by competing values." (1994:241).

1. A company positions itself on the market as top of the line. The staff members distance themselves from what they consider an "arrogant position" because they have seen the company's services decline drastically with respect to the chief competition. Within a period of two years, the number of not immediately resolvable complaints has increased nearly threefold. Employees at the desk advise customers to take their complaints to the upper management with the added comment, "They will not listen to us. Maybe they will listen to *you*." Within the ranks of the personnel the schism between pretense and practice give rise to so much anger and frustration that an atmosphere of resignation and passivity comes into being. "If the upper management wants the company to be the best, they will have to make the first move. Only then will we follow suit."

20. Visibility

Visibility of conduct can be further broken down into the visibility of the consequences of corporate conduct for the employees themselves and for the external stakeholders. Bovens makes this quality a condition for a responsible organization. "Within the organization, individual officials must have a real possibility to make a judgment about the nature and consequences of behavior of the organization as a whole and of their contribution to that in particular." (1990:158). The reason for this is supplied earlier in his thesis: "The nature of the risk is, in some cases, unknown or differs sharply from the risks they have been familiar with until now. Complex organizations bring new products into the world on the basis of production processes whose effects or manageability (certainly in the long term) are not always known or predictable. Examples of this are the risk of medicines like Softenon or DES that were unknown to users at the time, as was the nature of the deformations the products caused." (1990:23). If employees do not know what the consequences of their actions will be for others, they cannot modify or alter their conduct. Without direct feedback, no direct change in conduct is possible. The lack of visibility can partly be attributed to the result of the great distance between employee and stakeholder. According to Bovens (1990) many officials do not see, or see only after a long time has passed, the negative consequences of their actions because they are not involved with carrying out the policy or because the damage only becomes visible after a long time or across a great distance. This physical distance also leads to a great psychological distance. The individual official is hardly aware of the nature and the seriousness of the consequences of his actions, and is not invited by the organization to account for them. This conclusion fits with the results of the Milgram experiment discussed in Chapter 2. Fewer people would be prepared to go to the edge if they had more contact with the victim.[76] A bridgeable distance between employees and stakeholders reduces the likelihood of unethical behavior.

---

[76] For example, when the learner was placed in the same room with the teacher, the level of obedience dropped more than 20%. In another variation on the obedience to authority studies in which

1. One of a bank's accounting departments is responsible for manually entering funds transfer slips. The department's staff has no contact with the actual customers. Customers are therefore seen as numbers instead of human beings. The work is seen by the staff as a matter of entering a series of numbers and not as actually transferring funds from one account to another. Because of this depersonalization of customers and the alienation of the staff's actual activities, the staff shows little personal involvement in their work and with respect to customers. A relatively large amount of errors are made and no fuss is made about transfers that are not made on time. Customers whose funds are not transferred on time are thereby indirectly be duped.

2. The directors of an organization are so removed from the base of the company and its customers that they are not aware of the poor quality of services. Customers are increasingly cheated. The management only wakes up after the organization's market share drops by 30 percent within a half year's time.

3. A legal firm feeds its employees' dependence on the company by giving them high salaries, favorable mortgages, company cars and a feeling of family. In order to increase their financial dependence on the firm, employees are even encouraged to have offspring. Only when their full dependence has been achieved, the board informs the employees about the Mafia's share in the firm. After this message, the cooperation of employees is coerced. Internal whistle-blowing is therefore impeded while the external stakeholders are not made aware of the firm's criminality.

4. A chemical plant advertised itself as the cleanest chemical giant. The TV ads show the slogan "Better products for a better life," while a number of seals are applauding. Government investigation showed though, that in a period of three years, the company paid environmental fines and settlements of nearly one million dollars a month.

5. Management of an indoor swimming pool puts employees under pressure not to talk about the immoral practices (like discrimination of quests) at the pool. Several times, employees are physically threatened to make it clear to them that they should not even think about making the dirty business public.

Milgram varied the closeness of the learner victim to the teacher, when the teacher was asked to physically force the learner's hand onto the shock plate, the obedience level dropped another 10% (Trevino and Nelson, 1995).

21. Discussability

The last cell in the ethical content model concerns the quality of discussability forming part of the "dirty hands" dimension. This quality relates to the degree to which a corporation is open to criticism from stakeholders.

---

1. The explosion of a space shuttle could possibly have been prevented by heeding the criticism from outside the organization. Technicians from the company that produced large components of the rocket had repeatedly vented their concerns about possible problems arising from the sealing of the O-rings during cold-weather launches. This information did not reach the management of the organization who had to take the launch decision. The criticism was smothered by middle management so it would not reach the decision-making authorities. After the disaster, the management said the space shuttle would not have been launched if it had been aware of the technicians' criticism.

2. A frozen foods producer did not take complaints from retailers very seriously. "Dealing with complaints does not deliver any commercial gain and simply costs time," was always the response of the head of sales.

3. In a sauna producing company many items are made of wood to give an "earthy" impression. The sauna company simply throws away a lot of chemical refuse brushes, paint cans, empty cans of turpentine, and brush cleaners. The employees dare not to correct each other.

4. An employee from a company that cleaned oil tanks is told by his boss to dump the processed oil at a remote location. The employee knows that his action is illegal, but does not dare to refuse out of fear of losing his job.

5. The board of management of a multinational company flatly refuses to meet the request of a human rights organization for a meeting to discuss possible violations of human rights by certain of the company's subsidiaries. According to the human rights organization, the company makes large-scale use of child labor and the company consistently neglects the health and safety of its employees. The board of management's standard written response is that it does not see the point of such a meeting, since the company acts in line with the Universal Declaration of Human Rights. However, the human rights organization interprets the management's reaction as evidence that it is not taken seriously as a discussion partner. It was not until they organized a consumer boycott, that the company issued an internal investigation revealing that human rights are consistently being violated.

In this chapter, a differentiation is made between three fundamental moral dimensions and seven qualities. The tables below offer a brief overview.

Fundamental dimensions	Cause	Possible repercussions of failing context
"Entangled hands"	Because employees represent the organization, they have access to corporate assets which should be used for the company's purposes but which they may divert for their own use.	Carelessness use or misuse of: • time; • information; • funds; • authority; • equipment; • goods; and • staff.
"Many hands"	The organization consists of staff, departments and divisions, each with their own functional responsibilities which should be geared collectively and which should be furnished with the necessary assets for giving expression to the collective responsibilities.	• counter-productive competition between staff, departments and divisions; • responsibilities get lost; • unresolved collective problems; • responsibilities are shrugged off; and • tasks are not or only partially performed.
"Dirty hands"	The organization is confronted with (conflicting) expectations from stakeholders which should be realized or balanced adequately.	• stakeholders have legitimate reason to complain; • stakeholders are less willing to participate; • stakeholders remove themselves from the organization; and • "license to operate" expires.

Figure 4-3: Short description of the three dimensions of the ethical content.

Ethics management needs to guarantee the presence of those qualities required for organizing the three fundamental ethics issues in a responsible way. Twenty-one different qualities can be formulated with which the actual organizational context can be described in a moral sense.

Organizational dimensions / Criteria	"Entangled hands" - in regards to -	"Many hands" - within -	"Dirty hands" - on behalf of -
a) Clarity	1) It is clear how staff should handle the assets of the organization.	8) It is clear what functional responsibilities of employees are.	15) It is clear what stakeholders expect of employees.
b) Consistency	2) Referents make enough effort to handle the assets of the organization with care.	9) Referents make enough effort to fulfill their functional responsibilities.	16) Referents make enough effort to realize the expectations of stakeholders.
c) Sanctionability	3) If the assets are not handled with care deliberately, staff is sanctioned.	10) If the functional responsibilities are (not) realized deliberately, staff is sanctioned.	17) If the expectations of stakeholders are (not) realized deliberately, staff is sanctioned.
d) Achievability	4) The expectations regarding the handling of corporate assets can be realized.	11) The staff's functional responsibilities can be realized.	18) The expectations raised to stakeholders can be realized.
e) Supportability	5) The organization stimulates support for the careful use of the corporate assets.	12) The organization stimulates support for an adequate co-ordination between employees.	19) The organization stimulates support for the realization of the interest of stakeholders.
f) Visibility	6) (Consequences of) conduct regarding the handling of corporate assets can be observed.	13) (Consequences of) conduct regarding the realization of functional responsibilities can be observed.	20) (Consequences of) conduct regarding the realization of stakeholders' expectations can be observed.
g) Discussability	7) Dilemmas, problems, and criticisms regarding the handling of corporate assets can be discussed.	14) Dilemmas, problems, and criticisms regarding realization of functional responsibilities can be discussed.	21) Dilemmas, problems, and criticisms regarding the realization of stakeholders' expectations can be discussed.

Figure 4-4: Brief explanation of the Ethical Qualities Model.

Unethical behavior may occur if one or more of the above qualities is not fully embedded within the organizational context. An organization that seeks to work on improving its ethics can determine which ethics risks occur in this context. In the following chapter, I will demonstrate how a review can be implemented in practice.

Chapter 5

The Ethics Audit
in Practice

*"A shared vocabulary is essential
when trying to measure, observe,
describe and evaluate behavior in
situations characterized by a multiplicity of stakeholders, each with
multiple values and expectations."*
(Pruzan, 1997:11)

In Chapter 4, we observed what qualities can be used to describe and evaluate the
ethical content of corporations. In this chapter, we shall discuss how we can review
the ethical content in practice. We shall also discuss other parts of an ethics audit
more closely. The insight gained during an ethics review may serve as input for corrective measures and activities. The possible ethics measures to be adopted and activities to be undertaken will be discussed in chapters 6 and 7.

5.1   Six parts of an ethics audit: an elaborate discussion

In this section, the Qualities Monitor, Conduct Detector, Stakeholders Reflector, Measures Scan, Dilemmas Decoder, and the Individual Characteristics and Circumstances Assessment will be discussed. At the end of this section, I will present the Ethics Thermometer as a survey among employees for describing the perceived context, conduct, and consequences.

1. The Qualities Monitor

The assessment of ethical qualities can be carried out in the form of a written survey. It is often desirable to conduct several supplementary interviews in order to get a better understanding of the results obtained (Victor and Cullen, 1987). The ethical content can be quantified by requesting employees to give their opinion on a diversity of propositions on a Likert-type scale from 1 (disagree completely) to 5 (agree completely). Statistical analyses will then be possible. In Appendix 2, I discuss the pros and cons of a survey, a number of considerations in the formulation of questions, and a number of practical matters in conducting such a survey.

The questionnaire which has been developed consists of almost one hundred propositions. Each quality is being described with help of multiple propositions. An example: visibility in the "entangled hands" dimension encompasses the visibility among co-workers, the manager's view of his department, and the department's view of its manager. The propositions relating to this quality are:

		Disagree completely	Agree completely
•	If my co-worker does something wrong and tries to hide it, I or one of my other co-workers will certainly find out.		1-2-3-4-5
•	If my co-worker does something wrong and tries to hide it, my manager will certainly find out.		1-2-3-4-5
•	If my manager does something wrong and tries to hide it, I or one of my co-workers will certainly find out.		1-2-3-4-5

Figure 5-1: Three propositions of the Qualities Monitor.

The 21 qualities are applicable to every organization (with the exceptions named in Section 4.1). A quality that is not completely embedded in an organization implies moral risks. Some moral risks especially apply to certain forms of organizations. A bureaucratic type of organization has different moral risks (i.e. slow decision-making) than a matrix organization (i.e. disorder in responsibilities). The society a company operates in may also influence the ethical content. Companies in authoritarian societies will probably face moral risks which differ from those companies in egalitarian societies.

A survey among employees brings in view the actual organizational context as perceived by them. This perception is important because it guides the behavior of employees. Employees contribute to the perpetuation and change of the organizational context. A number of qualities can also be determined more objectively. For example, an auditor can determine how long it takes before unethical conduct is noticed by management (visibility). Some forms of unethical conduct (i.e. computer theft) could also be faked for this purpose. An auditor can also determine the forms and extent of unethical conduct in the corporation (Conduct Detector) and the degree to which the management is aware of these practices (visibility). It is not quite as easy to describe a quality, such as discussability, in objective terms. The degree to which management is open to criticism is largely determined by the opinion of the employees. Describing the ethical content objectively is sometimes so complex and time consuming, or even impossible, that the evaluation of the ethical content is necessarily based on the perceptions of employees. The perceptions of employees can be considered as an indication for the actual context. Sections 5.2, 6.3 and 7.9, and Appendix 2 discuss what fruitful information such a survey provides.

The completed questionnaires provide not only a score per question, but also a score per quality and per dimension. The results can be separated into department, hierarchical level, function, gender, and age. The relatively strong and weak aspects of the departments can be identified in order to take specific measures for each department.

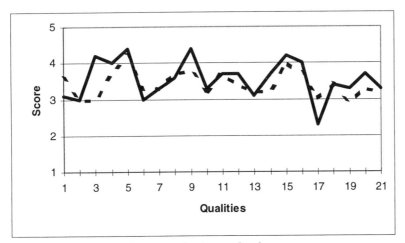

Figure 5-2: Ethics profile of an organization and a department.

2. The Conduct Detector

While the Qualities Monitor shows how an organization stimulates and hinders ethical conduct, the Conduct Detector reports the actual or perceived degree to which ethical or unethical behavior occurs. There are various methods for detecting conduct.

In the first place, the employees themselves can be asked, through interviews or questionnaires, what kind of unethical conduct occurs in their organization or direct work surroundings. Just as could be the case with the Qualities Monitor, this method calls on the employees' perception. In relation to the "entangled hands" dimension, employees can be asked about how much unjustified sick leave is taken in their department, whether there are any outside jobs that conflict with the interests of the organization, whether reckless use of company property is made, and whether confidential information is ever leaked. By also asking employees how morally acceptable they consider these practices, it is possible to determine the extent to which the practice deviates from the norm of the employees. If there is a discrepancy between norm and practice, employees indicate that the practice in question is an issue that requires attention.

The Conduct Detector in which the experience of the personnel is surveyed using a questionnaire does have the drawback of inquiring into subjective opinions. If fifty percent of the employees of a department indicate that they can cite an incident of declaring unreal expenses, it remains indistinguishable whether they are all thinking of the same incident or whether everyone have a different incident in mind. There is, however, always a problem if the respondents feel that expense claims are improperly handled in their own department. If the personnel has a good idea of what actually goes on in the department, they can prove that the organization is suffering financial damage from expenses which are claimed but not made. If employees incorrectly think that unacceptable practices occur in their work situation that obviously are not sanctioned, this offers a breeding ground for similar conduct from the employees themselves.

Another, rather direct method can be used by an auditor who himself lists the degree to which unethical conduct occurs. Figure 5-3 shows several measurement points with regard to the actual conduct relating to the "entangled hands" dimension.[77] The audit that measures conduct directly, a so-called fact investigation or fact-finding research, is significantly more time consuming than a written survey conducted among the personnel to measure the perceived conduct.[78] A detailed investigation is frequently required to get an idea of the degree to which bribes are accepted or con-

---

[77] See Huntington and Davies (1994) and Bologna and Lindquist (1995) for an elaborate discussion of some measurement points or warning signs with regard to internal fraud.

[78] Comer (1985) identifies a number of possible investigative techniques: analysis of documents, analysis of deviations, observations (visual and audio surveillance), forensic and technical examinations, pretext investigations, interviews with witnesses, and interviews with suspects.

Damage to company property.	Calculate the number of hours spent on repairing company property, the technical life span of property, and the frequency with which property must be replaced.
	Conduct visual checks on property damage.
	Analyze employee complaints regarding damaged or broken property.
Cheating on expense accounts.	Compute travel allowance by employee's overtime, compared to other employees, for specific task by employee, and by type of expense, i.e. rental car, hotel, and airfare.
Leakage of confidential information.	Investigate the number of times that the media or other external contacts report confidential information that could only have been obtained from employees of the corporation.
Theft of inventory.	Compute inventory at t=0 plus the production and purchase between t=0 and t=1, minus the sales and consumption between t=0 and t=1, and minus the inventory at t=1.
	Conduct surprise inventory counts.
	Use statistical sampling of sales invoices.
	Match sales invoices with customer orders.
	Compare customer names and addresses with employee names and addresses.

Figure 5-3: Some measurement points of the Conduct Detector.

confidential information is misused. Management may prefer an investigations of facts because it makes possible to track down those who have intentionally caused harm to the corporation or to the stakeholders. The Conduct Detector which investigates actual censurable conduct can be used in investigations into fraud and corruption, the so-called forensic investigation.[79] Such an investigation provides grounds for sanctioning offenders.

---

[79] See, for example, Comer (1985), Zier (1993), Huntington and Davies (1994), Bologna et al. (1995), and Thornhill (1995).

3. The Stakeholders Reflector

The Stakeholders Reflector is a protocol for examining the interests and expectations of stakeholders and the degree to which these expectations are realized. Some questions which need to be answered during such an assessment are: (a) who are the stakeholders, (b) what are their fundamental interests, (c) what are their expectations in regards to the organization, (d) how will be decided what the legitimate expectations are, (e) what are the indicators for measuring the extent to which these expectations are realized, (f) how will the stakeholders be approached, and (g) how will reliable and valid information be gathered in an efficient way? The most common techniques of consulting different stakeholder groups are: individual interviews, focus groups meetings, and questionnaires (Pearce et al., 1996). The choice between these techniques depends very much on the nature of the stakeholder group and resources available. Some stakeholders may be very costly to reach (Peace et al., 1996).[80]

I have worked out the interests and expectations from one stakeholder group below. Most of the questions can be presented on a Likert scale to the stakeholder concerned. The questions will often need to be adapted to the organization concerned.

Interests of the consumer

A product or service, or both, that fulfills the requirements of the consumer, has a reasonable price and is available at the right place and time and in the right amount.

Expectations of the consumer:

Product
1.   Does the product meet the expected quality standards?
2.   Does the product function as desired?
3.   Does the product meet the technical and economical longevity expectations?
4.   Is sufficient care taken to improve product quality?
5.   Is the product safe to use?
6.   Is the health of the customers ensured?
7.   Are the warrantee conditions reasonable?
8.   To what degree does the corporation take incorrect use of the product by the consumer into account?
9.   To what degree does the corporation take misuse of the product into account?
10.   Does the client receive sufficient assistance?
11.   How is service provided to customers who have already bought the product?
12.   Is the packaging in relation to the size of the product?

---

[80] According to Frederick et al. (1988), six major steps in stakeholder analysis are: (1) mapping stakeholder relationships, (2) mapping stakeholder coalitions, (3) assessing the nature of each stakeholder's interest, (4) assessing the nature of each stakeholder's power, (5) constructing a matrix of stakeholder priorities, and (6) monitoring shifting coalitions. For an exposition of how to do a stakeholder analysis, see also Freeman (1984) and Wheeler and Sillanpää (1997).

Promotion
1.   Does the corporation provide information about all of the features of the product which can influence the consumer's decision to buy the product?
2.   Is the customer actually familiar with this information?
3.   Does this information accurately reflect the features of the product?
4.   Are the names of the product and producer clearly legible?
5.   Does the corporation adequately inform the public about reductions in quality or quantity?
6.   Does the corporation advertise in a non-offensive way?
7.   Is the consumer pressured into buying the product? In other words, will the consumer regret his purchase within, for example, 48 hours?
8.   Do the advertisements promote responsible use?

Place
1.   Is the product reasonably available to sales outlets?
2.   Is the product always available? If not, does the corporation take enough care to meet the desires of the consumer?
3.   Is the sale of the product linked to the sale of another product from the same company?
4.   Is the sale of the product linked to the sale of the same product from the same company at a later time?
5.   Are there barriers to prevent the consumer from switching to a product from another company?

Price
1.   Is the profit margin reasonable or is the price too high?
2.   Is the price justified in comparison with what competitors are asking?
3.   If there are price fluctuations, are certain clients put at a disadvantage?
4.   Is there unreasonable price discrimination?
5.   Are bribes used in selling products?
6.   Are the payment conditions reasonable?

Complaints
1.   How many consumer complaints are there?
2.   What part of the product do the complaints relate to?
3.   Is there a complaints and information office for consumers?
4.   Do consumers know about this office?
5.   Is it easy for consumers to contact the office?
6.   Is making complaints encouraged?
7.   Are discussions carried out with consumer organizations?
8.   What is done with the complaints in regards to the consumer?
9.   What is done with the complaints in regards to the organization?
10.   Are lessons learned from justified complaints?
11.   Are possible complaints anticipated?

Figure 5-4: Some questions for a stakeholder analysis.

The disadvantage of the method above is that different questions must be posed for each stakeholder group. Furthermore, no standardized list for each stakeholder group can be created because stakeholders with the same interests often have different expectations in regards to the corporation. This problem can be avoided by first allowing the stakeholders themselves to formulate their substantial interests and expectations and then posing the questions relating to them. In addition, it seems to me that stakeholders have identical procedural expectations in regards to the moral trustworthiness of the organization. Some criteria, which will not be discussed further, include the following:

1. unity:	is the conduct of the corporate personnel consistent, both over time as among themselves?
2. openness	to what extent does the organization provide relevant information to the stakeholders and does the organization "listen" to criticism and ideas from the stakeholders?
3. honesty:	does the information provided by the organization give an accurate view of the actual situation?
4. liberty:	are the stakeholders free in their decision-making or does the organization put unfair pressure on them?
5. subsidiarity	does the corporation act at the right level of (de)centralization?
6. equality:	are stakeholders with comparable, relevant characteristics treated equally or are some stakeholders treated unfairly?
7. reciprocity:	does the organization apply the same standards to itself as it does to the stakeholders?
8. adequacy:	does the organization anticipate or react with appropriate speed or in an appropriate way when the interests of the stakeholders are potentially or actually harmed?
9. solidarity:	does the organization contribute to the resolution of social problems?
10. faithfulness:	does the organization fulfill expectations it has raised?
11. sustain-ability:	does the organization restore or compensate for unfair harm to interests?
12. readiness to learn:	does the organization learn from its mistakes or do the same mistakes occur more than once?

Figure 5-5: Criteria of the Stakeholders Reflector.

Linking the interests and expectations described by the respondents to the twelve criteria above will result in a standardized question list.

The Stakeholders Reflector holds a "mirror" up to the corporation from the surroundings and unravels the specific expectations stakeholders have of the corporation. The information obtained is relatively easy to translate into policy. By conducting such research, the corporation sends a clear signal to the stakeholders that it considers ethics important, that it is receptive to the opinions of the stakeholders, and that it is prepared to improve corporate ethics. A drawback of this method can be its time-consuming character if the auditor has to approach a representative group of each stakeholder category.

4. The Measures Scan

A Measures Scan examines the initiatives, activities, instruments, and rules that have already been undertaken to protect and improve the ethics of an organization. A Measures Scan charts the formal or explicit organizational context. The answers to the following questions can be filled into the Measures Chart.

1. Which?	In relation to which morally relevant aspects are rules formulated and other (supporting) measures taken?
2. By whom?	Who is responsible for the implementation, execution, and control of these measures?
3. For whom?	For whom are these measures intended?
4. Why?	Why were these measures taken?
5. What for?	What are the purposes of these measures?
6. When?	When were these measures first introduced and when were the last changes made?
7. Worth?	Are those who are responsible for the implementation, execution, and control of these measures satisfied with the effectiveness and efficiency of these measures?

Figure 5-6: Seven questions for describing existing measures.

For each moral dimension, a table can be created by placing the aspects of conduct in the left-hand column and filling in the various answers per row. An abbreviated view of the Measures Chart for the "entangled hands" dimension is shown below.

"Entangled hands"	Rules	Other measures	By whom?	For whom?	Why?	What for?	When?	Worth?
Family/private relationships								
Free time/outside jobs								
Gifts and gratuities								
Confidential information								

Figure 5-7: Some elements of a Measures Chart.

The auditor can evaluate the rules collected during this audit according to diverse criteria. Among these are clarity (is it clear what is written?), unequivocalness (do the rules conflict with one another?), flexibility (are discrepancies and nuances possible?), and achievability (can employees find their way with what is written and are the rules achievable in practice?).

The Measures Scan is valuable for formulating, scrapping or improving existing measures. Especially in large organizations, the Measures Scan provides management a better view of what has already been carried out with regard to ethics and who is responsible for it. It is conceivable that no one in the organization is completely aware of all the measures and activities in place. By charting the formal organization, new activities can be added to those already in place.

Another part of a Measures Scan concerns identifying the spots in the formal organization where inadequate measures create the chance for improper benefit of employees (or eventually external stakeholders). During this examination, the auditor is concerned with describing the assets employees have access to and which they can use in an improper way for their own purposes. Possible assets include cash, confidential information from the computer system, and goods from the inventories. Subsequently, the auditor investigates what measures are necessary to reduce the chances of improper benefit. For example: is the accounting and control of the cash done by different people, are there access procedures to enter the information system, and is there an inventory security system? In contrast with the Qualities Monitor, this examination leaves the stimulating and corrective workings of the informal context out of consideration. Such an examination consists of the following steps.

a. Flows

During the first phase, the auditor maps all the flows or processes which could be the object of improper use by employees. Examples of this are the products and service flows, information flows, and cash flows.

b. Possibilities of violation

During this phase an analysis is conducted of the opportunities employees have to use the various flows to their own improper benefit. The auditor asks himself: if an employee intends to act out of malice, what opportunities does he have to do so? Some positions (such as directors) and departments (such as purchasing) have a greater intrinsic, formal risk than other positions (such as doormen) and departments (such as R&D) have. Every position, however, carries the potential for infringement. Cleaners often have the place to themselves after closing, secretaries often have a lot of confidential information, and doormen can allow unauthorized people access to the building and premises.

c. Risks

The possibility of improper benefit should subsequently be analyzed with respect to (a) the reasonable chance and potential frequency of a possible break-in and (b) the repercussions for everyone of such theft. To this end, it will probably not be necessary to focus attention on such petty matters as the chance of someone stealing toilet paper from the rest rooms because (a) toilet paper do not often represent a "desired object" as such, and (b) if someone actually does steal it, the repercussions for the company's (financial) operations will be little.[81]

d. Desired measures

Based on the risks identified in the previous phase, the auditor determines the formal measures that are necessary to reduce the possible infringements to a minimum for each flow. The measures can be broken down into procedures, rules, controls, systems, and arrangements.

e. Actual measures

In this phase, the auditor describes the formal measures already taken within the organization to limit the possible violations of the risks indicated. An additional review can be made of the extent to which the staff is familiar with these measures and whether they are adopted and internalized.

f. Discrepancy

This audit ends with determining the degree of discrepancy between the desired measures and the actual measures. On the basis of this discrepancy, i.e. the extent to which the existing measures are insufficient, recommendations can be made as to implement new measures or to revision existing measures. One of the recommendations can be that the evaluation of proposals above a given amount should be done by several employees.

This part of the Measures Scan is a partial extension of the Qualities Monitor. Where, for example, the visibility in regards to the "entangled hands" issue is hardly embedded, employees have the possibility to hide improper use of the corporate assets from the view of management and co-workers. A drawback of this measures examination is that it is quite labor intensive to pass through all phases. It is also difficult to standardize the selection process of the desired measures so as to render the selection process strongly dependent on the knowledge and experience of the auditor. A bank, for example, faces quite different risks (i.e. embezzlement of money) than a university (i.e. committing fraud at exams).

5. The Dilemmas Decoder

First of all, a Dilemma Decoder lists the conflicting moral expectations employees face. When, for example, an employee is offered an expensive gift by a supplier, good customer relations (refusal can be interpreted as an insult by the supplier) are in

---

[81] According to Comer (1985), the relative attractiveness of the assets at risk should be assessed in terms of the following categories: cash and equivalents (0: highly vulnerable), secret business information (0), high value, low bulk items (1), normal products (2), stocks and raw materials (2), plant and machinery, small size (3), fixed assets (4/7), and buildings (10: barely vulnerable).

conflict with the norm that purchasers should remain independent (suppliers should be evaluated according to objective criteria). Secondly, the listed dilemmas can then be analyzed in order, for example, to write an ethics code of conduct. The dilemmas can be obtained during Dilemma Gathering Sessions, when the auditor invites the participants to formulate their own work-related dilemmas.[82] A dilemma is always a difficult choice. When a situation is felt to be a serious dilemma, the person involved feels torn between two norms or values. The norms and values in question are those which employees think ought to be respected within the organization. During Dilemma Analyzing Sessions, a discussion panel of employees will analyze the obtained range of actual dilemmas to determine (a) which norms and values are in conflict, (b) which risks are related to the options, (c) which principles, core values or considerations merit precedence, (d) what demands this makes on the employees, and (e) what organizational provisions are necessary. During a dilemma audit, actual insights, intuitions, and assumptions are revealed and made a subject of discussion. The auditor's function is to sharpen these intuitions. Section 6.3 discusses the process of decoding dilemmas and recoding them into a code of conduct in a more extensive way.

6. The Individual Characteristics and Circumstances Assessment

An Individual Characteristics and Circumstances Assessment maps out the morally relevant characteristics of individuals. Which moral criteria are relevant in examining the morality of employees and how can these be identified? Keeping in mind what has already been discussed in Section 2.2, three criteria can be stated as follows:

- intentions: does the employee have the will to behave morally?
- intuitions: does the employee have the moral awareness to behave responsibly?
- capabilities: does the employee have the ability and skills to realize his moral responsibilities?

An assessment of individual intentions will particularly be used for pre-employment screening. Such as audit can consist of, for example, a polygraph examination, a voice stress analyzer, a paper-and-pencil test, the Draw-a-Person test, a color preference test, handwriting analysis, a drug and alcohol test, and a background check. These methods vary in terms of costs and yields, and in terms of validity and reliability (Watson, 1994).

---

[82]   The dilemmas can be gathered using the KPMG game "Cards on the Table." This game consists of 50 different moral dilemmas. The dilemmas, which are taken from everyday business, place the players in difficult situations. In a group of four, the players have to "solve" a selection of these dilemmas. Often these dilemmas raise feelings of recognition during the game. After the game is over, the auditor invites the players to write these experiences down. Within ten minutes, most participants will often have written down two or three dilemmas. By playing the game within different parts of an organization, the auditor obtains a broad range of actual dilemmas.

The polygraph, or lie-detector, measures and graphs respiration, blood pressure, and perspiration while the applicant being tested answers questions. Doubts about the validity of the polygraph have led to legal restrictions on the use of polygraphs in the United States.[83]

A multiple-choice honesty test can be used to get an impression of the intentions of applicants. The commonly used paper and pencil honesty or integrity tests assess the likelihood of theft based on job applicants' thoughts, feelings, and expected behaviors in matters of honesty, theft, and the punishment of deviance, as well as admissions of past misbehavior (Cunnigham et al., 1994). Common areas of inquiry (Sacket and Harris, 1984) include beliefs about frequency and extent of theft in society (e.g. "what percentage of people take more than $1.00 per week from their employer?"), punitivenss toward theft (e.g. "should a person be fired if caught stealing $10.00?"), ruminations about theft (e.g. "have you ever thought about taking company merchandise without actually taking any?"), perceived ease of theft (e.g. "how easy would it be for a dishonest person to steal from his employer?"), likelihood of detection (e.g. "what percentage of employee-thieves are ever caught?"), knowledge of employee theft (e.g. "do you know for certain that some of your friends steal from their employer?"), rationalizations about theft (e.g. "an employer who pays people poorly is asking his employees to steal"), assessments of one's own honesty (e.g. "compared to other people, how honest are you?"), and admissions of theft (e.g. "what is the total value of cash and merchandise you have taken from your employer in the past?"). A test of individual intentions can also include in-depth questioning about other unethical activities (e.g. "which of the following list of activities have you engaged in in the past five years?"). A good test has a socially desirable answers- or 'lie'-scale. This involves the counting of the number of socially desirable but implausible responses (e.g., responding "no" to questions such as "have you ever in your life said something that was not true?").[84] Unfavorable attitudes and perceptions and acknowledgment of previous misconduct are expected to be predictive of the prospective candidates' future behavior. According to Sackett et al. (1989) and Bernardin and Cooke (1994) these, so-called, overt integrity tests are reasonably reliable and do seem to have some validity in identifying individuals who

---

[83] See The Employee Polygraph Protection Act, 1988.

[84] The Reid Report is an overt integrity test (Sacket et al., 1989) which involves two major factors: punitiveness and projectiveness (Cunningham et al., 1994). The punitiveness factor contains items that indicate that honest individuals tend to hold themselves to high standards of personal conduct and are relatively harsh toward those who act immorally. When asked a question such as, "Do you think that a manager should be fired if he used company money to pay his mortgage, even if he had replaced the money before the fact was discovered?", a high scorer on the Reid Report would be likely to indicate that the employee should be discharged. The projectiveness factor incorporates the idea that honest individuals project the image that they are honest and believe that most other people are as honest as they are. Dishonest people, by contrast, are more likely to admit that they think about committing crimes of theft and to see larceny in the hearts of others. Theft-prone individuals are likely to give a negative response to a question such as, "Do you think public officials are usually honest?" (Cunningham et al., 1994). The projectiveness factor is congruent with the classic finding of Katz and Allport (1931) that an individual's perception of the number of other students who were likely to cheat was closely related to the individual's own level of cheating.

have been caught for stealing in the past or will be caught stealing in the future.[85] The costs of these tests are relatively low with few administrative procedures required (Sims, 1991).

Another category of intention tests focuses more on general personality traits like reliability, conscientiousness, emotional stability, and agreeableness, rather than on specific attitudes toward dishonest behavior, and history of theft and other unethical activities. Personality-based integrity tests assume that certain general psychological traits distinguish unethical employees from ethical employees. These measures not only predict theft but also composite measures of other types of unethical behavior, such as abuse of sick leave, drugs use at work, aggression, rule-breaking, cheating on expense accounts, and engaging in unacceptable behavior to make a profit. For example, the Hogan Reliability Index, includes items dealing with hostility toward authority, thrill seeking, conscientiousness, impulse control, confused vocational identity, and social insensitivity (Hogan and Hogan, 1989, and Hogan and Brinkmeyer, 1997). Personality-based test do not have to contain obvious references to unethical practices and, thus, will be perceived as less offensive by employees than overt integrity tests.[86] Ones et al. (1991) found comparable levels of validity for the two categories of tests in their meta-analyses.

A background check can be done by checking the applicant's curriculum vitae, calling references and previous employers, requesting a municipal declaration of good conduct, and visiting the applicant at home. A full investigation can be quite expensive and may take up quite a lot of time. This can, however, be rewarding (Fletcher, 1997). A study in the United States shows that at least 30 percent of all curricula vitae contain falsehoods (Sims, 1991).

Personal intuitions can be identified by presenting employees with concrete dilemmas and asking them what they would do in these situations. The choices of employees can be analyzed in a number of aspects. Analyzing the arguments of employees with the Kohlberg model for example, shows the level of moral reasoning the employee uses and whether this matches the profile desired by the corporation. A questionnaire can be used to identify the level of moral reasoning of current employees (see, for example, Colby and Kohlberg, 1987, Weber, 1991, and Pearson, 1995).[87] For pre-employment screening, the following criteria may be used.

---

[85] Recurring themes in the reviews of intention tests are concerns about faking, the need for more follow-up research using an external, nonself-report criterion, and concerns about over-reliance on test scores in personnel decision-making (Sackett et al., 1989).

[86] Some integrity tests for use with current employees are, for example, the Reid Report, the Stanton Inventory, and the London House Employee Attitude Inventory (see Sackett et al., 1989).

[87] Kohlberg and others developed an instrument and scoring method to measure an individual's reasoning, the Moral Judgment Interview and Standard Issue Scoring respectively. The Moral Judgment Interview is designed to "...elicit a subject's (1) own construction of moral reasoning, (2) moral frame of reference or assumptions about right and wrong, and (3) the way these beliefs and assumptions are used to make and justify moral decisions" (Colby and Kohlberg, 1987:61). Questions are explicitly prescriptive so as to draw out normative judgments about what one should do, rather than descriptive or predictive judgments about what one would do. According to Colby and Kohlberg, interviews can be conducted in three ways: "(1) oral interviews (tape-recorded and

A set of dilemmas that are specific to the organization or position are made available to personnel officers. During an employment interview, one or more dilemmas are presented.[88] Because dilemmas often do not have black and white solutions, the officer should especially look at the arguments applicants give for their actions.

A number of relevant criteria with regard to the intuitions of applicants may include the following:

- The stakeholders that are recognized and acknowledged by the applicant in relation to the dilemma. (The more stakeholders are named, with reasons, the greater the ability of the applicant to realize the extent of a moral problem.)
- The degree to which the applicant is able to specify the interests of the stakeholders. (The more the applicant can specify the interests of the stakeholders, the greater the applicant's ability to realize the depth of the moral problem.)
- The degree to which the applicant feels responsible for solving the moral problem. (The less the applicant shoves off the problem onto others, the more the applicant will try to solve the moral problem himself.)
- The level at which the applicant argues: does he argue on the basis of (1) punishment, (2) reward, (3) social acceptance, (4) laws and rules, (5) principles which actually lay at the foundation of the problem and the system, or (6) principles which ought to lay at the foundation of the problem and the system? (The higher the level of reasoning (level 6 is the highest), the greater the ability of the applicant to choose a solution for the moral problem himself and the less the sensitivity to punishment, reward and peer pressure.)

The capabilities of an employee or applicant indicates his abilities or skills in carrying out his assigned responsibilities. If, for example, employees are burdened with tasks and responsibilities they are not fully able to handle, it has a negative effect on the quality of achievability in regards to the "many hands" dimension. Examining the abilities of employees and applicants is often a standard fixture of periodical job evaluations and employment interviews respectively. Especially for supervisory positions, it is important to evaluate candidates on the degree to which they are able to embed the ethical qualities within their departments. Questions regarding moral leadership are, for example: is the candidate able to discuss employees' unethical conduct with them, does the candidate have the ability to carry out moral discussions

---

transcribed); (2) oral interviews with responses written by interviewer; and (3) written interviews" (1987:152). The face-to-face, oral interview technique is preferred by Kohlberg due to the opportunity it provides for clarifying the subject's responses and to probe more deeply into the reasoning process.

[88] Weber (1990, 1991) found significantly higher moral stage responses for the remote dilemmas than for the more familiar dilemmas placed in a business context. The familiarity embodied in realistic dilemmas set in a corporate context will better elicit from the employees their actual type of moral reasoning.

within his department, and is the candidate able to stimulate a feeling of responsibility among his employees?

7. The Ethics Thermometer

The examination of perceived context, conduct, and consequences can be combined into a written questionnaire among the employees of a company. I would like to unite these audits under the term "Ethics Thermometer." Questions are then posed per dimension over the perceived actual organizational context and the perceived conduct. In addition, the questionnaire requests the employees to indicate to what extent they think that the stakeholders have a good reason to complain and which expectations are (not) realized. The concept of the thermometer refers to the notion of a short measurement period during which a quantitative view of the organization is compiled and by which the measurement results can be displayed on a standardized scale.[89] This combined examination provides extra information. By calculating the correlation between the qualities and the unethical conduct and consequences observed, key qualities can be outlined. Key qualities are the aspects of the context which contribute most to improving conduct. This is how the spearheads, central "buttons" or starting points for an ethics program can be found.

Which parts of the audit are to be used depends on the problems at hand, the means available, and the preferences of the principal. Each part of an audit can, in principle, be used separately. Carrying out more parts of an ethics audit may provide additional information. Analyzing the information from the Ethics Thermometer and the Stakeholders Reflector shows the discrepancies between the perceptions of stakeholders and the perceptions of employees. Comparing the results of the Ethics Thermometer with those of the Measures Scan shows to what extent the formal context and the actual context match up with each other. The next section shows how an ethics audit can be carried out in practice.[90]

---

[89] The Ethics Thermometer consists of approximately 200 propositions (the Qualities Monitor consists of 100 propositions, the Conduct Detector of 60 propositions, and the Stakeholder Decoder of 40 propositions). Completing the survey takes about 30 minutes.

[90] Organizations consulted so far expressed a preference for the combination of the Ethics Thermometer supplemented by several interviews, the Measures Scan and the Dilemmas Sessions. Until March 1998, nine of the 28 audited Dutch organizations preferred this combination. This combined review can be carried out reasonably quickly (the project turnaround time is three to four months), is not expensive (it takes about 80 to 120 hours in an organization of 2,000 employees for an experienced auditor), and provides plenty of information for focused measures. The Ethics Thermometer is also frequently used as the first review, after which, based on the results, decisions can be made as to what other reviews might still be necessary. Until March 1998, eleven of the 28 audited organizations preferred to start with the Ethics Thermometer.

5.2 Case X: the ethics audit at the Department of Justice[91]

The ethics review at the Dutch Department of Justice began in August 1995. The general goal of the project was "to provide a basis for forming a security policy and developing the integrity inside and outside the department." Initially, the Board of the Department and the members of the Integrity Coordinating Committee reduced the meaning of "integrity" to criminality, fraud and corruption. Furthermore, within the Department, there was a tendency to manage ethics by rules and procedures. Along the way, the relevance of the "dirty hands" and "many hands" dimensions and the organizational culture came into sight. The presentation of the findings to the Head of the Department took place in April 1996. Prior to our investigation a study had been done into the opportunities for improper benefit within the organization (partial Measures Scan). In addition, we made use of the annual reports of the national Ombudsman. The Ombudsman determined in his annual report for 1994 that the Department fell short in the areas of active information provision and the correction of mistakes (partial Stakeholders Reflector). Both sources were included in the description of the actual situation. The Individual Characteristics and Circumstances Assessment was not carried out, but was seen as a possibility for inclusion in future selection procedures.

In October 1995, Ethics Thermometer questionnaires were sent to the home addresses of 2,500 randomly chosen employees from the Department. In total, ten percent of employees received a questionnaire. The final response rate was 48 percent.[92] The results were presented to a panel of employees four weeks after receipt of the last questionnaire. The primary question at this meeting was whether the results matched their experiences or whether there were inexplicable scores among the results. The insiders saw no reason to doubt the picture arrived at. A number of aspects did merit further study. A large percentage of employees did not defend the Department when family or friends criticize the Department. On the basis of interviews, we attempted to determine what the personnel found indefensible, in concrete terms. From the statistical analysis, it appeared that there is a correlation between communicating policy decisions from management to the personnel and the degree to which employees can fend off criticism.

---

[91] All the data provided in this paragraph are also published in the public part of the report *Integriteitsontwikkeling van het Ministerie van Justitie: beschrijving, analyse en aanbevelingen*, J. van Berkel, C. Geluk, M. Kaptein, H. van Oosterhout and J. Wempe, Ethicon, Erasmus University Rotterdam, 1996.

[92] From telephone discussions with 22 non-respondents, it was learned that the reasons they gave for not filling out the questionnaire did not provide any information that would change the picture obtained from the survey. The organization reacted enthusiastically to the rate of response. In comparison with other surveys carried out within the department, this rate can be considered high. The conclusion was that the subject enjoyed broad interest. This was reinforced by the many personal comments written in the margins of the survey form. In addition, approximately 30 employees took the opportunity to tell their story by telephone. The response rate varied insignificantly per sub-department, age, and position.

The degree to which the 21 qualities are embedded in the Department is reflected in the graph below. A short explanation of the qualities is provided in Figure 4-4 at the end of Chapter 4. The interpretation of the scores follows later in this paragraph. The higher the score, the more the quality it relates to is embedded in the organization.

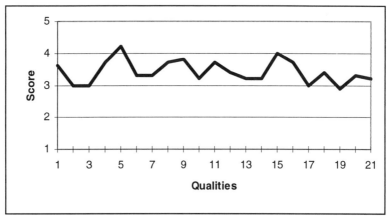

Figure 5-8: Ethics profile of the Department of Justice.

The Measures Scan is a search for all possible measures relating to the moral aspects that have been carried out over time. This examination was conducted by going through a large number of documents, brochures, laws, annual reports, meeting minutes, and lectures in search of what precisely was written about guaranteeing the three moral dimensions. This search began with people who have a broad view of the organization. These people gave the names of the employees who are knowledgeable about one or several aspects of the matrix in the subject under discussion. An interview with these employees provided information for the Measures Chart. These employees often knew co-workers who are involved with another aspect of the measures matrix. The Measures Charts were filled in by interviewing seventeen employees.

Ethical aspect	Rule	Person charged with carrying it out	Supporting activities/measures
Sexual harassment	Working conditions handbook, chapter 5, section 1 and 9 folder "Undesirable conduct"	Ms. Van Dongen, support-worker sexual harassment	Already in place: - victim assistance -- brochure "Sexual harassment" -- complaint investigation procedure Still to be done: - setting up network of women in higher positions -- establishing non- centralized contact person – development of complaints -- commission regulations -- developing registration -- system for complaints

Figure 5-9: One aspect of the Measures Chart.

Dilemmas Gathering Sessions began in the central office of the Department in the fall of 1995. At each session an average of 20 people took part. In total, approximately 200 different dilemmas were collected. A number of cases were presented to a panel in December 1995. The panel members first analyzed each dilemma individually after which the dilemmas were discussed in the group. By giving each of the members a different dilemma on the same theme (i.e. accepting gifts), the difficult facets of the moral dilemmas became clear. Based on the dilemmas formulated and the panel discussion, seven value clusters were formulated that set the current code of conduct. These value clusters are reliability, independence, helpfulness, decisiveness, uniformity, controllability, and efficiency. These value clusters regularly conflict with one another. One of the dilemmas in which helpfulness and uniformity come into conflict are as follows: "In order to carry out my tasks properly, I need to deviate from the policy followed by the Department. What should I do?"

Since it is undesirable and impossible to begin changing everything that should be improved immediately, the analysis of the information collected focused primarily on making the most salient issues clear for the Department. By integrating the analysis, four fields of attention (the so-called key qualities or spearheads) for the protection and improvement of the moral functioning became clear. The problem fields were obtained by calculating the underlying correlation between the relatively low-scoring propositions. Several interviews with employees were held to determine the degree to which these problem fields were considered to be cohesive clusters of questions and aspects. After some explanation, the problem fields and the cohesiveness of the subjects within the problem fields were generally recognized. These four problem fields form the spearheads for the development path. An abbreviated exposition of the spearheads that are relevant for the whole Department is set out below.

(1) The cooperation among sub-departments and between sub-departments and central office services ought to be improved. In order to achieve this, there ought to be a recognizable mission stated in the concrete tasks of the sub-departments and of the individual employees.

It appeared from the Measures Scan that internal cooperation receives virtually no attention. The job descriptions of employees relate only to themselves and not to others. Organizational charts are also lacking for some sub-departments, and the written mission is not communicated to those to whom it relates. Employees, therefore, have no clear overview of the organization and of their place and function in it, which makes assigning and fulfilling responsibilities difficult. From the Ethics Thermometer, it appears that employees find the cooperation between sub-departments and between hierarchical levels lacking. Twenty-four percent of the personnel experience the cooperation between sub-departments as good, while 14 percent are satisfied with the cooperation between central office and the other sub-departments. It appears that this can be blamed on an insufficiently clear division between the duties of the central office and the other sub-departments, and from the negligible encouragement employees receive within their own department to work with those outside their own sub-department. The Department of Justice is perceived by the employees as a fragmentary organization in which the sub-departments compete with one another. There is hardly, or not at all, a common goal. Poor cooperation means the persistence of problems both horizontally, among the sub-departments, as well as vertically, between the sub-departments and the central office. In addition, it leads to a poor exchange of information between the central office and the sub-departments. That goes some way towards explaining why only one-third of the employees indicate that they receive the necessary information in a timely manner to be able to carry out their tasks properly. It is noteworthy that, in the formulated dilemmas, there is virtually no indication of a department-wide objective. Apparently employees cannot see their own tasks along with those of the sub-department, the section or agency as concrete representations of the corporate mission.

(2) There needs to be more room created for contributions and constructive criticism from the employees.

Employees are able to discuss work problems (72%) and problems of conscience (79%) with co-workers and managers. The same does not apply to expressing criticism. Most employees (72%) experience pressure in greater or lesser degrees to conform to the opinion of the group. Expressing one's own opinion is, after all, not appreciated by co-workers or managers. When criticism is made, it is not clear to the employees what is to be done with it (73% have experienced this). A substantial part of the staff feels that contributions and criticism are not taken seriously by the organization. The negligible opportunity to express criticism and the lack of insight into what is then done with such criticism, brings, to a degree, a large number of employees to feel that management should apply higher norms. Because employees usually do not criticize each other, and as criticism, insofar as it is expressed, is not well received, abuses are not corrected. Only a quarter of the employees feel that fulfilling agreements, favoritism, co-workers' efforts and the careful handling of confidential information meet their own higher norms in practice. As regards the proper spending of budgets and the use of the organization's means, the percentage is slightly more favorable: 40 percent of employees say that practice meets the required norm. During the Dilemma Sessions, relatively many dilemmas were formulated that showed that it is difficult to criticize co-workers or managers. One of the dilemmas went as follows: "My co-worker's understanding of his position creates problems for me in carrying out my work properly. I have tried to discuss this with him. He laughed it off. Actually, I would like to discuss how this colleague functions with the management, but I feel that that would constitute gossip. The other co-workers would not appreciate it either. What can I do?"

(3) The organization should be more transparent.

The Ethics Thermometer showed that a substantial number of employees (69%) find that the Department raises too high expectations among outsiders. Due to these high expectations, external stakeholders are not adequately informed of matters that would be relevant to them. Other employees (44%) find that the Department would function completely differently if the parliament was fully aware of how things went on within the Department. The expectations which are too high harm the credibility of the Department among the employees. Employees are then unable to represent the Department in a positive manner. Due to the lack of openness between the Department and the external stakeholders, it is often quite difficult for outsiders to find the right person within the organization.

(4) The dominant motivation by rules and procedures should be limited and more room should be made for motivation from the management.

The Measures Scan showed that there are a lot of rules and guidelines within the Department. Some rules are characterized by complicated, legal language. An example: "The civil servant ought to refrain from revealing thoughts and feelings [...] if, by the exercise of these rights, the proper performance of his function or the appropriate execution of the pubic service, insofar as that relates to the performance of his function, could not reasonably be assured." The purpose of such rules is often unclear. A number of rules and regulations are so detailed that their proper execution is unlikely. Some rules, such as those relating to accepting gifts and outside jobs, differ substantially from sub-department to sub-department. The Ethics Thermometer shows that the actual organizational context differs sharply from the formal decision-making procedures. This is expressed, for instance, in the freedom to arrange things among one another and a high degree of old boys networks. Employees are primarily guided by rules, procedures, and budgets. The majority of the employees believe that these rules are too rigid. In addition, half the employees indicate that it is not always clear what the point of the rules and guidelines is. Because the formal organization is apparently inadequate, informal ways of doing things have evolved in order to ensure certain interests are protected. This issue returns repeatedly in the dilemmas collected. The fixation on rules and procedures that is necessary to guarantee objectivity and uniformity comes into conflict with the demand for access, helpfulness, and efficiency.

The report ends with a number of concrete recommendations for the improvement of the ethics of the Department. One of the recommendations was a code of conduct that can be formulated based on the value clusters encountered in the dilemmas. An explicit code offers cohesion between the existing rules and guidelines. A number of other recommendations included the reformulation of a number of rules, a graduated plan to improve the position of managers as moral guardians and communicators, a number of activities creating more room for criticism within the sub-departments, a rethinking of the too ambitious (absolute characteristics of) rules, and an orientation program for new employees. The report also recommends that the Department has to make clear, especially at the political level, what the Department does not stand for and what the stakeholders may expect from the Department in the short and long term.

This ethics audit explained to the decision makers that substantial improvement was needed on a number of levels. Due to the frank description of the deplorable present situation, both the top officials of the Department and the coordinating committee were quite satisfied with the study. "The report puts a finger right on the weak points of our organization," the Secretary General (the highest public servant of the Department) said. "The results do not surprise me..." one of the members of the co-ordinating committee said in the Personnel Newsletter, "...when I read the report, I experienced a sort of 'déja vu,' as if I'd known all along." The chairman of the co-ordinating committee wrote in the Personnel Newsletter that when he read the report, he recognized it point after point. Still, he was highly pleased that the report was issued. "Some people find only open doors in this report. But nobody kicked the doors in before." The fact that the report was not about individuals, but about the organizational context, appealed to the employees of the Department. The report did not attack anyone's position, but offered useful starting points for improving the organizational context. The Board of the Department, therefore, supported the report. It had been decided to treat the report as a public document. The report was subsequently sent to all executives. Other personnel were informed of the findings via the Personnel Newsletter.

Shortly after the report appeared, a new coordinating committee was established in order to ensure cohesion in the follow-up activities. The sub-departments themselves decided whether, and if so, how to undertake follow-up activities. At the end of 1996, follow-up activities were in progress in three sub-departments. Because an individual picture of the formal and the perceived organizational context can be formed per sub-department, the most relevant themes for each sub-department were determined. The results of the thermometer were also included in the reorganization of the top levels of the Department.

The ethics audit offered the Department sufficient starting points for the focused development of activities to improve its ethics. According to the policy makers of the Department, the ethics audit had been useful, both in the sense of validity (the audit gave an accurate view of the actual situation), relevancy (follow-up activities based on the audit have been carried out), and comparability (sub-departments can be compared in a simple manner). The results were reported in understandable and concise language. In addition, the Ethics Thermometer seems to be an efficient instrument because it formulates concrete areas of attention in a relatively short period of time and without making too great a claim on the resources of the organization. The Dilemma Sessions required more time from the participants than the Ethics Thermometer. However, fewer employees took part in these sessions than those who completed the thermometer. While the thermometer provided more quantitative information, the Measures Scan and the Dilemmas Session gave a more qualitative view of the organizational context. Because the thermometer consists of a standardized questionnaire, the method is also efficient for the auditor and making it possible for him to compare organizations with one another.

In this chapter, we have seen how an ethics audit can be implemented and executed in practice. The ethics audit provides both a description of the actual situation and a number of recommendations for improvement. The second central question of this study has, therefore, been answered. In the next passage, we shall see how the ethics of an organization can be developed.

PART III

DEVELOPING THE ETHICAL CONTENT

Chapter 6

The Ethics Process

"The rule in business ethics
was spray and pray."
(Mark Pastin)

Based on the results from an ethics audit, organizations can take concrete measures
and develop activities to improve the ethical content. In this chapter, a workable
ethics process will be discussed. The ethics process (or ethics project or ethics program) is a cluster of measures and activities used to protect and improve the ethics of
an organization. The measures and activities that can be implemented will come up
for discussion in the following chapter. During the ethical development process, a
number of difficult choices have to be faced. In this chapter, I describe these choices
as areas of tension which should be "relieved" during an ethics process. Ignoring one
or more of these conflicting issues or making a choice that has not been thought
through has consequences for the effectiveness of the process. In this chapter, a
vision of the management of ethics will also be discussed. This vision provides
guidelines for considering options in regards to the conflicting issues which have
been outlined. This chapter closes with a description of a number of simple ethics
project steps that have been taken in several organizations. In the introductory
chapter of this book it was already stated that hardly any explicit or implicit attention

is paid in business literature to the assumptions with regard to the management of ethics and the problems which can occur in this field.[93]

6.1   Conflicting issues during the ethics process

During the ethics process, a number of different problems could arise which require well-thought-out consideration. The conflicting issues discussed below come from diverse development projects in which I participated as consultant. Every time that the structure of the process was discussed within the process team, one or more of these conflicting issues were brought forward (explicitly or implicitly) by the team members. These conflicting issues are concerned with the choice of activities to be developed and measures to be taken by which each alternative has something important to contribute. These issues will be discussed separately below.

a.	speed	versus	intensity
b.	diversity	versus	unity
c.	pain	versus	ambitions
d.	formal	versus	informal
e.	status quo	versus	improvement
f.	targets	versus	ideals
g.	prohibitions	versus	guidelines
h.	free will	versus	coercion
i.	individual responsibility	versus	co-responsibility
j.	general pardon	versus	responsibility for past actions

Figure 6-1: Conflicting issues during the ethics process.

a. Speed versus intensity

There are some advantages if a company decides to adopt quickly a number of measures to prevent unethical conduct. One or more employees can be asked to think up some ideas within a short amount of time for the management to decide on. The employees can consult among themselves with respect to which measures should be proposed. If they take an energetic approach, results will soon follow. In a few days'

---

[93]   The description and comparison of the manner in which organizations organize ethics can be performed by mapping (a) the position taken with respect to the conflicting issues (Section 6.1), (b) the esteemed view of ethics management (Section 6.2), (c) the process steps which are taken (Section 6.3), and (d) the measures which are taken to improve the ethics of the organization (Chapter 7).

work a code of conduct can be written. As a consequence, much discussion can be avoided within the departments of the corporation and unacceptable practices can be tackled immediately. Should new forms of unethical conduct eventually arise, the management could write off its fault to the fact that they supposedly did all they could to prevent unethical conduct.

When only speed is prioritized, though, a number of issues are overlooked. First of all, the one or the few person who conceived the measures run the risk of not knowing exactly what concrete problems there are in the organization. Devising measures without first carrying out an ethics audit carries with it the danger that the process will be unsuccessful. In the second place, the result will be only a personal achievement of one or a few employees. Even if such a solo action were to result in exactly the same measures as a process in which all employees were involved, it still involves a different outcome. In the first case, only a personal view of the organization is concerned. In the second case, it involves a collective process that gets its result from consultation and deliberation. Thirdly, it is short-sighted to assume that simply implementing a number of measures will result in an increase of the ethical content of the organization.

Deciding to audit the whole organization and to discuss the measures to be taken should not lead, however, to an endless consultation of the employees. It is often impossible to attain complete unanimity about every item in the code of conduct. For very fundamental issues such approval is, of course, necessary (see the second and fourth conflicting issue). Speed in the development process is necessary to be sure that the progress of the process remains visible for employees. When employees do not see progress, attention to the process will slacken. Furthermore, the means available for the process (including time, money, and personnel) will always be limited.

b. Diversity versus unity

A second, quite fundamental issue concerns the extent to which the staff should have a shared set of moral norms and values. On the one hand, each employee should represent the corporation in a coherent and consistent way. A bank would have a fragmented image when its branches would have different policies in regards to accepting illicit funds. Also, as we saw in Chapter 2, outsiders can be alienated when some employees of a placement agency honor the discriminatory requests from clients while other employees from the same placement agency ignore such requests completely. On the other hand, this should not lead to the conclusion that employees should be programmed, without taking consideration of their own insights and beliefs (see the ethics management paradox discussed in Section 2.3). Too much emphasis on unity rewards conformity and punishes non-conformity and, in time, may lead to an organization that is not open for criticism. In addition, conformance can lead to an infringement on employees' individual responsibilities and rights.

c. Pain versus ambitions

When cases of fraud or corruption are the motivating factors behind the process, combating fraud and corruption could be chosen as the objective. This so-called negative approach, where "pain," expressed as costs or damage, is the motivation, can count on less enthusiasm among personnel than if the motives are expressed as the ambition to increase the moral appreciation of stakeholders and to strive towards a virtuous and excellent organization. A possible drawback of such a positive line of approach involves the less demonstrable or palpable ambitions and visible improvements of the process by which the perceived urgency to start a process decreases. A further disadvantage of a process driven by ambitions is the difficulty of constraining the process due to the broader scope of such a positively-based process. Moreover, ambitions may even have a counterproductive effect when they stand in a shrill contrast to common, deep-seeded unethical practices.

d. Formal versus informal

Rules and procedures can guarantee the above-mentioned conformity and consistency. In some cases, such conformity is necessary. Especially when there are great interests of the stakeholders at stake (such as security and health), a tight and clear line must be demanded by the organization. Furthermore, clarity is required whenever negative sanctions are linked to censurable conduct. The drawback of rules is that not all conduct can be encapsulated in them. In practice, every rule is coupled with the chance of avoiding it. There is frequently a gray area. Putting a limit of 25 dollars on accepting gifts can lead to the recipient requesting the gift-giver to split up the gift into units of $24.50. Trying, despite everything, to create an all-encompassing system of rules leads to a sort of Soldiers' Manual, which may have a rigidifying effect. A gift rule can be tightened up so that an employee may accept no more than one gift per supplier per year for no more than a total of 25 dollars. Even then, a new gray area is created. For example, may a gift worth one hundred dollars be shared among three colleagues? By making a new rule for each new gray area, the system of rules will grow out of proportion. This increases the chance of the totality of rules becoming inaccessible for the personnel due to extensive and complex formulations. Introducing a large number of organizational procedures to minimize the chance of unethical conduct makes the organization less transparent, more rigid, and less efficient. Adopting a large number of rules and procedures also sets a precedent for everything becoming permissible that is not bound to a rule or procedure. The fundamental problem with this vision of ethics management is that employees are gagged and relieved of their own responsibilities.

However, an organization that takes no formal measures to organize ethics runs the risk of exposing the staff to too many temptations or giving the staff too few stimulants to realize the company's responsibilities. A warehouse of expensive, easy-to-carry and easy-to-trade products "is asking for" company theft when, despite the presence of a strong culture in which stealing is absolutely unacceptable and where employees are very loyal to the organization, these products are not locked up nor subject to video security or an inventory system. Team meetings are usually a prerequisite for anchoring the quality of discussability in larger organizations. The right mix of formal and informal management of employees is essential. Too much focus on the formal side of the organization can draw important attention from the informal side. However, according to Van Luijk and Schilder, "even the hardest system crumbles when not supported by those who work within it" (1997:105).

e. Maintaining the status quo versus working towards improvements

A difficult and at the same time very fundamental issue concerns the question of who determines what behavioral standards are (un)acceptable. Employees who are regularly confronted with certain concrete moral dilemmas have developed a number of moral intuitions based on those dilemmas. Employees usually know what, according to them, is and is not acceptable and what should or should not be changed. But what to do if the intuitions diverge in regards to an important aspect of corporate behavior? The desired behavior is not necessarily the lowest common denominator. A code of conduct does not come into being by letting every employee vote on every standard. At some point, the desired norms may be inconsistent with the actual norms of some or many employees. Therefore, it is necessary to sharpen their moral intuitions or even alter them. However, paternalistic lecturing of employees disregards their own moral intuitions. The crucial question is: who decides what conduct is appropriate? Who has the legitimate position to determine the moral standards for the company: management alone, all employees, external stakeholders, and/or ethics experts?

f. Targets versus ideals

In organizing ethics, the management faces the choice of holding up ambitious ideals or realistic targets to the employees. Formulating ideals brings the future into vision and may motivate the personnel to work towards those ideals. If these ideals are too far removed from reality, they lose their motivating and stimulating effect. Slogans in a code of conduct can lead to the perception of the ethics management as a collection of hollow promises and self-justifications. Formulating realistic targets has the drawback that when they are reached, new ones must be formulated. Formulating realistic targets requires, therefore, more attention. Attempting to cause no damage to the environment is an ambitious ideal for many companies. In most cases, reduction of damage by, say, five percent for the coming year is more realistic. Such targets must be checked periodically, however, to see that they remain realistic.

The field of tension between ambitious ideals and realistic targets also arises in determining the number of activities to develop and measures to be taken. An ethics process may evolve in such a way that the corporate decision-makers immediately want to improve what could be improved. If the management or process team tries to improve all the moral qualities at the same time, it may be asking too much of the organization. In this way, it runs the risk that the whole process will end up being nothing. A coordinator or auditor may sometimes feel himself called upon to dampen the enthusiasm of the participants. It is, however, often not possible to implement measures one by one. Some measures do not lend themselves to separate implementation, but can only be implemented in conjunction with other measures. For example, implementing a code of conduct requires supporting activities to make employees familiar with the content and use of the code. "Revising a conduct code will have no impact on ethical behavior if corresponding modifications are not made in the incentive system to reflect less performance-based approaches to punishment and reward. Creating an ethics hot line or hiring an ombudsman will be seen as hypocritical by employees if top executives routinely promote managers who are known by peers and subordinates to bend the rules." (Cohen, 1993:351). It is, therefore, the challenge of the development process to achieve the greatest progress with the minimum of effort.

g. Prohibitions versus guidelines

In writing, for instance, a code of conduct, prohibitions can be applied as regards the conduct of employees. Prohibitions prescribe what employees absolutely should not do. A positive guideline can also be applied in which the corporate stand is clarified. Such expectations form a guideline for employees for what should be done. An important drawback of prohibitions or negative rules is that employees quickly perceive them as threatening. "A code that consists of 'thou shalt nots' is likely to alienate employees" (Ethics Resource Center, 1990:III-2). In addition, negative rules do not tell what in fact should be done. The disadvantage of positive guidelines is that compliance is less obligatory. It becomes only possible to impose negative sanctions when things are done which are not allowed. The drawback of punishment is that employees are not positively stimulated to adopt ethical conduct, but are only corrected with respect to unethical conduct. Imposing only positive sanctions for ethical conduct may have the drawback that employees do not regard ethical conduct as mandatory.[94]

h. Free will versus coercion

The issue of how to ensure compliance may also arise during an ethics process. On the one hand, the management will want to rely on the intuitions and intentions of employees. It is difficult, for example, to work in a context of mistrust. Still, it is quite legitimate to monitor in order to discover bent practices as quickly as possible. Unchecked unethical conduct, as we saw in Chapter 4, sends a powerful and undesirable signal. On the other hand, this must not lead to a situation where every action is checked by managers. A fanatic control may be seen as a vote of no-confidence by employees. The ethics management activities will be seen as a policy designed to

---

[94]   Section 7.6 discusses sanction mechanisms in more detail.

shackle employees and not as an expression of collective responsibility. Furthermore, over-organization leads to unworkable and inefficient relationships.

i. Individual responsibility versus co-responsibility

Given that it is impossible and also undesirable to incorporate all control of (un)ethical conduct into formal procedures, the corporate management will have to rely to a great extent on social control. Social control is a correction mechanism by which employees talk to one another about unethical conduct. Social control is based on the fact that employees collectively and cooperatively give expression to the organization's responsibilities. Someone who is proud of his organization will feel secure that co-workers elsewhere in the corporation deal with the interests and responsibilities of the corporation carefully. In addition, employees want to know they have the support of their co-workers for how their own moral problems are dealt with. This solidarity should not result in an out-of-hand, close model of supervision where everybody spies on everybody else to make sure that everything that happens is acceptable. The shared feeling of responsibility should not degenerate into a crippling lack of trust. It might be difficult to strike the right balance between individual responsibility, on the one hand, and co-responsibility, on the other hand.

j. General pardon versus responsibility for the past

A correction of the existing norms and values can usher in a new beginning. Old ways of doing things which are now forbidden may no longer serve as reference points for justifying conduct. "Why should I now all of a sudden be honest with my clients if my boss has never told the truth?" is an understandable but nevertheless unacceptable way of reasoning. The formulated standards are valid for everyone regardless of one's own past and the past conduct of co-workers and supervisors. However, this should not lead to a situation where all unacceptable conduct from the past is to be tolerated. The question then arises: what kind of unacceptable past conduct has to be sanctioned?

6.2   A view of ethics management

In order to make a thought-out deliberation relating to the conflicting issues mentioned above, the assumptions must be clear in regard to managing ethics. A number of the (hypothetical) assumptions below (such as C) have already been (implicitly) discussed in one of the earlier chapters.

a. a helping hand rather than an accusing finger
b. prevention rather than repression
c. a tailor-made approach rather than a uniform approach
d. total management commitment and communication rather than a task for a single manager
e. a process orientation rather than a product orientation
f. evolving rather than starting from nothing
g. integrated efforts rather than fragmented efforts
h. continuing attention rather than a single, clear-cut project

Figure 6-2: Some assumptions for ethics management.

a. A helping hand rather than an accusing finger

Organizing ethics is not only targeting the proverbial rotten apple which infects the whole barrel. Irresponsible conduct could become the occasion for paying broad attention to the ethical development of the whole corporation. An accident, internal theft, a bribery scandal, vagueness in regard to sideline activities, and other forms of conflicting interests may become a clear indication to the management that corporate ethics needs attention. Nonetheless, a lot of work has to be done on those "rotten spots." Rigorous measures may be required and employees might be fired. Tolerance of recurring unethical conduct is a breeding ground for other unethical practices. As soon as suspicions arise towards large-scale unethical conduct, such matters immediately should be taken care of, possibly with the assistance of forensic accountants, business investigators or criminal experts. At the same time, such measures should not endanger the positive aspects of the corporation. When all employees are treated as if they are potential criminals because of one or a few incidents, then an implicit expectation is being established as if employees are not able to bear responsibility for the organization. When employees look at their own functioning in the same way, the damage to morale may be enormous. A possible consequence of this negative self-image is that employees might start to behave according to this implicit expectation pattern. What managers expect from their employees is what they might get back from them. In order to climb out of the pit of unethical practices, this vicious circle of a decreasing trust should be broken.

The management of ethics mainly concerns offering a helping hand to the personnel. In normal circumstances, the majority of personnel, if not all, are to be considered as having honorable intentions. According to Goyder (1993:iix), "Most men and women at work want to be responsible." Ethics management should primarily focus on those employees who would rather behave responsibly and also want to work for a trustworthy corporation. In order to improve the ethics of an organization, it is advisable to call upon the positively developed moral intuitions of employees and to motivate employees to strive for the proper functioning of the corporation.[95] Employee support for an ethics process has the best chances of survival when the employees experience the process as something that is in their interest. Working for a corporation which is characterized by mutual trust has a much greater attraction than a corporation where employees constantly are out to get one another. Old boys networks, intimidation, and blackmail usually do not create a better working climate. Moreover, corporate ethics is not only about the duties of employees but also about their rights. As stakeholders, employees should be remunerated with fair salary systems and adequate opportunity for individual development.

Following a number of petty thefts, the security manager of a large production company decides to install video camera at strategic points on the premises. This creates such a suspicion-ridden atmosphere that the personnel become less dedicated to their work while various moral infringements start cropping up within the company (such as sick days taken for dubious reasons and unnecessary damage to company vehicles).

---

b. Prevention rather than repression

Fighting criminality and fraud may be approached from a repressive point of view: more control and heavier sanctions. In Chapter 4 we have seen that control (visibility) and sanctions (sanctionability) are important organizational qualities. Control and sanctions form important barriers to unethical conduct. An exclusively repressive approach, though, seems to be inadequate. The management will be continuously overtaken by events: it only takes action after it detects deviant conduct. According to Pijl (1991:53), in countries where large-scale police corruption is traditional (i.e. the United States, Italy, and Hong Kong), a repressive and aggressive approach to the phenomenon has unsatisfactory results in the long term. A number of arguments give plausibility to the application of prevention rather than repression. A repressive approach implies that action is taken on the grounds of unethical conduct in which stakeholders' interests have already been damaged. Seen from the corporation's moral responsibility to realize the expectations of the stakeholders and to protect the staff members from themselves, it is morally reprehensible to refrain consciously from developing preventative practices. So prevention is morally better than repression. Second, an organization that adopts a repressive approach relies on the assumption that all unethical conduct becomes visible. Everything that is kept secret from the immediate work environment can proliferate as a result. The final argument against a purely repressive approach concerns the disruption that stands to be caused by the implementation of such a policy. Tracing an offender quickly leads to an atmosphere of accusation which has a negative impact on the work climate. Despite the absence of gripping problems, putting energy into ethics management can,

---

[95]   According to Solomon (1992b), business ethics is too often conceived as a set of impositions and constraints, obstacles to behavior, rather than the motivating force of that behavior.

therefore, be justified. Furthermore, a repressive policy cannot be neatly separated from a preventive policy. For a successful repressive policy, it is important to make clear what is acceptable (to determine the extent of infringement and the grounds for calling someone to account) and to bring the conduct of referents into line with the desired ethical standards (with respect to the consistency and possible (legal) validity of sanctions).

c. A tailor-made approach rather than a uniform approach

Corporations have their own past, stakeholders, ethical dilemmas, and organizational context (see, for example, Victor and Cullen, 1987, and Robin and Reidenbach, 1991). Where the ethics process steps (see Section 6.3) and audit methods can be standardized to a great extent, there seems to be no measure which in advance has to be implemented in every organization. Therefore it is very risky to implement measures without an understanding of the actual unique situation (Cohen, 1993). Not every organization should have a written code of conduct. In some cases, a written code of conduct may have a rigid making effect. Even if it were necessary for every organization to have a written code of conduct, the substance of a code of conduct depends on the specific moral problems and dilemmas which employees are confronted with. The level of education of employees may also influence the level of abstraction of a written code.

Even within the same corporation, the ethical content of departments can vary to such an extent that a single mix of corporate measures and activities might not be suitable. Nevertheless, steps should be taken to prevent a tailor-made approach leading to a fragmented approach with absolutely no consistency in the organizational measures and activities. With each of the ethics programs described in Section 6.3 and 7.10 it was decided to standardize the tools implemented to a great extent. However, the way in which the tools were used provided sufficient leeway for the specific needs of each department and team. In these organizations, a standardized and, at the same time, flexible approach was taken.

> The middle management of both a sales organization and a production company were functioning poorly. Based on the analysis of the results of the ethics audit, it appeared that the sales organization would most benefit by increasing the role of the middle management. For instance, the middle management needed to become more visible to those at the bottom of the organization and to take more of a stand. At the production company, the recommendations went another way completely. The role of middle management needed to be significantly decreased. The middle management denied all the employees their feelings of responsibility by delegating very little. Responsibilities needed to be moved to lower levels in this production company to make the personnel feel more involved in the organization. Employees on the shop floor needed to be given more autonomy.

d. Total management commitment and communication rather than a task for a single manager

An effective process needs sincere support of the management (Cohen, 1993). The conduct of management is, as was discussed in Chapter 4, of crucial importance for the ethical content. The credibility and consequently the effectiveness of the process will decrease if the management does not support the process fully. Employees may use the misconduct or hidden agenda of one or more managers to rationalize their inactive or hostile attitude towards the process. The management support is translated not only into visible and sincere communication at the beginning of the project, but also into the role of initiator and instigator during the development of activities within one's own department or division. Despite the fact that one member of the board may have the ethics portfolio, it will be the responsibility of the entire management to propagate their commitment to the employees.

e. A process orientation rather than a product orientation

Organizing ethics is not primarily about what measures are adopted. In other words, it is not mainly about what is to be decided on paper. Ethics management tries to improve the actual organizational context. An explicit code and a training program can be appropriate instruments to achieve this. A well-written code can remind employees of their responsibilities (see also 7.4). Such a document is often a must, especially in large organizations with multiple, relatively independent operating divisions or subsidiary companies. However, the practice of ethics management is often more about beginning a focused, organization-wide process. Among other things, ethics management should focus on the creation of conditions within which an organization-wide consciousness-raising effort and internal interaction can take place. In this instance, "organization-wide" means that every employee contributes to the ethical development of the organization. Collective insights can arise from organization-wide discussions. In the first place, these will be focused on understanding one another's problems and dilemmas within the organization and getting insight into the different opinions that employees have. That will quickly lead to the growth of new insights that those involved will experience as an enrichment. Having the employees to do the coding rather than having the employees themselves coded is the key to the process. To put it more forcefully: a code is nothing, coding is everything. Employees should be involved in the execution of an extensive development program because the ethical content of a corporation takes form in their conduct. The point of view to opt for, therefore, is ethics management for and by every employee. The ethics of the organization is important for every employee, as we saw in the first assumption. Ethics management by everyone means that all employees could be involved in the ethical development, although some employees will play a greater role than others.

f. Evolving rather than starting from nothing

Improving the organizational context does not mean by definition a radical break with the past. The morale of the corporation is to evolve from what already works well, already exists as motivations, and already exists in the form of moral intuitions.

The ethics of the corporation is to evolve from what already works well. During the development process, attention should not only be paid to what the organization lacks, but also to where the organization functions well. These examples of "best practices" demonstrate that some aspects of the corporation actually run well and that the staff has a reason to be proud. Departments can thereby learn from each other's successes (without copying each other's approaches indiscriminately).

The ethics of the corporation is to evolve from those motivations and suggestions which already exist within and outside the organization. A company which incorporates the desire to improve its ethics makes apparent the presence of at least a small number of employees who are willing to change the current situation. The employees' will to change means that they have a (partial) overview of the current situation and that they apply standards which the organization apparently does not meet.

The ethics of the corporation is to evolve from the existing positive moral intuitions of the employees. Writing a code of conduct is usually an improvement upon the norms and values already exist, even if these norms and values are unconsciously or not very well developed. A reaction such as "the code of conduct does not include anything new" is not surprising but rather a sign that the code fits in with intuitions which are already present. A proper code gives a good fit of the dilemmas with which employees of the corporation are confronted. Largely, intuitions have already been developed of how employees should deal with these dilemmas. Among other things, ethics management focuses on letting implicit normative frameworks which are already present in the organization function better through careful guidance and intervention. Where necessary, ethics management creates formal conditions for improvement.

g. Integrated efforts rather than fragmented efforts

The preceding section concedes that rules and procedures are no panacea. Nevertheless, rules and procedures can make a significant contribution to improving and safeguarding the ethical content of a corporation. Implicit or informal norms and values are also an important building block for the ethical company. Accordance between formal and informal systems is important in order to create an adequate organizational context. Formal and informal systems should support one another, while they also should compensate for each other's weaknesses. The exact relation between the two depends on the specific situation in which the corporation finds itself. According to Trevino and Nelson (1995), the best programs aim to focus on commitment first and foremost, supported by just and fair enforcement of the rules.

Corporations should also try to avoid implementing new measures which conflict or overlap with existing measures. Measures should be linked with one another as much as possible. It would be more confusing than enlightening if an ethics ombudsman were appointed when there is already an ombudsperson for discrimination and an ombudsperson for sexual harassment.

Risk managers, controllers, security personnel, public affairs employees, strategists, and personnel managers concern themselves with topics which are as well of concern for ethics management. The variety of officers each with their own fields of interest requires an integrated approach because independent measures may undermine each other and may lead to undesired side-effects at the corporate level. Integrative ethics management requires an interdisciplinary approach by which the functional areas are seen in coherence.

The business units of a multinational company are required to run through a number of different projects which have been developed by all sorts of corporate project teams. The business units are to pay attention to commercialization, customer-friendliness, the new company code, fraud prevention and staff satisfaction. While there is absolutely no communication between the project teams, they are all involved in competing for the favor of the business units. The effectiveness of all the projects is low because the employees are not able to recognize any relation between the projects. Most of the managers begin within their teams by paying attention to commercialization and customer-friendliness. However, the staff members are difficult to mobilize because they feel that their positions have been taken advantage of too often. Too much attention is focused on the instrumental (and therefore threatening) nature of fraud and too little to embedding fraud prevention within the core values of the organization. The staff members experience the code as a farce because it runs counter to the actual daily practice. The code is also seen as window dressing because it is so abstract that the desired rate of conversion into concrete targets in the field of personnel policy, quality policy and security policy is unattainable.

---

h. Continuing attention rather than a single, clear-cut project

The ethical development of an organization is a never-ending process. Conditions inside and outside the organization change. Forces within the organization will put a pressure on the ethical content. Due to the division of tasks and specialization of labor, the inclination of employees to neglect collective responsibilities will continue. Due to the entry of new personnel and other working arrangements, the quality of the organizational context may decline. Due to changing circumstances, like new markets and product technologies, moral dilemmas will change and will require new "answers." Although a project team could be discontinued after a period of time, ethics management is a never-ending process of verifying and re-verifying.

The next section will illustrate how the assumptions discussed above can be translated into practice.

6.3   Case Y: the ethics process at Amsterdam Airport Schiphol

This section gives an overview of the ethics process at the Amsterdam Airport Schiphol (AAS) that I participated in together with Johan Wempe. How the conflicting issues were dealt with regarding the substance of the written code of conduct will be set out in Section 7.4. Four important developments encouraged the airport to start an ethics process in the summer of 1993.

a. Glass house

Within the airport authority, there was a growing awareness of the fact that the airport's public image implied a continuing process of accounting for the corporate conduct. The CEO of the airport authority expressed this as follows in the corporate magazine: "We are a national airport, which means that we are public property. This demands a lot of our company activities and of our conduct. Everything we do at Amsterdam Airport Schiphol is weighed on a golden scale. In the glass house we live in, I consider it therefore of great importance that our conduct be impeccable and able to withstand the test of criticism."

b. External developments

The goal of the airport's board of directors is to create the best mainport of Europe. To this end, expanding the airport with a fifth runway is considered necessary by the management. The CEO described the need for a trustworthy organization as follows: "In order to be the best mainport, Schiphol must not only provide the best facilities. It is also important that it be trustworthy. Being trustworthy means that the stakeholders are convinced that Schiphol respects their interests and realizes them. Schiphol is trying to contribute to the Dutch economy by ensuring a good infrastructure for the future. Besides that, the environment must be protected and the interests of nearby residents must be safeguarded. Stakeholders should trust that, indeed, we carefully consider their interests. A code of conduct should document our efforts."

c. From civil service to private

Amsterdam Airport Schiphol was to be transformed from a public authority to a commercial company. In order to function effectively and efficiently as a corporation, a wide-ranging reorganization took place in the 1980's. At the start of the ethics project, the corporate structure consisted of three divisions which had to operate result oriented. As a negative side effect, the cooperation among the divisions was perceptibly deteriorated. Reorientation towards the collective purpose would contribute to improving the cooperation among the divisions.

d. Looming uninsurability

At the start of the ethics process, the employees were rather careless and nonchalant in regards to the assets of the company. The insurance company holding AAS's policy threatened to declare the airport uninsurable. The damage to company vehicles was unacceptably high. Reckless driving cost the airport one million dollars per year. In addition, the distinction between mine and thine seemed to have become somewhat hazy. Company property was used for private ends on a great scale.

The attempt at improving the coordination of conduct with respect to the three moral dimensions, with the aim of becoming a trustworthy partner, led to the process which centered on the formulation of a code of conduct. The ethics process at AAS consisted of the following global steps.[96]

> a. orientating
> b. planning and fine-tuning
> c. communicating visible support of management
> d. setting up platform
> e. auditing: describing and analyzing
> f. developing measures and activities
> g. changing organizational context
> h. monitoring ethical developments
> i. adopting new measures and activities

Figure 6-3: Steps during an extensive ethical development process.

These steps do not have to occur sequentially and may even overlap. More often than not, a developing process is non-linear and recursive.

a. and b. Orientating, planning and fine-tuning

During the orientation phase we determined the airport authority's initial problems and desires on the basis of information and materials obtained during a number of meetings with employees. There were no signs of unethical practices of such a scope that, in order to be able to start a development process, a preliminary repressive study would have to be made. Moreover, it quickly became apparent to us that the process was no window-dressing. The upper management had sincere intentions to improve the ethics of the airport authority. The action plan was formalized in a proposal specifying expected benefits, the audit methods to be used, the project steps to

---

[96] These steps have also been taken by a number of other ethics projects, such as in the Department of Justice.

be taken, the time schedule, the cooperation expected from the airport, and the staff and facilities to be supplied by us as consultants. Based on discussions with our contact person (the security manager) and the management regarding a concept plan, we adjusted the proposal.

c. Communicating visible support of management

After the proposal was approved, the management of the airport communicated to the entire staff the management's unconditional support for the process. The CEO wrote about the importance, the motivation, and the expected results of the process in the company magazine. In addition, he made clear what contribution was expected from every employee throughout the process. By informing employees in a proper and timely fashion about the intent of the process support was won for improving corporate ethics.

d. Setting up the platform

The process was coordinated by a platform in which seven employees from different departments participated. These employees participated out of their own interest and on their own behalf. The chairman of the platform was directly responsible to the CEO. The platform fulfilled five different roles. It functioned as:

a. guardian: the platform accompanied the process and was the visible supporter of the process within the corporation. As external consultants, we were not the ones carrying out the process. Our role was limited to providing the instruments and giving support.

b. touchstone: within the platform, all steps were extensively discussed to ensure organization-wide support and to optimize the chances for success. How do people from the different backgrounds feel about the various steps to be taken?

c. sounding board: the platform also functioned as a sounding board for the signals from within the organization. The signals were picked up by the platform. The members of the platform had extensive knowledge of the organization. Their numerous feelers within it gave them the needed familiarity with the organization.

d. panel: within the platform the ethical dilemmas were analyzed and organizational bottlenecks were identified.

e. ambassador: finally, the members of the platform were the translators and the presenters of the process to their co-workers and they answered questions regarding the ultimate text of the code.

During the course of the process, the platform met at least once a month. Due to the different roles of the platform, a lot of attention was paid by platform members at the beginning of the process to make them familiar with the approach, concept, and methods.

e. Auditing: describing and analyzing

In order to chart the current situation, the ethics audit consisted of the Ethics Thermometer, the Measures Scan and the Dilemmas Decoder. Due to the exemplifying role of the top management, three meetings were held for them. From the results of the thermometer, it appeared the following qualities scored relatively low: clarity in regards to the "entangled hands" dimension, discussability in regards to the "entangled hands" and the "dirty hands" dimension, and supportability in regards to the "dirty hands" dimension. In addition, employees had little encouragement to cooperate with employees outside their own department. The most typical dilemmas as formulated during the Dilemma Sessions were presented in the corporate magazine. Employees were invited to react to these dilemmas. The reactions were included in the analyses made by the platform. The dilemmas were clustered according to subject. Various ways of clustering were possible, for instance according to dimension ("entangled hands," "many hands," and "dirty hands"), stakeholder (such as passengers, personnel, suppliers, the people living in the neighborhood, and government), activity (such as purchasing, sales, planning, and accounting) and asset (such as time, information, physical means, money, and colleagues). Differences in moral intuitions were made visible by having the platform members first analyze the dilemmas per cluster individually (according to the protocol described in Section 5.1) and subsequently to discuss them within the platform. As consultants, it was our task to expose differences and similarities and to make them subject of discussion while searching for areas where agreement could be made. As soon as agreement was achieved, it was our task to present other dilemmas which could lead to differences of opinion with respect to the newly agreed standpoint. By means of this iterative process (process of decoding and recoding) the intuitions were sharpened and the desired corporate code of conduct came into being. Within five sessions, a code of conduct was written by the members of the platform (Section 7.4 discusses this code). Based on the Ethics Thermometer a plan of approach was developed to embed the code within the organization. Every month the corporate magazine published an article on the progress of the process.

f. and g. Developing measures and changing organizational context

After the code had been written, it was presented to the management and to the employees council. After approval, the CEO introduced the code of conduct to the personnel in his New Year's speech. Distributing the code took place seven months after the start of the ethics project. In addition, almost all external parties received a copy of the code with an accompanying letter.

An important part of the implementation process consisted of showing and discussing five videos. These videos were developed around a core value that was described in the code of conduct. These videos portray, in a concrete way and using everyday examples, how these values can be threatened. These videos were produced to enhance the effectiveness of team meetings. By showing and discussing the videos, it became possible to address issues that were not easy to discuss, such as, for example, the criticism to the employees from their neighbors about their employer. Thanks to the discussions of these difficult issues, employees acquired a better insight into how to deal with these situations. Furthermore, employees began to understand that the underlying problems can be discussed within the organization. These discussions made it possible to examine one's own moral intuitions with the code. Furthermore, a number of posters were made. Citations from the code were presented in a forceful way. All new videos were announced with posters which were hung in every hallway. As a consequence, employees asked their manager to show this new video. Indirectly, managers were stimulated to discuss the new subject.

The team meetings had a central place in keeping the code alive. Moral issues that employees were confronted with had to be discussed there first. The managers were also equipped for this task through information and training. During the annual performance reviews, the code was discussed with each employee. During employment interviews, candidates were asked if they were willing to agree to the code.

An ombudsman was appointed to deal with extremely difficult or confidential issues. In the wake of the introduction of the code, a number of small practical decisions were taken. For example, every employee received a mug so as to curtail significantly the use of plastic cups. Furthermore, employees could buy at prime cost office and coffee supplies for private use.

h. and i. Monitoring ethical developments and adopting new measures and activities

As the guardian of the continuous process, the platform remained, under the leadership of the ombudsman, in operation. In order to determine when new activities need to be developed, it has been decided to regularly repeat the Ethics Thermometer. Using the Ethics Thermometer, positive and or negative developments can be signaled at an early stage.

In the following chapter, we shall see which specific measures can be taken on the basis of the results of the Ethics Thermometer.

Chapter 7

The Ethics Mix

*The art of policy making
is setting priorities.*

There are all kinds of measures available for the development of the ethical content of a corporation. Publications regarding the "implementation of ethics" usually pay attention to the instruments with the name "ethics" in them (such as Weber, 1981, Center for Business Ethics, 1986, Hoffman and Moore, 1990, and Stead et al., 1990). The three most discussed ethics instruments are roughly speaking a code of conduct, an ombudsman, and a training program. These instruments are usually only briefly discussed. The Ethics Resource Center (1987) and the Institute for Business Ethics (1990) discuss codes of conduct extensively. In this chapter, a great many instruments will be reviewed. Some instruments will be discussed in depth. Section 7.7 shows which measures may best be applied to improve each moral quality in order to make a tailor-made mix of measures possible. Section 7.8 presents an example of the recommendations made for the Dutch Furniture Factory (fictitious name) on the basis of the results of the Ethics Thermometer. This chapter closes with a summary of some important decisions for the well-considered ethical development of an organization.

7.1   An ethics office

An ethics platform, ethics committee, ethics project group, or integrity coordinating committee are different names for a structural relationship of one or more people who are responsible for making policy for the development, perpetuation and protection of the morally relevant aspects of the corporation. The ethics office is a general term for these institutions.

How the ethics office takes form depends on the roles it is assigned. In addition to the five functions of a platform discussed in Section 6.3, an ethics office can also have the following roles:

Initiator	The ethics office stimulates the organization of ethics. The ethics office is the driving force and motivator behind keeping the process of ethical development and safe-guarding going.
Coordinator	The office coordinates activities relating to ethics management and with other management activities taking place within the organization. The ethics office creates synergy and cohesion in the measures and activities to be undertaken.
Channeler	The office creates communication channels between the corporation and its surrounding, between employees and management, and among departments. The office can serve as a point of contact for complaints,[97] problems, solutions, and ideas, both for employees as for other stakeholders. In this sense, the office is an intermediary, a Janus-head, or a problem-and-solution broker.
Advocate	The ethics office follows corporate policy critically and positively. The ethical advocate is someone whose job is to think of and raise the right ethical question.[98] In this way, policy alternatives can be evaluated according to the 21 moral qualities. In this role, the ethics office acts as the devil's advocate.[99]
Facilitator	The ethics office realizes the pre-conditions in which the ethical development may take place. For example, the ethics office can offer instruments which departments can use for their ethics programs.
Mediator	Finally, the ethics office mediates in both internal and external conflicts.

In addition to the usually applicable conditions for the proper functioning of a project group[100] there are several specific requirements for an ethics office.

---

[97]   Weiss (1994) limits the role of an ombudsman to listening to and resolving complaints.
[98]   See, for example, Solomon and Hanson (1985).
[99]   De Hosson (1995) warns here that a Quasimodo may never become a Don Quixote.
[100] Including adequate financial support, sufficient authority, availability of personnel, sufficient secretarial support, links to existing structures, short lines to relevant information sources, and familiarity among the personnel.

It is generally preferable to assign the ethics portfolio to someone in the top of the corporation so as to guarantee the support and establishment at the highest levels. In this way, the communication lines from upper management to the ethics office are kept as short as possible. It is, however, undesirable that someone from upper management become part of the ethics office if this would impair the trustworthiness of the office. The office's credibility is especially important in situations where the office serves as a reporting point for unethical conduct. In relation to the position of ombudsman there is a specific requirement that employees may in no way be dependent upon the ombudsman, in terms of compensation, promotion, or otherwise. In this case, it is preferable to have a staff official rather than a line manager fill this position.[101] In addition, a well-functioning ombudsman must be able to guarantee complete anonymity to employees if they insist on it.[102] It is crucial for the ombudsman that his position is not combined with another staff position which could possibly turn against the interest of the employees. The position of ombudsman loses credibility if the same person is also responsible for internal investigations into corruption, fraud, and criminality.[103]

The functions of touchstone, sounding board, panel, and, to a lesser degree, ambassador require a broad and representative composition of the participating employees. Personal characteristics which could influence the moral intuitions of employees include: position,[104] work experience,[105] age,[106] gender,[107] religion,[108] and nationality.[109]

A major risk of institutionalizing an ethics office is the chance of employees shoving off moral issues and responsibilities onto the ethics office. An ethics hot line can decrease the discussability of a department rather than increase it. Critical remarks of employees can be cut off by their co-workers and managers by directing them to the hot line. An employee might also make himself less vulnerable out of fear that the co-workers he trusted will turn him in.

---

[101] Moreover, the ombudsman should have an unblemished company record, know how to listen to others, and be able to present problems quickly and pointedly.

[102] A "defendant," therefore, has no right to know who has complained about him. If this right did apply, employees' willingness to complain might decrease because reprisals by the person they complained about would be possible.

[103] The effectiveness of the performance of an ombudsman cannot be deduced from the number of punishments meted out because of his actions. Weiss (1994) gives General Electric as an example, where 30,000 contacts within five years led to 1,419 punishments, 165 suspensions, 58 cases of financial compensation, 26 firings, and 10 cases that were handed over to the police. Much punishment may indicate a failing organizational context. If the only measures are repressive, there will be, as already discussed in Chapter 6, insufficiently stimulus for ethical conduct, and this can lead to even greater problems. An ombudsman who, as De Hosson (1995) postulates, is responsible for tracking down censurable and punishable conduct within the organization occupies a lack-of-trust position rather than a position of trust.

[104] See, for example, Dubrinksy and Gwin (1981).

[105] See, for example, Kidwell (1987).

[106] See, for example, Kohlberg (1982).

[107] See, for example, Gilligan (1982), Kidwell et al. (1987), and Dawnson (1995).

[108] See, for example, Behrman (1981).

[109] See, for example, Hofstede (1991).

7.2   Training

An ethics training program is another instrument to improve and safeguard the ethics of an organization. Some specific functions of ethics training could include:
-    teaching employees to recognize and acknowledge the moral components in their conduct;
-    explaining the importance of ethics for stakeholders and the organization;
-    providing methods of outlining, analyzing, resolving, and implementing moral issues;
-    avoiding or reducing ambivalence about who is responsible for what and to what degree;
-    generating, discussing, and resolving actual moral issues;
-    communicating, reinforcing, clarifying, tightening, and developing the code of conduct and other ethics measures; and
-    explaining and testing out the use of instruments that can be applied during the development process.

The simplest training program consists of an external expert conducting a lecture followed by a question and answer session. A rather interactive form of training is a workshop in which, in addition to a lecture, time is set aside to discuss cases. According to Velasquez (1988), the most successful workshops are not led by external trainers or staff employees, but by managers. These managers, on the other hand, will be trained by external trainers. This "train the trainer" method offers two advantages. First of all, the management shows that it takes moral considerations with respect to the company's economic activities seriously. Secondly, the management's learning curve is greater because they have to teach others. A drawback is the time that managers lose in preparing and conducting the training program. In addition, there is the possibility of the desired discussability not being achieved because the manager himself is perceived as part of the current problems or the participants fear that what is said will later be used against them. The advantage of an outside trainer is that he is often specialized in giving such training programs, has practical expertise in the field of business ethics, and is not seen as a threat by the employees. Training by staff-employees is an in-between option, with the accompanying advantage that these employees can develop into ombudsmen within the organization.[110]

Training sessions are ideally suited for discussing cases. Cases are fictional or actual descriptions of practical problems for which participants should find solutions. Because there is often a whole range of possible solutions, the participants often take different point of views. The exchange of these point of views will lead to fruitful discussion characterized by a high degree of solidarity.[111] Points of view may con-

---

[110]   Ethics training programs can also be integrated into the general company orientation for all new employees. In addition, ethical subjects can be interwoven into existing courses on functional subjects.

[111]   According to Stead et al. (1990), employees in every workshop should be encouraged to participate actively.

verge or diverge on a case-by-case basis. A good discussion of a case will lead to a situation where the standpoints of the participants will be better founded and sharpened. The higher the "real life content" of the cases, the more the employees learn to discover the practical implications of norms and values, giving the message being transmitted more strength. This individual and collective development consist of four stages, which together form a cycle.

Every participant relates (1) concrete experience with moral issues. By (2) critically reflecting on this experience, it can become clear which characteristics are unique to these specific problems and dilemmas, which norms and values play a role in the decision-making, and why each alternative was chosen at the time. During this phase, the different experiences can be compared with one another for similarities and differences. From this reflection, (3) a rule or consideration can be extracted by which the alternative selected in phase two is generalized. The rule or consideration can furthermore (4) be applied to other situations as a basis for new experience after which it can be modified or sharpened. At the same time, employees can train themselves in translating abstract principles into difficult practical situations. Fictional cases can be applied in phase four, while actual cases brought up by employees can be used in phase one. In general, case discussions can create a room for generating norms and values (from phase 1, via 2 to 3: the inductive side of the cycle), after which norms and value can be translated into practice (from phase 3, via 4 to 1: the deductive side of the cycle).

Case studies constitute a flexible training tool. They can also be used in role playing where the participants imagine themselves in different positions and have to communicate with one another from there. The European Institute for Business Ethics uses the Colleagues Consultation System as part of its dilemma training sessions. A participant presents an ethical dilemma to two other participants. These two participants assist their colleague in looking for options and in reflecting on the pros and cons. The rest of the group observes the discussion among the three. From time to time, as determined by the trainer, the group gives feedback.

Harrington strongly criticizes the use of case studies, because these do not lead to improved decision-making. "Employees are still on their own in reasoning through the alternatives." (1991:25). In order to meet this criticism, a training of employees must be considered not as individual but as a collective event, in which the group dynamic is pivotal. In addition, participants may be given a number of methods to help them in analyzing the cases.

There are various methods to approach moral issues systematically, such as those of Blanchard and Peale (1988), Center for Business Ethics (1990), Nash (1990), Steiner and Steiner (1991), Van Luijk (1993), and Werhane (1994). These methods offer the user a number of considerations to come to a sound decision. Blanchard and Peale pose three questions in their Ethics Check: (1) "Is it legal?", (2) "Is it balanced and justified?", and (3) "How do I feel about it?" The Center for Business Ethics has six test questions: (1) "Is it fair?", (2) "Is it honest?", (3) "Who is harmed?", (4) "Would you feel comfortable if the details were published on the front page of the local newspaper?", (5) "What would you tell your child to do?", and (6) "How do you feel about it?" Steiner and Steiner give seven tests, including the "test of ventilation" ("Can the problem be discussed with others?") and the "test of the purified idea" ("Is the choice based on the opinion of someone in authority or is the choice independent of the opinions of others?"). Such methods are relatively simple and easy to use. Few detailed and complicated processes are necessary to be able to pass the most important concepts on to participants. However, there is a risk that reality becomes oversimplified and that insufficient account is taken of the complexity of most moral issues.

Other themes that can be handled during an ethics training program are the rationalizations that are used for unethical conduct (Gellerman, 1989), how ethics can be embedded in day-to-day functioning, and how ethics can be managed. Managers can be trained to identify (un)ethical conduct and ethical dilemmas in their departments based on symptoms or indicators and subsequently to develop focused activities.

Delaney and Sockell (1992) substantiate that ethics training has a significant influence on the perceptions of conduct of employees.[112] A strong point of the training programs is that participants distance themselves from the day-to-day course of business and systematically exchange concrete experiences. For all that, training consisting solely of case studies and methods of analysis is incomplete, according to Nielsen (1988), because it pays too much attention to moral reasoning and participants do not concentrate enough on actual conduct. An Ethics Team Test, such as is discussed in Section 7.5, copes with this criticism. The next section sets out a number of tools for stimulating dilemma discussion in training programs and departmental consultations.

7.3   Dilemma discussions

The discussion of potential or actual dilemmas has several purposes. Discussing dilemmas that are not specifically related to the experiences of employees may (a) break through the taboo of talking about such subjects, (b) help them to reflect on their own conduct, (c) teach them to express themselves and to argue, (d) teach them to listen to the convictions and arguments of others, (e) help them to understand other's points of view, (f) help them to see that sometimes consensus is necessary, (g) show them that consensus is achievable, and (h) also help them to see that sometimes diversity of opinion is desirable.

Discussing dilemmas which employees face themselves is more directed at (a) finding out if other employees face similar dilemmas, and (b) learning from the insights of other members of the group, so that (c) each employee achieves a well-

---

[112]   It is noteworthy that Delaney and Sockell (1992) do not mention the substance and structure of the training program in their article, while they determine the effectiveness of it.

thought out position and (d) the group achieves a shared view. Simply placing a number of strongly similar dilemmas next to one another creates the possibility for participants to fine-tune or clarify their intuitions. The advantage of discussing relatively general dilemmas is that those involved do not have to worry about becoming (implicitly or explicitly) the topic of discussion. Two advantages of discussing specific dilemmas are that employees have the necessary background information and that the practical value is increased (the chance is greater, after all, that employees are confronted with similar dilemmas in their work situation).

Videos

Five videos were made for the ethics process at Amsterdam Airport Schiphol. The first is an introductory video that follows two airport employees in their car on the way to work. Discussing day-to-day private and work situations, they conclude that norms and values apply to everyone from top to bottom, and real norms and values can be "read" from the behavior of individual employees and from the organization as a whole. Subsequently the CEO explains what a code is, what subjects it includes and why the airport authority wished to have such a code. This video was presented to the upper management with the request to play the video during work meetings. Four short videos each discuss a core value from the code. The video on loyalty shows an employee who is asked by his neighbors, while the ear-deafening roar of an airplane overhead is heard, if "it can't fly a little more quietly." This video reflected the dilemma employees faced on how to react to external criticism of sound disturbances caused by air traffic.

Posters

A large number of posters were distributed in the buildings of a regional Dutch police force within the framework of an integrity project. In a non-patronizing way, various propositions were designed to give the police officers food for thought. The posters were signed "Devil's Advocate." Periodically, the posters were replaced by others with different sayings on them. Some examples of the poster sayings were: "Better a cap on your head than guilt on your conscience...," "Silence means approval...," "Which hat do you wear?...," and "Where do you get your donuts?..." Sayings like this connect with the police culture and make police officers stop and think about bad habits. The simple posters caused a lot of reactions and discussion. In addition, some employees wrote their reactions on the posters themselves. Some posters were filled up in a very short time.

Employee Journals

The employee journal of the Amsterdam Airport Schiphol presents and discusses an actual dilemma each month. Employees are invited to react to these dilemmas. The following journal presents an anthology of the reactions. The ethics office provides commentary on both dilemmas and reactions.

Games

For some corporations, the ethics game "Cards on the Table" (see Footnote 82) has been transformed into an organization-specific game, consisting dilemmas that are obtained during Dilemma Gathering Sessions. Employees can play the game without supervision.

Cards

Another possibility for stimulating discussion is to send employees reply cards. On the card, a dilemma is described with the request that employees send their opinions in. In a regional Dutch police force, employees received a reply card with the proposition "I find the police force honorable/dishonorable because..." At the Amsterdam Airport Schiphol, employees received thirty postcards with different messages and images on them. The postcards contained various messages, like "I'm standing behind you," "I rate you a 10," and "Thanks for your co-operation." The postcards were send to co-workers, supervisors and upper management.

7.4   A code of conduct

There is a multitude of types of codes of behavior which may apply to corporations. Codes can be divided by the level they apply to. There are codes at international, supranational, national, sectoral, company, professional, and individual level. A corporate code of ethics is distinguished from the other codes in that the content and the use of the code are determined by the company itself.

A written corporate code of conduct fulfills a number of communicative functions. Internally, a code may have (a) an orientation function: it increases awareness in relation to the moral aspects of activities, (b) an explanatory function: a code gives clarity in regard to responsibilities, (c) a committing function: a code imposes a minimum number of expectations that apply to everyone, and (d) a correcting function: a code creates checks and balances in that employees can call each other to account in living up to the code's requirements. Externally the code may have (e) a distinguishing function: a code increases the recognizability of the corporation for the stakeholders, (f) a legitimizing function: a code presents reasons for the existence of the corporation and provides thereby grounds for stakeholders to participate in the corporation, and (g) a correcting function: a code creates checks and balances in that stakeholders can call the company to account in living up to the code's requirements.[113]

---

[113]   In spite of a number of studies into the effectiveness of corporate codes of ethics strong empirical evidence for or against their effectiveness is lacking at this time. See, for example, Brenner and Molander (1977), Mathews Cash (1987), Weller (1988), Touche Ross (1988), and the Ethics

Both the substance of an explicit code and the process of compiling, writing, communicating, safeguarding and enforcing it are important in achieving an effective code. The process of coding has already been discussed in Chapter 6. As regards the substance, I would like to say only a few things.

The substance of a code of conduct may consist of the following elements: a mission, rules, considerations, definitions, and examples. The diagram below shows the relationship among these elements, which will be explained afterwards.[114]

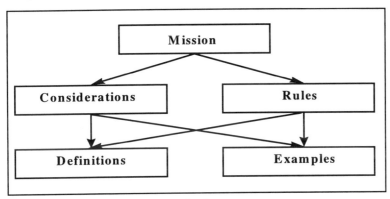

Figure 7-1: Relationship diagram of code elements.

The corporate mission answers the question of what a corporation stands for. Considerations provide a basis for employees in decision-making when they find themselves in situations in which black and white rules are impossible or undesirable. There are three types of considerations that can be distinguished in codes (Ethics Resource Center, 1990): considerations regarding employee conduct in general,[115] considerations by which employees are requested to ask for advice or provide information to a person or group in certain situations,[116] and considerations as rules of thumb.[117] Definitions and examples attempt to clarify the considerations and rules.[118]

Resource Center (1994). As mentioned in previous chapters and as elaborated in Appendix 1, the effectiveness of a code can be determined, for instance, on the grounds of longitudinal measurements with the assistance of the Ethics Thermometer.

[114] The Ethics Resource Center (1990) uses a relationship diagram that has a lot in common with Figure 7-1.

[115] Such as in the code of General Motors Netherlands: "Each employee is expected to avoid doing anything which could imply selection of a supplier on any basis other than the best interest of General Motors, or which could give any supplier an unfair advantage over another."

[116] An example in the Texaco code is: "If employees find themselves in conflict with the policy rules, they are advised to contact the department head."

[117] A noteworthy rule of thumb can be read in the Xerox code: "If you have to make an immediate decision and have any doubts about what you are doing, do not do it." Rules provide a basis for decision-making when either-or choices are possible.

[118] An example of a definition is: "A conflict of interest is an obligation to or relationship with any person or organization which competes or does business with General Motors that could affect an employee's judgment in fulfilling his or her responsibilities to General Motors."

What code of conduct did the Amsterdam Airport Schiphol project (outlined in Section 6.3) lead to and what choices were made in regard to the conflicting issues (outlined in Section 6.1)?

The code of conduct, printed in a convenient and accessible brochure of eight pages and about 800 words, is called "Together we lay our cards on the table." It consists of three parts: the airport's mission, the corporation's responsibilities towards stakeholders and employees' responsibilities in regard to the corporation. Seven general considerations/values are central to the code: respect, discussability and independence for the "dirty hands" dimension, and loyalty, collegiality, meticulousness and credibility for the "many hands" and "entangled hands" dimensions. These considerations require a commitment of effort from employees. What these considerations mean and why they are important for every employee is repeatedly clarified. One or two concrete examples are provided for each consideration. In regard to the responsibilities towards the environment, the code provides examples such as "filling gas tanks without spilling" and "making double-sided copies when possible."

The code contains both general principles and concrete norms. The seven general considerations offer long-lasting reference points for the code, while examples can be adapted with no problem for changing circumstances. The code explains to the reader that these are only examples and that considerations must not be limited to these examples. The code makes up a coherent whole of mission, considerations, rules, definitions, and examples.

The code is to become a common ground, a document that must be supported by every employee. The code formulates not only the duties but also the rights of employees. The positive approach means that the code does not express a lack of confidence in the personnel. It is precisely the collective internalization of the considerations that ensures a better corporation, according to the code. The code is concerned with the mutual advantage of all those involved. Mutual interest can be seen from the following passage: "No one appreciates working with second-hand tools or to have to drive in a dirty car with almost no fuel. Therefore, please return all company property as you found it." The confidence in the employees is demonstrated by the fact that the code emphasizes that it is an aid and a guide for conduct. The code is not a replacement for individual intuitions but builds on employees' personal intuitions. Diversity is tolerated and even encouraged up to a certain level. "Your co-workers' different opinions must be respected and no one is required to carry out an action which runs counter to his or her conscience." Nevertheless, unity and uniformity is desirable when fundamental interests are at stake. As such, there is the rule that agreements should be kept under all circumstances.

The positive approach is apparent from the fact that only two rules are formulated in a negative sense. Such as: "Employees should not shove off their responsibilities on co-workers." Only once a rule with a negation is used without resorting to absolute applicability: "Company assets (such as tools, cars, etc.) may not be used for private ends, unless the employer gives permission for such use. "Although the code does present some targets that cannot be realized immediately, it is a realistic document. One reads in the code that "...not all interest can be realized at the same time...because all interests are not always equal." The code does not propose that environmental pollution be reduced to zero. That does not remove the responsibility to take utmost care of the environment. If doubts remain in spite of the help the code offers, the employee should consult their own manager or the ethics officer. "Two heads are better than one, after all."

It is also possible to create a set of considerations in the form of a checklist in regard to serious dilemmas employees face. An ethics checklist of conduct stimulates the autonomy and individual responsibility of employees even more than a full written code does, and at the same time ensures that upright employees follow the crucial reasoning steps. An example of a checklist I developed for a Dutch regional police force regarding a gift-acceptance policy is presented on the next page.

A written code or an ethics checklist can be a section of a handbook or brochure. A brochure of ethics could contain an introduction by the CEO or ethics office (or both), an overview of salient dilemmas, a discussion of one or more examination methods that the group can carry out itself, an outline of the function of the ethics office, a description of methods for analyzing dilemmas, and a discussion of the ethics measures.

7.5   The Ethics Team Test

Periodically, a team examination or department examination can be carried out by the employees themselves. The results can then be discussed during a meeting. Carrying out such a test is an attempt to make the organizational context among a group of employees, who regularly work with one another, open for discussion. The team becomes the auditor.

An Ethics Team Test involves the following. Using a computer program, every employee individually answers a selection of questions from the Ethics Thermometer. If the Thermometer has already been used among a selection of the personnel, the questions scoring relatively high or relatively low can be selected. This makes it possible to make a separate test for each team. By making participation in the test mandatory, a high response rate is guaranteed. Each employee is forced to think about his own organizational context and to form his own opinion. In addition, every respondent contributes to the team score and a collective result is thereby achieved. Answers are anonymous. A person from inside or outside the organization process the data and, using the computer program, determines the group score, the high score and the low score, the standard deviation and the positive or negative deviation from

---

WHEN SHOULD I (NOT) ACCEPT A GIFT?

Everyone likes to receive something from someone else as an expression of appreciation, a pat on the back or as a sign of goodwill. Gifts can improve relationships and sometimes means extra resources for the police force. But gifts also have another side to them. The police belongs to everyone and serves everyone. That is why people should not be shown favoritism for something that was received from them in the past or for what is laid away for them in the future. Every employee must be aware that gifts from others touch their independence. That is why every police officer swears or affirms that he or she "...will accept promises or gifts from no one, now or later, that could affect his or her action or lack of action." Nevertheless, translating this oath/affirmation into practice is not always easy. In order to give this principle some strength, a number of criteria relating to accepting or refusing a gift are given below. If you have doubts about whether you should accept a gift, you should look for the answer that is most relevant to your situation. The answers to the right of the scale indicate meticulousness, reluctance or absolute refusal.

Nature of the gift:	service - consumables - discounts - goods - money
Absolute size of the gift:	small - medium - large
Relative size of the gift:	smaller than average - average - above average
Initiative:	giver takes initiative - police employee takes initiative
Time:	independent of - after - during the provision of a service/activity
Frequency:	once - now and then - often
Recipient:	force - department - employee at work - employee at home
Intentions of giver:	friendly gesture - gratitude - requirement to return the favor

If one of the following questions is answered with "yes," the gift should not be accepted:
• By accepting the gift are others put at a disadvantage?
• If I accept the gift, will I no longer be able to defend fully my objectivity and freedom of conduct towards those outside the organization?
• Do I need to be careful about whom I tell that I accepted the gift?

If you decide to refuse a gift, this should always be done carefully in order to prevent, as far as possible, the giver perceiving the refusal as an insult.

Figure 7-2: An example of an ethics checklist.

the score of the entire corporation per question. The scores form the basis of the group discussion. Supervisors may be trained for managing these discussions. Because sensitive topics are brought up in a collective discussion, employees learn that sensitive subjects can be discussed.[119] After this discussion, a number of proposals can be reviewed that can help to improve the "team score" in the future. If possible, a plan of approach can be formulated that can be evaluated after a period of time and modified or expanded if necessary. Proposals for measures beyond the scope of the team can be passed on to the ethics office. Supervisors can be held accountable for the results of the team test: did the test take place, what plan of approach was developed, and what were the follow-up activities?

		completely disagree	completely agree
-	I regularly get reactions from my colleagues over my work.		1 - 2 - 3 - 4 - 5
-	My supervisor knows what I did at work last week.		1 - 2 - 3 - 4 - 5
-	Within the past month, I was openly criticized.		1 - 2 - 3 - 4 - 5
-	Within the past month, I have brought something up in my team that I thought was unethical.		1 - 2 - 3 - 4 - 5
-	The organization provides sufficient means to resolve the problems I encounter in my work.		1 - 2 - 3 - 4 - 5
-	Within our team, problems sometimes remain unresolved because no one feels responsible for resolving them. I can give an example.		1 - 2 - 3 - 4 - 5
-	During periods of heavy pressure, I find it difficult or impossible to carry out my tasks carefully.		1 - 2 - 3 - 4 - 5
-	The way I am evaluated takes into account how I have performed in all aspects of my tasks.		1 - 2 - 3 - 4 - 5
-	I can give an example that occurred within the past month which shows that the organization encourages cooperation among employees.		1 - 2 - 3 - 4 - 5

Figure 7-3: An example of the Ethics Team Test.

After a period of time, the team can decide to carry out a team test with other questions. If the following team test also has the same questions as the previous test, a comparison of the scores can be made to give a picture of the effectiveness of the

---

[119] In order to have a constructive and effective discussion, discussion protocols can be distributed. A discussion protocol helps employees to think about (a) examples of (un)ethical practices, (b) the (potential) negative consequences for the organization and the stakeholders, (c) the importance of working on improvement, (d) the causes of (the continuation of) these unethical practices, (e) the correlation in organizational causes, and (f) the possibility to improve the current situation by the employee himself as well as the team and the organization as a whole.

activities deployed in the interim. The strength of such a team test lies in the fact that the employees themselves examine their own situation, propose improvements, give these improvements shape, evaluate improvements, and determine the tempo at which the different team tests follow one another. In conjunction with the proposed assumptions of ethics management, the team test process increases the support for ethical behavior, requires that the team takes more responsibility, and makes it possible to do tailor-made work in order to improve the ethics of an organization.

7.6   Sanction mechanisms

In Chapter 4, I made a distinction between positive sanctions (rewards) and negative sanctions (punishments). The criteria used for sanctioning are relevant to how employees are motivated.

In Chapter 6 we saw that not all desired conduct from employees can be encapsulated in enforceable, controllable, and sanctionable rules. An attempt to establish values purely in rules quickly leads to a law book situation. How can a balance be found between rules and controls, on the one hand, and considerations and free will, on the other hand?

Rules whose violations are not sanctioned lose their credibility. In situations where rules are possible and desirable, measures of control ought to be included. Management must opt for rules with controls and sanctions or none of the three. In choosing for rules, the controls should be as efficient and friendly as possible so as to minimize the chance of employees seeing the controls as a motion of no-confidence. At the same time, leaving sanctions out of situations where employees are aware of censurable conduct leads to a loss of credibility of the good intentions of the corporation.

The conflicting issue above is, however, not so black and white as I have just outlined. Considerations can also be controlled, but not as control is usually understood. In addition to the formal control systems, informal or social controls can also be mobilized. Social control puts the pressure on employees to keep each other under control. It goes without saying that too much is demanded of employees if they are required to correct every type of censurable conduct in the organization. They also have to deal with loyalty towards the co-worker in question and cannot bear co-responsibility for everything and everyone. In addition, employees at the lower end of the corporate hierarchy do not have authority to punish formally. Supervisors are the first level of authority to do that. A supervisor also weakens his authority if he only takes repressive measures at the instigation of his personnel. The immediate co-workers are sometimes able to ascertain censurable conduct earlier than their supervisor do, such as in cases of discrimination and insufficient work effort. Social control is, however, no panacea. Employees can, for example, decide to cover up each other's unethical conduct. For the sake of efficiency, employees may also have to work entirely alone.

The commitment of supervisors for the morally responsible functioning of their departments can be stimulated by holding them accountable for the unethical conduct of all their employees. Kornblum (1976) cites the example of a police force in the US where a similar assignment of responsibilities applies. If a police officer conducts himself unethically, his superior is held equally responsible if he was aware of the misconduct but took no action or if he was unaware of the misconduct but should have known about it. The danger is great, though, that superiors will assist in covering up censurable conduct of their staff when they are responsible for everything that goes on in their departments. The crucial criterion for holding supervisors responsible is whether they have taken sufficient action to prevent and correct unethical conduct.

Social control has also to do with immaterial sanctions. Rewards for ethical conduct are especially founded in a good working atmosphere, company pride, appreciation and compliments from the stakeholders, and a clean conscience.[120] Unethical conduct comes at the cost of these items. Censurable conduct may be condemned by co-workers. Therefore, co-workers will be reluctant to develop collective activities with the offender (the offender cannot be completely trusted after all). These softer forms of sanctions are usually undervalued or overlooked (see, for example, Metzger et al., 1993) as effective tools in realizing ethical behavior. In addition, formal sanctions have a higher burden of proof than social sanctions do. So informal sanctions can often be used in an earlier stage.

Stead et al. (1990) and Di Toro (1995) recommend rewards for moral behavior. There are, however, some reservations to this. If a corporation rewards moral conduct too much, it may create the impression that morally responsible conduct is not mandatory. A reward is given for extra performance, which implies that such extra performance is not mandatory.[121] A corporation should, therefore, ensure that at least unethical conduct be punished always and that ethical conduct be punished never.[122] Formal and informal controls should complement each other.[123]

---

[120] Conduct that deviates from the norm can lead to a restless feeling by the perpetrator. An employee said in an interview that his regular, deviant conduct troubled his conscience, causing him to become restless. "The fact that I could no longer look myself in the mirror ate at me and compelled me to tell the whole story to my boss."

[121] As General Motors says in its code: "Good ethics is more or less a given. There is no positive reinforcement with respect to ethical behavior. You are only punished if you are caught out of line. All rewards, on the other hand, are for economic performance." Or, as the code of Mark Twain Bancshares states: "Business ethics serves more as a veto than an extra. A person is expected to be honest and ethical; as a result, his conduct cannot be used as a factor in job evaluation except where a decision must be made on terminating the relationship."

[122] Punishments for unethical conduct should be just, measured according to the severity and the frequency of the violation and with an eye to possible apologies or mitigating circumstances. It is important that punishments be consistent and unbiased.

[123] The need for an integrated approach can partly be explained by the fact that fear of punishments (depending on the size of the punishment and the likelihood of detection) is not sufficient to ensure

7.7   Other measures

In addition to the measures discussed above, some other ethics measures will be summarily discussed in this section. This overview will illustrate the wide variety of ethics measures which can be taken.

7. Recruitment and selection procedures

In addition to the organizational context, the personal characteristics of the employees influence corporate conduct. It is, therefore, important for a corporation to consider carefully who it hires. The recruitment and selection procedures determine which applicants will or will not be hired. The Individual Characteristics and Circumstances Assessment can be used to evaluate the morality of applicants.[124]

8. Agenda item for team meeting

Time is periodically set aside during the team and departmental meetings for discussing ethically relevant and related subjects.

9. Meeting techniques

There are several techniques available to prevent conformance or group-thinking in meetings. Members can be asked to put their own ideas about a given theme down on paper. The chairman can also make sure that dominant persons do not immediately get the floor by first asking the most reticent employees or lowest persons in the hierarchy for their opinion. The placement of the tables and chairs and the seating arrangement can also influence the exchange of ideas.[125] There are also computer programs available for people to communicate with one another without knowing who is on the other end. These computer programs stimulate a discussion on the basis of arguments rather than on the basis of authority. Corporations can also use outside experts, a second opinion or a second-chance meeting. In the latter case, a period of reflection is given after a decision is taken. During a second meeting, participants can retract the earlier decision.

10. Minutes

Minutes are a kind of black-on-white collective memory of what was decided at a meeting. Good minutes prevent employees from carrying out the wrong things and keep the same topics from coming up repeatedly for discussion. In addition, the absent members of the meeting are well informed.

---

ethical conduct. According to Nash (1990), many business cases make it clear that even when immoral conduct over a long period is discovered, knowledge of it does not necessarily prevent employees from conducting themselves unethically over the short term.

[124] The employment interview is an opportunity to make it clear to the applicant what the corporation expects from him in moral terms. Giving the applicant a copy of the code of conduct and discussing it can strengthen the message.

[125] Employees who sit on a corner or at the far end of a conference table are more readily taken less seriously than those who sit at the head or in the middle.

11. Variety in personnel

In order to echo social developments internally, the corporation can ensure that the composition of the personnel is a reflection of society. Some relevant characteristics of employees are: residence, national origin, marital status, family structure, level of education, gender, political sympathies, religion and product preferences. According to Husted (1993:765), a broad personnel composition increases the ability to find alternative solutions to problems.

12. Supervisor as primary responsible person

Due to the fact that responsibility can seep away when employees cooperate, supervisors can be considered as those primarily responsible for noticing issues which remain unsolved, for picking them up, and for ensuring they are carried out. Without removing the staff's responsibilities, supervisors are not enabled in this case to hide themselves behind the responsibilities of their team members.

13. Micro management

To increase accessibility and mutual trust, supervisors should know what their subordinates are up to and what motivates them. A supervisor can set aside time weekly or daily to make contact with his personnel. Common lunch or coffee breaks are simple ways to break down hierarchical barriers to communication. In large corporations, the management can regularly pay a visit to a department or business unit to discuss moral questions.

14. Conflicting interests register

To prevent the staff from using conflicting interests as an excuse, and to limit conflicting interests themselves, potential conflicting interests can be reported. Employees may be obliged to report sideline activities, private ownership of shares and gifts received. Making reporting mandatory makes employees more careful and brings this sort of conflict out into the open. Supervisors, ombudsmen, or compliance officers can examine any conflicting interests for their moral acceptability.

15. Segregation of duties

A job which contains conflicting tasks could be split up. According to Cornwall (1994), corporations should ensure that, for example, making payments, receiving goods, releasing goods, and receiving payments are never part of the job of one and the same person. Checking one's own expense accounts should also be impossible.

16. Adequate division of responsibilities and work

Management could periodically review how much the tasks assigned to people, committees, departments, and divisions match the available time, means, authority, knowledge, skills, and information. The employees themselves can also make periodic reports on their activities and the time required for their performance. On that basis, management could decide to deploy more workers during peak periods, to institute flexible work, or to reassign responsibilities and tasks.

17. Job rotation

Job rotation means that employees switch jobs to prevent them from "rusting" or developing such expertise or networks that their functioning no longer can be overseen. In addition, job rotation facilitates internal cooperation as well as the degree to which employees can empathize with those in other positions.

18. Replacement procedures

An adequate organizational structure includes the need to incorporate replacement procedures for necessary positions in case of illness, leave, vacation, or other reasons for absence.

19. Detailed job profiles

Uncertainty regarding jobs, tasks, and activities by employees should lead to more accurate job profiles to make it clear what is expected from employees. Job profile forms and regular updates of the job profile are important necessities in this regard. The job profiles and task descriptions can be distributed to (potential) co-workers.

20. Flat structures

A flat organizational structure makes the assignment of responsibilities more obvious, shortens the lines between management and the shop floor, and makes it less easy for employees to hide behind structures. On the other hand, limiting the number of management levels removes many control possibilities because the distance between the management and the floor becomes greater.

21. Contract management

In contract management, departments or employees are assigned a large responsibility for how they should carry out certain tasks or objectives. Prior to a given contract period, clear objectives, and the scope within which these objectives are to be realized (i.e. budgets) are formulated. At the end of the period it is determined whether the department fulfilled the agreement. Such agreements explicitly state what can be expected from the "contractees" and increases the feeling of responsibility and solidarity.

22. Matrix organization

A matrix organization can be used in interdisciplinary and multiple-stakeholder issues, around which management draws employees who each approach the problem from different perspectives. In this way, the multiplicity and diversity of problem definitions, information, and solution choices are made evident.

23. Information distribution

The proper distribution of information ensures that employees and external stakeholders are aware of relevant developments. Current and future developments within the field of information technology offer countless possibilities in this regard. Supervisors can contribute to good information distribution by explaining management decisions to workers and passing suggestions and criticism from the work floor on to the management.

24. Mistakes register

In order to learn from mistakes and near mistakes during work, these (near) mistakes can be registered, analyzed, and discussed.

25. Complaints system

A complaints system stimulates the openness of an organization for the complaints of stakeholders. A complaint system may record the complaints of stakeholders, the time and place complaints are received, the employee who handles the complaint, the handling period, the differences and similarities between complaints, and the corporate reaction to the complaints.

26. Performance feedback mechanism

In performance feedback mechanisms, the effects of and satisfaction with the behavior of employees is played back to them. So employees are able to modify or correct their actions. Feedback can take place formally (i.e. in the form of work group discussions and evaluation discussions) and informally (i.e. in the corridors or while performing actual work). Employees can also investigate the effects of their own performance by systematically calling up or paying a visit to stakeholders.

27. Backward policing

With backward policing (Coleman, 1982) responsibility is not partial, but cumulative. Control no longer occurs from above, but backwards, from the end product. Each department or employee is wholly responsible for reporting mistakes that took place earlier. This assigning of responsibilities is especially well suited to production processes in which each department approves the parts supplied by another department, and thereby retains the right to refuse the parts. The premiums a department can earn depend on the quality of the products delivered..

28. Personification of products and actions

When products are delivered, the names of those who made or checked the product can be displayed. Personification increases the involvement of the personnel because their contribution is clearly recognizable. Furthermore, personification of products and actions notifies stakeholders whom they can call if there are questions, complaints, and comments.

29. Multiple decision-making

Multiple decision-making decreases the chance of unethical decisions. An example of a double-check is a double signing system, in which several people have to sign for a purchase. Several employees engaged in important negotiations with suppliers is another example. This principle of collective or double responsibility can be named as the four-eyes principle. The chance of mistakes in a system declines when the redundancy factor increases (Landau, 1969).[126]

30. Social stimuli

In order to improve mutual relationships, management can draw on a number of measures, such as drinking coffee together, celebrating festive and commemorating important moments in employees' lives. In that way, attention is paid to the person behind the employee, the division between private life and work is lessened and the involvement of the personnel in the organization may increase.

31. Contribution to idealistic goals

Identification with and solidarity of employees can be increased by making contributions to social "good causes" (i.e. the homeless, addicts, disaster victims, orphans, and famine victims) in the form of sponsorship, donations, gifts, and making other corporate means available (i.e. production time and office space).

32. Symbols

Certain moral expectations can be expressed by symbols. A police force used an open visor as a symbol for its ethics process to illustrate the open attitude of the organization. Another corporation adopted a crystal as a symbol. A crystal stands for clarity and transparency. Furthermore, a crystal is precious and its many facets reflect the many sides of a moral dilemma.

33. Buildings and interior

The design and colors of buildings and their interiors create certain expectations among employees. To express the open culture at Amsterdam Airport Schiphol, the new head office was designed with lots of glass and soft colors.

34. Administration

Under administration falls the organization of, for example, keys, money, inventory, equipment (i.e. office supplies and tools) and access to certain rooms, information systems and documentation. An adequate inventory control prevents employees from

---

[126] Husted (1993) points out, however, that as the number of redundant groups or structures increases, the incentives to act responsibly may be lost. Jongsma (1992) also points out that double-signing in practice has led to the conclusion that the first one to sign should bear the primary responsibility. If both signers are equally responsible, there is a chance that both will think the other is being more careful than he is.

stealing supplies, semi-manufactured goods or end-products. Keeping journals makes it possible to maintain good financial control. A "clean desk" policy is another form of administration. When employees are absent, they should bring all confidential documents and computer disks to safety.

35. New-employee orientations

Newcomers are ideally able to recognize practices which slowly have been declined. If newcomers are not, or only barely, listened to, this leads to the newcomers either adapting to the collective or distancing themselves from it after a while. Attention could be paid to new employees to give them the opportunity to raise declining practices.

36. Exit interviews

Parting employees could be interviewed for getting valuable information about the corporate ethics.[127]

Each of the measures discussed above can be applied to enhance one or several moral qualities of the organization. The matrix in the next section shows which measures can best be applied for improving certain qualities.

7.8   The Qualities-Measures Matrix

Organizing ethics involves composing a mix of measures and activities which contribute to the ethical development of the corporation. As we saw in the previous chapter, setting priorities is required. In Chapter 5, it was shown how the spearheads for an ethics process can be distilled from the results of the Ethics Thermometer. The composition of the measures mix depends on the qualities which need to be improved first. The relationship between the information collected from the other examination methods and the measures to be taken will not be considered. In this study we are concentrating on improving the ethical content. However, the other examination methods can be applied in the selection and execution of the measures to be taken. If clarity needs to be improved, the Dilemmas Decoder provides information for what the code of conduct should contain. The Measures Scan is used to select those measures which have not yet been taken by the corporation. The measures which are chosen on the basis of the Ethics Thermometer should be set next to the measures already in place. The choice of the measures for improving visibility can be better grounded using the part of the Measures Scan which traces the opportunities for improper benefit. From a perspective of prevention, the Conduct Detector is especially valuable for gaining better insight into the ethical context. From a

---

[127]   According to Huntington and Davies (1994), the employees concerned should be interviewed by someone other than their normal supervisor in order to ensure maximum discussability.

perspective of repression, the Conduct Detector is especially valuable when there are so many serious unethical practices that a development project will only make sense if offenders are punished first or rumors of unethical practices are stamped out. The Stakeholders Reflector primarily provides information for focused activities and measures in regards to the "dirty hands" dimension. The Individual Characteristics and Circumstances Assessment is used to select the right applicant and employee in order to improve or safeguard the ethical content.

The matrix below shows the most obvious measures by quality. The numbers in the matrix match the measures discussed in this chapter. A frequent position rotation can improve inter-departmental cooperation, but can also decrease the sense of long-term responsibility. The degree to which measures have detrimental effects on other qualities is not given in the matrix because the negative side effects are to a large degree dependent on how the measures are applied and on the specific situation in which the corporation finds itself. In compiling a package of measures, the peripheral effects need to be well thought out.

Dimensions Qualities	"Entangled hands"	"Many hands"	"Dirty hands"
a) Clarity	1): 1, 2, 3, 4, 5, 13, 32, 33	8): 1, 2, 3, 5, 10, 12, 13, 18, 19, 26	15): 1, 2, 3, 4, 5, 7, 11, 13, 25, 26
b) Consistency	2): 1, 2, 3, 4, 5, 6, 7	9): 1, 2, 3, 4, 5, 6, 7, 21	16): 1, 2, 3, 4, 5, 6, 7, 12
c) Sanctionability	3): 1, 4, 5, 6, 7, 12, 13, 34	10): 1, 4, 5, 6, 7, 10, 12, 13, 17, 19, 20, 21, 22, 27, 28	17): 1, 4, 5, 6, 7, 10, 12, 13
d) Achievability	4): 1, 2, 3, 4, 5, 13, 35	11): 1, 2, 3, 4, 5, 7, 13, 16, 23	18): 1, 3, 4, 5, 23
e) Supportability	5): 2, 3, 4, 5, 6, 7, 13, 30, 31	12): 2, 3, 4, 5, 6, 7, 13	19): 1, 2, 3, 4, 5, 23, 30, 31
f) Visibility	6): 1, 2, 5, 7, 13, 14, 16, 29, 34, 36	13): 1, 2, 5, 10, 12, 13, 15, 16, 17, 20, 24, 26, 27, 28, 29, 36	20): 1, 5, 9, 10, 11, 13, 23, 25, 26, 27, 28, 36
g) Discussability	7): 1, 2, 3, 4, 5, 7, 8, 9, 13, 35	14): 1, 2, 3, 4, 5, 7, 8, 9, 12, 13, 24, 29, 35	21): 1, 2, 3, 4, 5, 8, 9, 13, 25, 35

Figure 7-4: The Qualities-Measures Matrix.

The above matrix represents a first attempt towards indicating which measures per quality are most eligible for improvement.[128] Empirical research should show the extent to which the relationships between qualities and measures that are assumed in the matrix actually apply in practice.[129]

The seven instruments which are described in detail (office, training, dilemma discussions, code of conduct, Ethics Team Test, recruitment and selection procedures, and sanction mechanisms in Section 5.1) can each be deployed to improve a large number of qualities. An ethics office can, for instance, contribute to the improvement of many of the qualities. A code may bring a large number of qualities explicitly to the attention of the employees and a training course, discussion of dilemmas and an Ethics Team Test may, via groups processes, also contribute to the improvement of most of the qualities. In addition, selection and sanction mechanisms ensure that staff that make a positive contribution to the improvement and perpetuation of the ethics of the organization are appointed and retained, while staff making a negative contribution to the corporate ethics are reprimanded or, in the last extremity, dismissed. Some measures, however, apply to one or a small number of qualities. A register for conflicting interests of employees can particularly contribute to an increase in visibility with regard to the "entangled hands" dimension. Personification of products and services can contribute to an increase in visibility with regard to the "many hands" and "dirty hands" dimension, thus ensuring that employees can be called to account for reprehensible conduct (sanctionability) at an earlier stage.

The wide availability of some instruments does not mean that an examination of the current situation is superfluous in view of the considerable chance of these instruments being deployed anyway. After all, the ethics audit also provides information about the way in which these measures can be deployed and with respect to which specific qualities. From the analysis of the actual organizational context it may, for instance, appear that it is desirable to create an ethics office with the sole function of helping staff who have questions about dilemmas which they are confronted with (improvement of discussability and clarity). What appears from the data gathered in the matrix is that each quality at first glance has a specific set of measures and that each measure can be linked to at least one quality. Furthermore, there are all kinds of measures which can conceivably improve the ethics of an organization. The ultimate choice of the ethics mix depends upon the assessment of preferences of those who are involved in the decision-making process. Because the interrelationship of the measures is important and may also differ per ethics program, it is sometimes preferable for one division or department to be used as a pilot project in order to test the proposed measures there. The following section gives an example of how the results of the Ethics Thermometer can be used to compose an ethics mix.

---

[128] According to Volberda (1992), most diagnostic instruments in the field of business administration have no concept of control and are not able to provide recommendations for future performance.

[129] Every measure suggested for improving a certain quality can be formulated as an hypothesis for empirical research. For example: H(0): An ethics office can improve the clarity of the organizational context regarding the dimension of the "entangled hands."

7.9   Case Z: recommendations for the ethical development of the Dutch Furniture Factory

The Dutch Furniture Factory employs 1200 workers. Production and sales offices are spread throughout the Netherlands. Because of several small incidences of fraud in 1996, the management decided to examine the ethics risks of the organization. In January 1997, the Ethics Thermometer was sent to 300 randomly selected employees. The response rate of completed questionnaires was 56 percent.

Based on the statistical analysis of the results of the Ethics Thermometer, five spearheads for the improvement were:
1. improving the information dissemination between management and lower levels;
2. stimulating better cooperation;
3. increasing the visibility of unethical behavior;
4. promoting an open attitude in regards to accepting criticism; and
5. increasing the insight into or the flexibility, or both, of rules and procedures.

These spearheads are briefly discussed below.

(1) improving the information dissemination between management and lower levels and (2) stimulating better cooperation.

Half of the personnel felt the cooperation among departments within a division to be inadequate. The personnel was somewhat more positive regarding the cooperation among departments in different divisions. Three quarters of the staff were satisfied with the cooperation among personnel within their own departments. Figure 7-5 presents the causes and effects (Pearson, $r > 0.35$).

The coordination among departments reported as inadequate was fed largely by (a) employees seeing inadequate stimulus to cooperate with others outside their departments and (b) the fact that the coordination between upper management and the lower levels was felt to be insufficient. Only a quarter of the employees were satisfied with the coordination between central and local management, on the one hand, and those at the lower levels, on the other hand. The inadequate coordination between management and lower levels was largely blamed on the inadequate information dissemination. The information dissemination was inadequate in both directions, upwards and downwards. As a result, only a quarter of respondents felt that management knows what goes on "at the bottom" of the organization. The consequence of the reported inadequate coordination among departments is that (a) it is very difficult for external stakeholders to find the right person within the organization, (b) urgent problems remain not dealt with, and (c) personnel receive insufficient information to carry out their jobs properly.

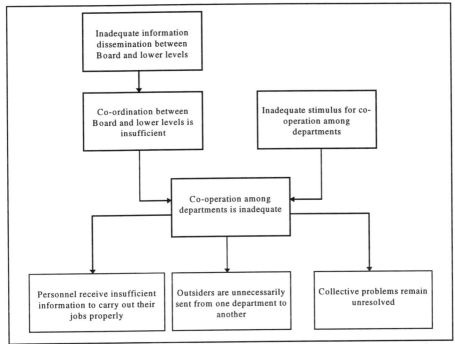

Figure 7-5: Improving the information dissemination between management and lower levels and stimulating better cooperation.

(3) Increasing the visibility of unethical behavior and (4) promoting an open attitude in regards to accepting criticism.

Opinion was unanimous that a large number of issues (such as discrimination, moonlighting, reckless use of property, and calling in sick when one is not ill) are not acceptable. Over the following issues, however, opinion diverged widely (the standard deviation is, on a five-point scale, greater than 1.2): on giving and receiving gifts valued at above 25 dollars, use of company resources for private ends, taking premiums/business gifts for own use, and use of working hours for private ends. According to a substantial part of the personnel, practice in their departments deviates from their own standards in regards to the following issues:

- misuse of power (according to 62%),
- not fulfilling agreements (30%),
- insufficient effort of supervisors to carry out tasks (30%),
- insufficient effort of employees to carry out tasks (24%),
- booking off sick days unfairly (24%),
- lying within the company (23%),
- reckless use of company resources (15%),
- inappropriate use of budgets (11%), and
- careless handling of confidential information (11%).

The most important explanatory factors are shown in the figure below.

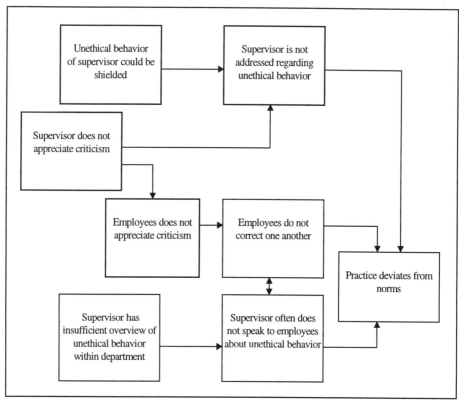

Figure 7-6: Increasing the visibility of unethical conduct and stimulating an open attitude in regards to accepting criticism.

The most important explanation for the discrepancy between standard and practice lies, on the one hand, in the fact that the immediate supervisors and co-workers have an insufficient overview of unethical conduct within their departments and, on the other hand, in the fact that, to a certain degree, the context does not lend itself to employees discussing one another's unethical behavior. Only 44 percent of the personnel have the opinion that managers have a sufficient overview of unethical behavior within their departments. As a consequence employees often are not spoken to by their supervisors regarding unacceptable behavior. Analysis of the results seems to show that when supervisors do speak to employees about unethical conduct, it leads to a context in which co-workers also correct one another. Only 45 percent of employees indicated that if a direct co-worker were to do something unacceptable, this would be noticed by a co-worker. One in three employees said that, if they had evidence of unethical conduct by a co-worker and wanted to discuss it privately with him, the co-worker would appreciate this criticism. As a consequence, co-workers often do not talk to one another about unacceptable behavior. In achieving a context in which employees are addressed with respect to their unacceptable conduct, it is important to increase the degree to which supervisors appreciate criticism of their performance. Analysis has shown that if a supervisor shows himself to be open and, thereby invites possible criticism from his staff, it has an impact on the behavior of the employees. If the company wants to increase the social control, then mutual oversight of the collective activities of the department must also be increased. Seventy-five percent of the respondents are of the opinion that immoral behavior of their supervisors could be shielded from the sight of the employees.

(5) Increasing the insight into or flexibility, or both, of rules and procedures.

Nearly 80 percent of employees find that their department handles the interests of stakeholders carefully. Still, 60 percent of the employees find that there are opportunities within the organization to improve the relationships with external stakeholders.

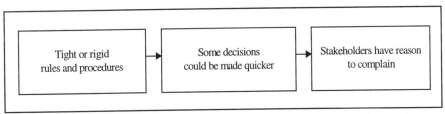

Figure 7-7: Increasing insight into or flexibility, or both, of rules and procedures.

Nearly 60 percent of the personnel find that some decisions in their departments could be made significantly earlier. A deeper explanation for this is that half of the personnel feel that external stakeholders have reason to complain to greater or lesser degrees due to tight and rigid rules and (decision-making) procedures.

After discussing the results within the process team, the following suggestions were made to improve these five spearheads.

a. Discussion of results

The results can be systematically raised in all work teams. The members of the teams can themselves make proposals for improving their own context. A discussion of the results increases the awareness and collective insight of the employees.

b. Information transmission (spearhead 1)

Supervisors should explain more frequently and carefully to their personnel what is decided at the higher levels of the company. Supervisors have to find out how to improve feedback from the contributions of their staffs. Important decisions may be communicated via the internal computer network.

c. Improving internal customer and supplier relationships (spearhead 2)

Collective meetings involving two departments can be organized at which attention is paid to concrete issues which arise between the two departments. Other suggestions in regards to the improvement of cooperation include increased job rotation and allowing employees to be temporarily attached (a sort of internship) to departments they have to deal with in their jobs.

d. Training programs (spearhead 3)

The ability of supervisors to recognize symptoms of immoral behavior at an early stage can be sharpened by means of training programs.

e. Micro management (spearhead 3)

Increased presence of supervisors in their teams is desirable or, if that is not possible, an assistant supervisor should be appointed to keep an eye on the activities of the personnel.

f. Room for criticism and discussion of dilemmas (spearhead 4)

Using, among other things, an ethics game, supervisors can themselves work on increasing the openness to mutual criticism within their departments.

g. Rules and procedures (spearhead 5)

The current rules and procedures that are relevant for external stakeholders should be made less rigid or better explained. The purpose and the content of the rules and procedures should be better communicated in order to reduce the chance for friction. A Measures Scan is recommended to determine which rules and procedures are suitable for improvement.

h. Code of ethics

The last suggestion relates to the development of a policy in regards to the private use of resources of the company, accepting and giving gifts, and handling confidential information. A corporate code of conduct is a valuable instrument to increase employees' insight into the moral risks involved. A written code may be embedded by means of departmental meetings, performance reviews, and employment interviews, and may also be provided to, for example, suppliers and business partners.

After the results and suggestions discussed above were presented to the management and the employees council, it was decided to ask each department to provide follow-up on the suggestions. Furthermore, the following program was undertaken in order to integrate a number of activities and measures.

After a draft of the code of conduct has been written and additional communication instruments have been made, the following sessions can take place within one year. The process team coordinates the activities within the departments.

A. Kick-off with the Board, discussing impact of ethics process for strategy, structure and culture, training in the giving of a good example and carrying out team session 1 and 2 (see below for description).

B. Training of supervisors, preparing them to lead at least three sessions with their team and improving their capacity to recognize symptoms of unethical conduct.

C. Team sessions

Session 1: playing ethics game, discussing dilemmas of participants, presenting method for handling dilemmas, discussing code of conduct, comparing code of conduct and formulated dilemmas, and making suggestions for corrections to code of conduct.

Session 2: analyzing and discussing the results from the Ethics Team Test in order to formulate a plan for improvement.

Session 3: at least one sessions involving two teams to discuss specific collective issues in order to improve cooperation.

D. Supervisors collect plans of teams and decide together with the Board about follow-up measures and activities.

E. Second Ethics Thermometer or other Ethics Team Tests and follow-up activities.

Figure 7-8: The ethics program for the Dutch Furniture Factory.

7.10   The Ethics Management Wheel

The above description of the Dutch Furniture Factory shows how -- taking account of the conflicts, assumptions and process steps described in Chapter 6, and based on the Ethics Thermometer -- a large number of instruments can be deployed in a coherent, specific and focused manner in order to improve the ethics of an organization.

The preceding chapters can be summarized in the figure below. This figure can serve as a guideline for the management of the ethical development of a corporation.

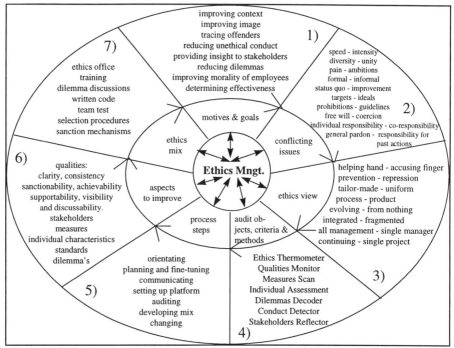

Figure 7-9: The Ethics Management Wheel.

There is a wide range of decision alternatives during the management of corporate ethics. The results of these decisions influence the direction and the extent of the ethical development. Each phase of decisions and its following activities yield particular results (such as goals, insights, points of departure, methods, criteria, process steps, improvement directions, and changes) on the basis of which the following phase can be started. In practice, the process will usually be non-linear with activities shifting back and forth between the phases rather than proceeding sequentially. The process is characterized by continuous feedback and iteration with findings at later phases generating a need for new search activities at earlier phases. The recursive nature of the process implies that each phase has its own primary and secondary objects which contribute to the work of other phases (see also Volberda, 1992). The ethics manager is especially involved in the phase he is in at a particular moment. However, the ethics manager also deals with all phases simultaneously. The ethics manager uses the results of the previous phases to make decisions in the current phase, which in turn are relevant for the following phases. At the same time, the ethics manager will need to highlight and correct the results from the previous phases. It is, for instance, desirable to provide clarity at the beginning of the process with respect to the aims and the assumptions. In response to, for instance, the results of the process or unforeseen conflicting issues which occur during the process, the aims or assumptions, or both, can be either extended or changed. However, the presented phases have a particular order so that it is only possible to go through one particular phase after a certain choice has been made about the previous phases. It only makes sense to choose an audit method after it has been (provisionally) determined what the objectives are. By depicting the decisions in a wheel, the process-like character of ethics management is emphasized.

The role of ethics management can be visualized as the core or axle of the wheel. The decisions to be taken "revolve" around the staff responsible for the management of ethics. Furthermore, the movement of the wheel starts from the axle, indicating that particularly the staff responsible for the management of ethics will put much energy into the ethics process.

There can be many reasons for paying attention to ethics management such as cutting costs, increasing turnover, improving corporate identity and image, preventing crises, covering for penalties for possible unethical practices, and anticipating or preventing legislation. This study considers the improvement and protection of the corporate ethics as a moral duty. The selection of motives and objectives, complemented with existing (unsubstantiated) insights into improvable organizational aspects, makes it possible to determine the direction of the process (for instance, improving context or tracing one or a few offenders).

Phases 1 (determining motives and goals) and phase 2 (listing conflicting issues) have to be completed (partially) before a view can developed with respect to the way in which ethics will be organized. Based on the discussion of conflicting issues which may occur, a (temporary) point of view will be taken which can be reviewed or highlighted on the basis of information obtained from later phases.

Depending upon what should be achieved, it is possible to determine which audit part will be used (in the first instance). The Conduct Detector can, for instance, be used for tracing unethical conduct. If the organization is interested in the formal risks (for instance, to make visible where hostile staff can encroach upon the interests of the company), the Measures Scan should be used. After the audit parts and methods (including questionnaires, interviews, focus groups, desk research, and direct observation) have been chosen, it is possible to choose the evaluation criteria and the aspects (such as specific stakeholders or corporate assets) to be evaluated.

Depending upon the chosen parts of the audit, the process steps may be further substantiated. After all, a repressive approach requires a different project setup than a preventative approach. The audit process may provide information regarding the dilemmas which should be dealt with and information regarding the improvement of the organizational qualities, relationships with stakeholders, characteristics and conduct of employees, and organizational measures. As already stated, it is desirable to set a priority to the objects and aspects to be improved.

The desired measures and activities can be selected on the basis of the spearheads obtained. For instance, a code of conduct can be selected if individual opinions about fundamental matters vary widely. The openness can particularly be increased by training managers and their employees. The presented Qualities-Measures Matrix provides a first impulse for linking measures to qualities.

The results of the activities and measures can be established by performing a further review of the current situation. Based on the new findings, new activities can be developed. In this way, the process of the ethical development remains on the move in a focused manner.

Chapter 8

Summary and conclusions

Business ethics (as a professional field) and the ethics of business (as a practice) have been shown quite a lot of interest lately. In general, the term ethics has a positive connotation, but its substantiation is often caught up in abstract terms, high and mighty ideals, or purely descriptive and relativistic notions. Moreover, ethical judgments are usually related to individual decisions or officials. The question that often remains is how the ethics of business itself can be determined, evaluated, and improved.

This study is characterized by a practical approach based on theoretical and empirical research. The objective of this study was to develop a conceptual model of the ethical content of organizations and a method for its review and improvement. This objective has a scientific, social, and managerial ground, and led to the following three central research questions:

1. What is an adequate definition of the ethical content of a corporation? (Part I)

2. How can the ethical content of a corporation be diagnosed or measured? (Part II)

3. How should the ethical content of a corporation be developed? (Part III)

In **Part 1**, according to a Socratic, Platonic, and Rawlsian line of reasoning, the corporate mission is defined in order to be able to develop the desired moral organizational dispositions. **Chapters 1 and 2** discuss the rationale of the corporation from an ethical point of view. Based on the Kantian categorical imperative, two key concepts of a corporate mission can be distilled: mutual advantage and respect. Corporations are instruments with which stakeholders attempt to realize an advantage and by which other stakeholders can be put at a disadvantage. A corporation's management in particular bears the moral and irreplaceable responsibility to effect organizational conditions such that the best corporate attempt is made to realize the interests and expectations of stakeholders and, where conflicting interests and expectations are at play, to ensure that such conflicts are resolved in a balanced and just manner. The corporate mission lays down the moral grounds for determining (a) the willingness of the stakeholders to participate in and to support the corporation and (b) the corporate "license to operate." Mutual advantage and respect cannot be fully guaranteed by market mechanisms, legislation, and social opinion. As the sophistication of the relationship between the stakeholders and the corporation increases (from transaction via contract to bond), the moral trustworthiness of the corporation -- all things being equal -- will become more important. A corporation's moral trustworthiness is the extent to which stakeholders are convinced that the efforts of the corporation will succeed in realizing or protecting their interests. The moral trustworthiness of a corporation is communicated to the stakeholders by, for instance, the honesty, equality, adequacy, openness, and reciprocity of the corporation within the relationships with stakeholders. The moral trustworthiness should be organized where external mechanisms fall short and where the moral intuitions, intentions, and abilities of the personnel are not sufficient to guarantee unequivocal trust. Moreover, the organizational context by nature exerts a downward pressure on the morale of the employees. Ethics management is the systematic and coherent development of activities and the emplacement of measures to improve and safeguard the ethics of an organization. When are we justified in speaking of an improvement or decline in a corporation's ethics? When is a corporation moral?

In **Chapter 3,** a discussion of various misconceptions paves the way for locating the ethical content of a corporation. A corporation can be called ethical when the actual organizational context fully stimulates and facilitates the employees to realize the fundamental and justified expectations of the stakeholders and to balance conflicting expectations in an adequate way. The ethical content concerns the moral excellence or virtuousness of the company itself, and consists of neither the sum nor average, of the individual or collective, intentions or moral intuitions of the staff, nor of the formal and explicitly developing pattern of expectations. The ethical content can be described and evaluated by means of a number of moral virtues or qualities. Organizational virtues or qualities are the desired moral characteristics of the organizational context. By investigating which characteristics of the context can stimulate or hinder the stakeholders in their careful attempts to weigh and balance their (conflicting) interests and expectations, universally applicable qualities can be established. The extent to which the organization embodies these qualities can be charted by an ethics audit. In addition to a review of the organizational qualities, by means of a so-called Qualities Monitor, an ethics audit can consist of a Stakeholders Reflector, Conduct Detector, Measures Scan, Dilemmas Decoder, and Individual Characteristics and Circumstances Assessment.

Part II investigates which qualities are applicable to organizations and how such qualities can be made operational. On the grounds of the analysis made in **Chapter 4** of a large number of real case studies in which stakeholders are let down and the actual organizational context is in a shambles, seven qualities have been obtained, each of which are applicable to the three moral dimensions of the organizational context. The seven qualities are clarity, consistency, sanctionability, supportability, achievability, visibility, and discussability. The three moral dimensions by which the ethical content can be described are the degree to which employees are stimulated to deal carefully with the corporation's assets (the "entangled hands" dimension), the degree to which employees are stimulated to carry out their jobs and tasks in a responsible way (the "many hands" dimension), and the degree to which employees are directly stimulated to express the responsibilities of the corporation in regards to the stakeholders (the "dirty hands" dimension). The three dimensions stand for the coordination of the responsibilities of the staff "with respect to," "within," and "on behalf of" the organization. The conceptual model of the moral content consists of twenty-one qualities and is applicable to every form of organization where the staff acts on behalf of the stakeholders, where staff activities should be geared to one another, and where the staff has the potential of misusing the assets which have been placed at its disposal (such as information, time, and equipment). The ethical development of an organization takes place with respect to one or more of these twenty-one qualities.

Chapter 5 represents an initial attempt at making the six separate parts of an ethics audit operational. One or more of these components of the audit can be deployed depending on the issue at hand, the preferences of the principal, and the means available. The Ethics Thermometer is the name of a survey with which the perceptions of the personnel in regard to the actual context, conduct, and consequences can be mapped out. A case study at the Dutch Department of Justice illustrated how an ethics audit can be carried out and what valuable information it can provide for the development process. As the thermometer consists of a standardized list of questions which can be used in any organization, this method is efficient for the auditor and makes it possible to compare the ethical content of organizations.

In **Part III**, a description is made of the process along which the ethical content of an organization can be improved. **Chapter 6** begins with a discussion of the various conflicting issues which can manifest themselves during the development process. These tensions, such as between prevention and repression, speed and intensity, formal and informal systems, unity and diversity, pain and ambition, and between free will and coercion require sound decisions. To facilitate a well-founded decision, eight hypothetical assumptions for ethics management have been formulated. For example, "a helping hand rather than an accusing finger" and "a process orientation rather than a product orientation." Chapter 6 closes with a description of the phases of an ethics process at Amsterdam Airport Schiphol. A platform plays thereby a crucial role as guardian, touchstone, sounding board, panel, and ambassador. The Dilemmas Decoder provided the airport authority with building blocks for a specific code of conduct. Recommendations for improving the conditions for imbedding the code were obtained with the Ethics Thermometer.

Finally, **Chapter 7** indicates for each quality which measures and activities can contribute to improving the ethical content of corporations. The measures and activities vary from a training session and an ethics officer to job rotation and meeting techniques, to cite a few examples. Based on the assumptions of ethics management, two new measures have been developed: an ethics team test and an ethics checklist of conduct. The case of The Dutch Furniture Factory shows us how, based on a correlative analysis of the results of the Ethics Thermometer, spearheads for development can be designated and specific recommendations can be made for these spearheads. The Ethics Management Wheel gives a summary of the considerations which have been discussed and which are relevant for the ethical development of organizations.

Among other things, the results of this study include a model for reviewing and developing the ethical content of corporations. With help of it, a corporation's ethics can be defined, measured, and improved. The Ethical Qualities Model is founded upon a conceptual and empirical basis. Nevertheless, the suggested model and methods should be further tested and the ethical instruments need to be further developed and elaborated. In **Appendix 1**, a number of suggestions are formulated for follow-up research. On the basis of a multi-case longitudinal study, the effectiveness can be determined of the assumptions which haven been applied, the activities which have been adopted, and the measures which have been taken. Another important research question is the degree to which a factor analysis may reveal the same qualities as the twenty-one which have been outlined in this study.

Because of the great responsibilities which corporations bear and the internal decentralization of duties, authorities and responsibilities, and the vulnerability to unethical conduct which increases as a result, the Ethical Thermometer could be used by a corporation's management to monitor the ethical performance of its departments periodically. Moreover, the thermometer may provide the corporation with specific information for managing ethics from the bottom to the top. Because of the great responsibilities which corporations bear, the increasing sophistication of business operations, and the critical stance of stakeholders, an ethics (annual) report can provide the stakeholders with insight into the formal and factual efforts of the organization, the consequences of its actions, and the actual dilemmas. The Stakeholders Reflector, the Conduct Detector, Measures Scan, the Ethics Thermometer, and the Dilemmas Decoder can be deployed consecutively to obtain relevant information for the preparation of an ethics report and a review by an ethics auditor.

The success of the discipline of business ethics will be determined by the extent to which it succeeds in providing the business community with the motives and instruments to ingrain ethics in business. It is exactly in the provision of effective and efficient instruments to managers and ethics officers in particular that an important and highly-appreciated future role for business ethics professionals is guaranteed.

References

- Aguilar, F.J., *Managing Corporate Ethics - Learning from Americas Ethical Companies: how to supercharge business performance*, Oxford University Press, New York, 1994
- Akaah, I.P. and E.A. Riordan, "Judgments of marketing professionals about ethical issues in marketing research: a replication and extension," *Journal of Marketing Research*, vol. 26, no. 1, 1989, pp. 112-120
- Andeweg, R.B., "Overheid of overhead: de bestuurbaarheid van het overheidsapparaat," in M.A.P. Bovens and W.J. Witteveen (eds.), *Het Schip van Staat: beschouwingen over recht, staat en sturing*, Zwolle, 1985, pp. 207-224
- Andrews, K.R., "Ethics in practice," *Harvard Business Review*, 67, September-October 1989a, pp. 99-104
- Andrews, K.R. (ed.), *Ethics in Practice: managing the moral corporation*, Harvard Business School Press, Boston, 1989b
- Ansoff, H.I., *Strategic Management*, MacMillan, London, 1981
- Arendt, H., "Organized guilt and universal responsibilities," 1948, in L. May, S. Hoffman (eds.), *Five Decades of Debate in Theoretical and Applied Ethics*, Rowman & Littlefield, 1991, pp. 273-283
- Arendt, H., *Eichmann in Jerusalem: a report on the banality of evil*, The Viking Press, New York, 1964
- Arlow, P. and T.N. Ulrich, "Business ethics and business school graduates: a longitudinal study," *Business and Economic Review*, 16, 1988, pp. 13-17
- Arrow, K.J., *The Limits of Organization*, Norton, New York, 1974
- Asch, S.E., *Social Psychology*, Englewood Cliffs, Prentice-Hall, New York, 1952

- Baarle, B., *Corruptie bij de Nederlandse Politie*, Katholieke Universiteit Leuven, Faculteit Rechtsgeleerdheid, 1994
- Badaracco, J.L., "Business ethics: four spheres of executive responsibility," *California Management Review*, Spring 1992, pp. 64-79

- Baier, K., "Guilt and responsibility," in P.A. French (ed.), *Individual and Collective Responsibility: the massacre at My Lai*, Cambridge, Mass., 1972, pp. 37-61
- Baier, A., "Trust and antitrust," *Ethics*, 96, 1986, pp. 231-260
- Bar-on, A.Z., "Measuring Responsibility," 1985, in L. May and S. Hoffman (eds.), *Five Decades of Debate in Theoretical and Applied Ethics*, Rowman & Littlefield, 1991, pp. 255-271
- Barnard, C.I., *The Functions of the Executive*, Harvard University Press, Cambridge, 1938
- Baumhart, R.C., "How ethical are businesses?," *Harvard Business Review*, 39, June-August 1961, p. 6
- Behrman, J.N., *Discourses on Ethics and Business*, Oelgeschlager, Gunn & Hain Publishers, 1981
- Bekke, A.J.G.M., "Integriteit en organisatie," *Bestuurswetenschappen*, 5, November-December 1995, pp. 426-446
- Berenbeim, R.E., *Corporate Ethics*, Research Report No. 900, The Conference Board, New York, 1988
- Bernardin, H.J. and D.K. Cooke, "Predicting theft among convenience store employees," *Stores*, October 1994, pp. 1-3
- Bishop, J.D., "The moral responsibility of corporate executives for disasters," *Journal of Business Ethics*, 10, 1991, pp. 377-383
- Blaauw, J.A., "Een corrupte diender is de pest voor het hele korps," *Justitiële Verkenningen*, vol. 17, no. 4, 1991, pp. 33-52
- Blake, D., W. Frederick and M. Myers, *Social Auditing: evaluating the impact of corporate programs*, Preager Publishers, New York, 1976
- Blanchard, K. and N.V. Peale, *The Power of Ethical Management: why the ethical way is the profitable way in your life and in your business*, Morrow, New York, 1988
- Bok, S., *Lying: moral choice in public and private life*, Pantheon Books, New York, 1978
- Bologna, G.J., and R.J. Lindquist, *Fraud Auditing and Forensic Accounting: new tools and techniques*, Wiley, 1995, second edition
- Bovens, M.A.P., *Verantwoordelijkheid en Organisatie: beschouwingen over aansprakelijkheid, institutioneel burgerschap en ambtelijke ongehoorzaamheid*, Tjeenk Willink, Zwolle, 1990
- Bowie, N.E., "The paradox of profit," in N. Dale (ed.), *Papers on the Ethics of Administration*, Provo, Utah, University of Brigham Young Press, 1988, pp. 97-118
- Brand, A.F., "Bedrijfskunst," *Bedrijfskunde*, vol. 61, no. 4, 1989, pp. 322-326
- Brenner, S.N., "Ethics programs and their dimensions," *Journal of Business Ethics*, 11, 1992, pp. 391-399.
- Brenner, S.N. and E.A. Molander, "Is the ethics of business changing?," *Harvard Business Review*, 55, January-February 1977, pp. 57-71
- Brigley, S., "Business ethics research: a cultural perspective," *Business Ethics*, 4, January 1995, pp. 17-23
- Brinckmann, E., "Gaten boven de vloedlijn: over de vraag naar de blijvendheid van organisaties," *Filosofie in Bedrijf*, 3, Winter 1991, pp. 15-19
- Brons, Th. and H. van der Lee, *Ethiek als Managementinstrument*, NIVE, Zeist, 1989
- Butler, J.K. and R.S. Cantrell, "A behavioral decision theory approach to modeling dyadic trust in superiors and subordinates," *Psychological Reports*, 55, 1984, pp. 19-28

- Carmichael, S. "Countering employee crime," *Business Ethics: A European Review*, 1, July 1992, pp. 180-184

- Carroll, A.B., "Linking business ethics to behavior in organization," *Advanced Management Journal*, vol. 43, no. 3, 1978, pp. 4-11
- Carroll, A.B., *Business and Society: ethics and stakeholder management*, South-Western Publishing Co., Ohio, 1989
- Carter, D.L., "Drug-related corruption of police officers, a contemporary typology," *Journal of criminal justice*, 18, 1990, pp. 85-98
- Center for Business Ethics, "Are corporations institutionalizing ethics?," *Journal of Business Ethics*, 5, 1986, pp. 85-91
- Chandler, A.D., *Strategy and Structure: chapters in the history of the industrial enterprise*, Cambridge, Mass., 1962
- Chewning, R.C., J.W. Eby and S.J. Roel, *Business through the Eyes of Faith*, Apollos, Leicester, 1992
- Cohen, D.V., "Creating and maintaining ethical work climates: anomie in the workplace and implications for managing chance," *Business Ethics Quarterly*, vol. 3, no. 4, 1993, pp. 343-358
- Colby, A. and L. Kohlberg, *The Measurement of Moral Judgment: theoretical foundations and research validations*, Volume 1, Cambridge University Press, Cambridge, Mass., 1982
- Coleman, J.S., *The Asymmetric Society*, Syracuse, 1982
- Comer, M.J., *Corporate Fraud*, McGraw-Hill, London, 1985, second edition
- Cook, J. and T. Wall, "New work attitude measures of trust, organizational commitment, and personal need nonfulfillment," *Journal of Occupational Psychology*, 53, 1980, pp. 39-52
- Cooke, R.A., "Business ethics at the crossroads," *Journal of Business Ethics*, 5, 1986, pp. 250-263
- Cooke, R.A., "Danger signs of unethical behavior: how to determine if your firm is at ethical risk," *Journal of Business Ethics*, 10, 1991, pp. 249-253
- Cornwall, H., *Data Theft*, Heinemann, London, 1994
- Coye, R., "Individual values and business ethics," *Journal of Business Ethics*, 5, 1986, pp. 45-49
- Crisp, R. and M. Slote, "Introduction," in R. Crisp and M. Slote (eds.), *Virtue Ethics*, Oxford University Press, 1997, pp. 1-25
- Cullen, J.B., B. Victor and C. Stephen, "An ethical weather report: assessing the organizations ethical climate," *Organizational Dynamics*, 1989, pp. 50-62
- Cunningham, M.R.., D.T. Wong and A.P. Barbee, "Self-presentation dynamics on overt integrity tests: experimental studies of the Reid Report," *Journal of Applied Psychology*, vol. 79, no. 5, 1994, pp. 643-658
- Cyert, R.M. and J.G. March, *A Behavioural Theory of the Firm*, Prentice Hall, Englewood Cliffs, 1963

- Darley, J.M. and B. Latane, "Bystanders' intervention in emergencies: diffusion of responsibility," *Journal of Personality and Social Psychology*, 8, 1968, pp. 373-383
- De George, R.T., *Business Ethics*, McMillan, New York, 1990
- Deal, T.E., and A.A. Kennedy, *Corporate Cultures: the rites and rituals of corporate life*, Reading, Addison Wesley, 1982
- Delaney, J.T. and D. Sockell, "Do company ethics training make a difference: an empirical analysis," *Journal of Business Ethics*, 11, 1992, pp. 719-727
- DeLeon, L., "As plain as 1, 2, 3, ... and 4: ethics and organization structure," *Administration & Society*, vol. 25, no. 3, November 1993, pp. 293-317
- Deutsch, M., "The effect of motivational orientation upon trust and suspicion," *Human Relations*, 13, 1960, pp. 123-140

- Donaldson, T., *Corporations and Morality*, Prentice-Hall, 1982
- Donaldson, T., *Case studies in business ethics*, Englewood Cliffs, Prentice Hall, 1984
- Donaldson, T. and T.W. Dunfee, "Toward a unified conception of business ethics: integrative social contracts theory," *Academy of Management Review*, vol. 19, no. 2, 1994, pp. 252-284
- Donaldson, T. and T.W. Dunfee, "Contractarian business ethics: current status and next steps," *Business Ethics Quarterly*, vol. 5, no. 3, 1995, pp. 173-186
- Donaldson, T., "Values in tension: ethics away from home," *Harvard Business Review*, 74, September-October 1996, pp. 48-62
- Downs, A., *Inside Bureaucracy*, Boston, 1967
- Drucker, P.F., *Management*, Harper's College Press, New York, 1977
- Dubinsky, A.J. and J.M. Gwin, "Business ethics: buyers and sellers," *Journal of Purchasing and Materials Management*, Winter 1981, pp. 97-103

- Edelman Bos, J.B.M., *Bezwijkende Muren*, Faculteit der Bedrijfskunde en Faculteit der Geneeskunde en Gezondheidswetenschappen, Rotterdam, 1990
- Ermann, M.D. and R.J. Lundman, *Corporate and Governmental Deviance: problems of organizational behavior*, Contemporary Society, 1982
- Ethics Resource Center, *Creating a Workable Company Code of Ethics*, Washington, D.C., 1990
- Ethics Resource Center, *Ethics in American Business: policies, programs and perceptions. Report of a landmark survey of US employee*, Washington, D.C., 1994
- Evans, W.A., *Management Ethics: an intercultural perspective*, Nijhoff, The Hague, 1981

- Falkenberg, L. and I. Herrenans, "Ethical behaviors in organizations directed by the formal or informal systems?," *Journal of Business Ethics*, 14, 1995, pp. 133-143
- Ferrell, O.C. and L. Gresham, "A contingency framework for understanding ethical decision making in marketing," *Journal of Marketing*, Summer 1985, pp. 87-96
- Fiedler, R., *Die Moral der Manager: Dokumentation und Analyse*, Seewald, Stuttgart, 1977
- Fijnaut, C., *Politiële Corruptie in Nederland: een impressie van veertien gevallen*, Gouda Quint, Arnhem, 1993
- Fletcher, C., "Not all candidates are who they say they are," *People Management*, 17 April 1997, pp. 51-53
- Follet, M.P., *The New State*, Gloucester, Mass., 1918
- Ford, R.C. and W.D. Richardson, "Ethical decision making: a review of the empirical literature," *Journal of Business Ethics*, 13, 1994, pp. 205-221
- Frederick, W.C., "Corporate social responsibility in the Reagan era and beyond," *California Management Review*, vol. 25, no. 3, 1983, pp. 145-157
- Frederick, W.C., K. Davis and J.E., Post, *Business and Society: corporate strategy, public policy, ethics*, McGraw-Hill, Singapore, 1988
- Freeman, R.E., *Strategic Management: a stakeholder approach*, University of Minnesota, Pitman, Boston, 1984
- French, P., *Collective and Corporate Responsibility*, Columbia University Press, New York, 1984
- Friedman, M., *Capitalism and Freedom*, University of Chicago Press, Chicago, 1962
- Friedman, M., "The social responsibility of business is to increase its profits," *The New York Times Magazine*, September 13, 1970
- Fritzsche, D.J. and H. Becker, "Ethical behavior of marketing managers," *Journal of Business Ethics*, 2, 1983, pp. 291-299

• Fukuyama, F., *Trust: the social virtues and the creation of prosperity*, Free Press, New York, 1995

• Gambetta, D.G., "Can we trust trust," in D.G. Gambetta (ed.), *Trust*, Basil Blackwell, New York, 1988, pp. 213-237

• Gauthier, D. *Morals by Agreement*, Oxford University Press, Oxford, 1986

• Gellerman, S.W., "Why 'good' managers make bad ethical choices," *Harvard Business Review*, 64, 1986, pp. 85-90

• Gellerman, S.W., "Managing ethics from the top down," *Sloan Management Review*, Winter 1989, pp. 73-79

• Gilbert, D.R. and R.E. Freeman, *Corporate Strategy and the Search for Ethics*, Prentice Hall, Englewood Cliffs, 1988

• Gilligan, C., *In a Different Voice: psychological theory and women's development*, Harvard University Press, Cambrigde, Mass., 1982

• Goodpaster, K.E. and J.B. Matthews, "Can a corporation have a conscience?," in W.M. Hoffman and J.M. Moore (eds.), *Business Ethics: readings and cases in corporate morality*, McGraw-Hill, 1982, second edition, pp. 184-194

• Goodpaster, K.E., "Business ethics and stakeholder analysis," *Business Ethics Quarterly*, vol. 1, no. 1, January 1991, pp. 53-72

• Goyder, G., *The Just Enterprise: a blueprint for the responsible company*, Adamantine Press, 1993

• Grijpink, J.H.A.M., *Interne Criminaliteit: managementvraagstuk voor bedrijfsleven en overheid*, SMO-informatief, 1, 1995

• Gunsteren, H.R. van, *Denken over politieke verantwoordelijkheden*, Rijksuniversiteit Leiden, Alphen aan de Rijn, 1974

• Hardin, G., "The tragedy of the commons," *Science*, 162, 1968, pp. 1243-1248

• Hardin, R., *Morality within the Limits of Reason*, University of Chicago Press, Chicago, 1988

• Harington, S.J., "What corporate America is teaching about ethics," *Academy of Management Executive*, vol. 5, no. 1, 1991, pp. 21-30

• Hart, H.L.A., *Punishment and Responsibility: essays in the philosophy of law*, Clarendon Press, New York, 1968

• Hegarty, W.H. and H.P. Sims, "Some determinants of unethical decision behavior: an experiment," *Journal of Applied Behavior*, 63, 1978, pp. 451-457

• Hill, C.W.L, "Cooperation, opportunism, and the invisible hand: implications for transaction cost theory," *Academy of Management Journal*, 15, 1990, pp. 500-513

• Hill, J.W., M.B. Metzger and D.R. Dalton, "How ethical is your company?," *Management Accounting*, July 1992, pp. 59-61

• Hirschman, A.O., *Exit, Voice, and Loyalty: responses to decline in firms, organizations and states*, Harvard University Press, Cambridge, Mass., 1970

• Hoffman, W.M. and J.M. Moore, *Business Ethics: readings and cases in corporate morality*, McGraw-Hill, New York, 1990

• Hofstede, G, *Cultures and Organizations: software of the mind*, McGraw-Hill, London, 1991

• Hogan, J. and R. Hogan, "How to measure employee reliability," *Journal of Applied Psychology*, 74, 1989, pp. 273-279

• Hogan, J. and K. Brinkmeyer, "Bridging the gap between overt and personality-based integrity tests," *Personnel Psychology*, 50, 1997, pp. 587-599

- Hoogstraten, J., "De weerslag van corruptie op de organisatie en de uitvoering van het politiewerk," in *Strategiën voor Corruptiebeheersing bij de Politie*, E.W. Kolthoff (ed.), Gouda Quint, 1994, pp. 47-56
- Hosmer, L.T., *The Ethics of Management*, Irwin, Homewood, Illinois, 1991
- Hosmer, L.T., "Trust: the connecting link between organizational theory and philosophical ethics," *Academy of Management Review*, vol. 20, no. 2, 1995, pp. 379-403
- Hosson, G.J. de, "Vertrouwenspersoon en bestuurlijke integriteit," *Bestuurswetenschappen*, 6, November-December 1995, pp. 447-456
- Hummels, G.J.A., *Vluchtige Arbeid: ethiek en een proces van organisatie-ontwikkeling*, Eburon, Delft, 1996
- Hunt, S.D., L.B. Chonko and J.B. Wilcox, "Ethical problems of marketing researchers," *Journal of Marketing Research*, 21, 1984, pp. 304-324
- Huntington, I., and D. Davies, *Financial Fraud: a guide for business*, The Institute of Chartered Accountants in England and Wales, 1994
- Husted, B.W., "Reliability and the design of ethical organization: a rational approach," *Journal of Business Ethics*, 12, 1993, pp. 761-769
- Hyman, M.R., R. Skipper and R. Tansey, "Ethical codes are not enough," *Business Horizons*, March-April 1990, pp. 15-22.

- Institute for Business Ethics, *Company Philosophies and Codes of Business Ethics: a guide to their drafting and use*, London, 1990
- Izraeli, D., "Ethical beliefs and behavior among managers," *Journal of Business Ethics*, 7, 1988, pp. 263-271

- Jackall, R., *Moral Mazes: the world of corporate managers*, Oxford University Press, New York, 1988
- Jennings, M. M., *Case Studies in Business Ethics*, West Publishing Company, 1996, second edition
- Jones, T.M., "Ethical decision making by individuals in organizations: an issue-contingent model," *Academy of Management Review*, vol. 16, no. 2, 1991, pp. 366-395
- Jongsma, K., *Administratieve Organisatie en Interne Controle van Banken*, NIBE, Amsterdam, 1992

- Kant, I., *Groundwork of the Metaphysics of Morals*, trans. H.J. Paton, Harper & Row Publishers, New York, 1971
- Kanter, R.M., *The Change Masters*, Simon & Schuster, New York, 1983
- Katz, D. and F. Allport, *Student Attitudes*, Syracuse, New York, 1931
- Kelman, H.C. and V.L. Hamilton, *Crimes of Obedience: toward a social psychology of authority and responsibility*, New Haven, 1989
- Kidwell, J.M., R.E. Stevens and A.L. Bethke, "Differences in the ethical perceptions between male and female managers: myth and reality," *Journal of Business Ethics*, 6, 1987, pp. 489-493
- Kimman, E.J.J.M., *Deugden in de Directiekamer*, Van Gorcum, Assen, 1989
- Kirrane, D.E., "Managing values: a systematic approach to business ethics, *Training & Development Journal*, vol. 44, no. 11, November 1990, pp. 53-60
- Knapp-commission, *Report on Police Corruption*, George Braziler, New York, 1973
- Knouse, S.B. and R.A. Giacalone, "Ethical decision-making in business: behavioral issues and concerns," *Journal of Business Ethics*, 11, 1992, pp. 369-377
- Kohlberg, L., *The Philosophy of Moral development: moral stages and the idea of justice*, Harper & Row, San Francisco, 1981

- Kohlberg, L., *The Psychology of Moral Development: the nature and validity of moral stages*, Harper & Row, San Francisco, 1984
- Kornblum, A.N., *The Moral Hazards: police strategies for honesty and ethical behavior*, Lexington, Massachusetts, 1976
- Kuitert, H.M., *Het Algemeen Betwijfeld Christelijk Geloof: een herziening*, Ten Have, Baarn, 1992

- Laczniak, G.R. and E.J. Interrieden, "The influence of stated organizational concern upon ethical decision making," *Journal of Business Ethics*, 6, 1987, pp. 297-307
- Laczniak, G.R. and P.E. Murphy, "Fostering ethical marketing decisions," *Journal of Business Ethics*, 10 , 1991, pp. 259-271
- Ladd, J., "Morality and the ideal of rationality in formal organizations," *The Monist*, 54, 1970, pp. 488-516
- Landau, M., "Redundancy, rationality and the problem of duplication and overlap," *Public Administration Review*, 29, 1969, pp. 346-358
- Levi, P., *The Drowned and the Saved*, Summit Books, New York, 1986
- Linowes, D.F., *The Conference Board Record*, Elsevier Sciences, Amsterdam, 1972
- Lorsch, J., "Managing culture: the invisible barrier to strategic change," *California Management Review*, 28, 1986, pp. 95-106
- Luijk, H.J.L. van, *Om Redelijk Gewin: een oefening in de bedrijfsethiek*, Boom, Meppel, 1993
- Luijk, H.J.L. van, and A. Schilder, *Patronen van Verantwoordelijkheid; ethiek en corporate governance*, Academic Services, Schoonhoven, 1997

- Madsen, P., "Managing ethics," *Executive Excellence*, 7, December 1990, pp. 11-12
- Mahoney, J., *Teaching Business Ethics in the UK, Europe and the USA: a comparative study*, The Athlone Press Ltd, London, 1990
- March, J.G. and Z. Shapira, "Managerial perspectives on risk and risk taking," *Management Science*, 33, 1987, pp. 1404-1418
- Mathews Cash, M., "Codes of ethics: organizational behavior and misbehavior," *Research in Corporate Social Performance and Policy*, JAI Press Inc., 9, 1987, pp. 107-130
- Mayer, R.C., J.H. Davis and F.D. Schoorman, "An integrative model of organizational trust," *Academy of Management Review*, vol. 20, no. 3, 1995, pp. 709-734
- McCoy, C.S., "The parable of the Sadhu," in *Harvard Business Review*, 61, September-October 1983
- McCoy, C.S., *Management of Values: the ethical difference in corporate policy and performance*, Pitman Publishing Inc., Marshfield, Mass., 1985
- Metzger, M., D.R. Dalton and J.W. Hill, "The organization of ethics and the ethics of organizations: the case for expanded organizational ethics audits," *Business Ethics Quarterly*, vol. 3, no. 1, 1993, pp. 27-43
- Michalos, A., "The impact of trust on business, international security, and the quality of life," *Journal of Business Ethics*, 9, 1990, pp. 619-638
- Milgram, S., *Obedience to Authority*, Harper en Row, New York, 1974
- Morgan, G., *Images of Organizations*, Sage Publications, Beverly Hills, 1986
- Mulder, A.M., "SAFER: een veiligheids management tool voor de staalindustrie," *NOBO*, 6, 1993, pp. 131-140
- Mullighan, T.M., "The moral mission of business," in T.L. Beauchamp and N.E. Bowie (eds.), *Ethical Theory and Business*, Englewood Cliffs, Prentice Hall, New York, 1983, pp. 65-75

- Murphy, P.E., "Implementing business ethics," *Journal of Business Ethics*, 7, 1988, pp. 907-915

- Nash., L.L., *Good Intentions Aside: a managers guide to resolving ethical problems*, Harvard Business School Press, Boston, 1990
- Niebuhr, R., *Moral Man and Immoral Society: a study in ethics and politics*, Scribners Sons, New York, 1932
- Nielsen, R.P., "What can managers do about unethical management?," *Journal of Business Ethics*, 7, 1987, pp. 309-320
- Nielsen, R.P., "Limitations of ethical reasoning as an action (praxis) strategy," *Journal of Business Ethics*, 7, 1988, pp. 971-979

- Ophuls, W., "The scarcity society," Harpers Magazine, 1974, in T.J. Donaldson and P.H. Werhane (eds.), *Ethical Issues in Business*, Englewood Cliffs, New York, Prentice Hall, 1988
- Orwell, G., *Decline of the English Murder and Other Essays*, Penguin Books, 1965
- Ostapski, S.A. and D.G. Pressley, "Moral audit for Diabco Corporation," *Journal of Business Ethics*, 11, 1992, pp. 71-80
- Ottoson, G.E., "Winning the war against corporate crime," *Ethicos 2.4*, January-February 1989

- Paradice, D.B. and R.M. Dejoice, "The ethical decision-making processes of information system workers," *Journal of Business Ethics*, 10, 1991, pp. 1-21
- Parfit, D., *Reasons and Persons*, Clarendon Press, Oxford, 1984
- Pastin, M., *The Hard Problems of Management: gaining the ethics edge*, Jossy-Bass, San Francisco, 1986
- Pastin, M., "Lessons form high-profit, high-ethics companies: an agenda for managerial action," in W.M. Hoffman and J.M. Moore (eds.), *Business Ethics: readings and cases in corporate morality*, McGraw-Hill, 1990, second edition, pp. 624-628
- Paul, K. (ed.), *Business Environment and Business Ethics: the social, moral, and the political dimension of management*, Cambridge, Mass., Ballinger, 1987
- Paul, K. and S.D. Lydenberg, "Applications of corporate social monitoring systems; types, dimensions and goals," *Journal of Business Ethics*, 11, 1992, pp. 1-10
- Pearce, J., P. Raynard and S. Zadek, *Social Auditing for Small Organisations: a workbook for trainers and practitioners*, New Economics Foundation, 1996
- Pearson, G., *Integrity in Organizations: an alternative business ethic*, McGraw-Hill Book Company, London, 1995
- Pijl, D., "De bestrijding van politiële corruptie," *Justitiële Verkenningen*, vol. 17, no. 4, 1991, pp. 53-74
- Pijl, D. and P. Muijen, "Integriteit is geen modebegrip," *Algemeen Politieblad*, 16, August 1994, pp. 14-16
- Porter, M.E., *The Competitive Strategy: techniques for analyzing industries and competitors*, The Free Press, New York, 1980
- Posner, B.Z. and W.H. Schmidt, "Ethics in American companies: a managerial perspective," *Journal of Business Ethics*, 6, 1987, pp. 383-391
- Pruzan, P, "Reflections on three themes: performance, ethics and accountability," *AccountAbility Quarterly*, 5, 1997, p. 11
- Punch, M., *Dirty Business: exploring corporate misconduct*, SAGE Publications, London, 1996

- Raiborn, C.A. and D. Payne, "Corporate codes of conduct: a collective conscience and continuum, *Journal of Business Ethics*, 9, 1990, pp. 879-889
- Rappaport, A., *Creating Shareholder Value: the new standard for business performance*, Free Press, New York, 1986
- Rawnsley, J., *Going for Broke*, Harper Collins Publishers, 1995
- Rion, M.R., "Training for ethical management at Cummins Engine," in W.M. Hoffman and J.M. Moore (eds.), *Business Ethics: readings and cases in corporate morality*, McGraw-Hill, 1990, second edition, pp. 109-116
- Robin, D.P. and E.R. Reidenbach, "A conceptual model of corporate moral development," *Journal of Business Ethics*, 10, 1991, pp. 273-284
- Rotter, J.B., "A new scale for the measurement of interpersonal trust," *Journal of Personality*, 35, 1967, pp. 651-665

- Sacket, P.R. and M.M. Harris, "Honesty testing for personnel selection: a review and critique," *Personnel Psychology*, 37, Spring 1984, pp. 221-245
- Sacket, P.R., L.R. Burris and C. Callahan, "Integrity testing for personnel selection: an update," *Personnel Psychology*, 42, Autumn 1989, pp. 491-529
- Schwartz, S.H., "Words, deeds and the perception of consequences and responsibility in action situations," *Journal of Personalities and Social Psychology*, 10, 1968, pp. 232-242
- Sethi, S.P. and C.M. Falbe, *Business and Society: dimensions of conflict and cooperation*, Lexington Books, Lexington, 1987
- Shaw, R.B., *Trust in Balance: building successful organizations on results, integrity, and concern*, Jossey-Bass Publishers, San Francisco, 1997
- Sherman, L.W., "Becoming bent: moral careers of corrupt policeman," in F. Elliston and A. Feldberg (eds.), *Moral Issues in Police Work*, Pottzoa, New Jersey, Rowman & Allanheld publ., 1985, pp. 253-265
- Shrivastava, P., "Technological and organizational roots of industrial crisis: lessons from Exxon Valdez and Bhopal," *Technological Forecasting and Social Science*, 45, 1994, pp. 237-253
- Sims, R.R., "The institutionalization of organizational ethics," *Journal of Business Ethics*, 10, 1991, pp. 493-506
- Smith, A., *The Wealth of Nations*, Oxford University Press, 1993, first edition: 1776
- Solomon, R.C. and K. Hanson, *It's Good Business*, Atheneum, New York, 1985
- Solomon, R.C., *Ethics and Excellence: cooperation and integrity in business*, Oxford University Press, New York, 1992a
- Solomon, R.C., "Corporate roles and personal virtues: a Aristotelean approach to business ethics," *Business Ethics Quarterly*, vol. 2, no. 3, 1992b, pp. 317-340
- Solomon, R.C., *The New World of Business: ethics and free enterprise in the global 1990s*, Rowman & Littlefield Publishers, Inc., 1994
- Stark, A., "What's the matter with business ethics?," *Harvard Business Review*, 71, 1993, pp. 38-48
- Staw, B.M. and E.I.O. Szwajkowski, "The Scarcity-munificence component of organizational environments and the Commission of Illegal Act," *Administrative Science Quarterly*, 20, 1975, pp. 345-354
- Stead, W.E., D.L. Worrell and J.G. Stead, "An integrative model for understanding and managing ethical behavior in business organizations," *Journal of Business Ethics*, 9, 1990, pp. 233-242
- Steiner, G.A. and J.F. Steiner, *Business, Government, and Society: a managerial perspective*, John Wiley & Sons, New York, 1991

- Steinmann, H. and A. Lohr, *Grundlagen der Unternehmensethik*, Poeschel, Stuttgart, 1992
- Stone, C.D., *Where the Law Ends: the social control of corporate behavior*, Waveland Press, New York, 1975
- Sturdivant, F.D., *Business and Society: a managerial approach*, Homewood, Irwin, 1985

- Thompson, D.F., *Political Ethics and Public Office*, Cambrigde, Mass., 1987
- Thornhill, W.T., *Forensic Accounting: how to investigate financial fraud*, Richard D. Irwin, 1995
- Torabzadeh, K.M., D. Davidson and H. Assar, "The effect on the recent insider-trading scandal on stock prices of securities firms," *Journal of Business Ethics*, 8, 1989, pp. 299-303
- Toro, P. Di, "Building an ethical organization," *Business Ethics: A European Review*, vol. 4, no. 1,, January 1995, pp. 43-51
- Touche Ross, *Ethics in American Business*, New York, 1988
- Trevino, L.K., C.D. Sutton and R.W. Woodman, "Effects on reinforcement contingencies and cognitieve moral development and ethical decision making behavior: an experiment," paper presented at the Annual Meeting of the *Academy of Management*, San Diego, 1985
- Trevino, L.K., "Ethical decision making in organizations: a person-situation interactionist model," *Academy of Management Review*, 11, 1986, pp. 601-617
- Trevino, L.K. and S.A. Youngblood, "Bad apples in bad barrels: a casual analysis of ethical decision-making behavior," *Journal of Applied Psychology*, 74, 1990, pp. 378-385
- Trevino, L.K. and K.A. Nelson, *Managing Business Ethics: straight talk about how to do it right*, John Wiley & Sons, 1995
- Tsalikis, J. and D.J. Fritzsche, "Business ethics: a literature review with a focus on marketing ethics," *Journal of Business Ethics*, 8, 1989, pp. 695-743
- Tucker, J., "Employee theft as social control," *Deviant Behavior*, 4, 1989

- Vaughan, D., *Controlling Unlawful Organizational Behavior: social structure and corporate misconduct*, Chicago University Press, Chicago, 1983
- Vaughan, D., "Autonomy, interdependence, and social control: NASA and the Space Shuttle Challenger," *Administrative Science Quarterly*, 35, 1990, pp. 225-257
- Velasquez, M.G., "Why corporations are not morally responsible for anything they do?," *Business and Professional Ethics Journal*, 2, Spring 1983, pp. 1-17
- Velasquez, M.G., "Corporate ethics: losing it, having it, getting it," in P. Madsen and J.M. Shafritz (eds.), *Essentials of Business Ethics*, 1990, pp. 228-243
- Velasquez, M.G., *Business Ethics: concepts and cases*, Englewood Cliffs, New York, 1992, third edition
- Verstraeten, J. and J. van Gerwen, *Business en Ethiek*, Lannoo, Tielt, 1994, second edition
- Victor, B. and J.B. Cullen, "A theory and measure of ethical climate in organizations," *Research in Corporations Social Performance and Policy*, 9, 1987, pp. 51-71
- Victor B. and J.B. Cullen, "The organizational basis of ethical work climates," *Administrative Science Quarterly*, 33, 1988, pp. 101-125
- Volberda, H.W., *Organizational Flexibility: change and preservation*, Wolters-Noordhof, Groningen, 1992

- Wahn, J., "Organizational dependence and the likelihood of complying with organizational pressures to behave unethically," *Journal of Business Ethics*, 12, 1993, pp. 245-251
- Walker, O.C., G.A. Churchill and N.M. Ford, "Where do we go from here?," in D. Albaum and G.A. Churchill (eds.), *Critical Issues in Sales Management*, University of Oregon, 1979
- Warren, R.C., "Loyalty as an organizational virtue," *Business Ethics: A European Review*, vol. 1, no. 3, July 1992, pp.172-179
- Waters, J.A. and F. Bird, "The moral dimension of organizational culture," *Journal of Business Ethics*, 6, 1987, pp. 15-22
- Waters, J.A. and F. Bird, "Attending to ethics in management," *Journal of Business Ethics*, 8, 1989, pp. 493-497
- Watson, T., "Recruitment & selection," in K. Sisson (ed.), *Personnel Management: a comprehensive guide to theory and practice in Britain*, Blackwell, 1994
- Weber, J.A., "Institutionalizing ethics into the corporation," *MSU Business Topics*, vol. 29, no. 2, 1981, pp. 47-52
- Weber, J.A., "Managers moral reasoning: assessing their responses to three moral dilemmas," *Human Relations*, 43, 1990, pp. 687-702
- Weber, J.A., "Adapting Kohlberg to enhance the assessment of managers' moral reasoning," *Business Ethics Quarterly*, vol. 1, no. 3, 1991, pp. 293-318
- Weber, J.A., "Institutionalizing ethics into business organizations: a model and research agenda," *Business Ethics Quarterly*, vol. 3, no. 4, 1993, pp. 419-436
- Weiss, J.W., *Business Ethics: a managerial stakeholder approach*, Wadsworth, Belmonth, Cal., 1994
- Weller, S., "The effectiveness of corporate codes of ethics," *Journal of Business Ethics*, vol. 7, no. 5, 1988, pp. 389-395
- Wempe, J.F.D.B. and K. Melis, *Management & Moraal*, Stenfert Kroese, Leiden, 1991
- Wempe, J.F.D.B., *Market & Morality*, Rotterdam School of Management, thesis, 1998
- Werhane, P.H., *Persons, Rights and Corporations*, Englewood Cliffs, Prentice Hall, 1985
- Werhane, P.H., "Moral character and moral reasoning," in T.J. Donaldson, and R.E. Freeman (eds.), *Business as Humanity*, Oxford University Press, New York, 1991, pp. 98-106
- Wheelen, T.L. and J.D. Hunger, *Strategic Management and Business Policy*, Addison-Wesley, 1995, fifth edition
- Wheeler, D. and M. Sillanpää, *The Stakeholder Corporation: a blueprint for maximizing stakeholder value*, Pitman Publishing, London, 1997
- Wijffels, H.H.F., "Idealen voor de toekomst," *Filosofie in Bedrijf*, 3, Winter 1991, pp. 37-41
- Wimbush, J.C. and J.M. Shepard, "Towards an understanding of ethical climate: its relationship to ethical behavior and supervisory influence," *Journal of Business Ethics*, 13, 1994, pp. 637-647
- Witkin, H.A. and D.R. Goodenough, "Field dependence and interpersonal behavior," *Psychological Bulletin*, 1977, pp. 661-689
- Wood J.A., J.G. Longenecker, J.A. McKinney and C.W. Moore, "Ethical attitudes of students and business professionals: a study of moral reasoning," *Journal of Business Ethics*, 7, 1988, pp. 249-257

- Zand, D.E., "Trust and managerial problem solving," *Administrative Science Quarterly*, 17, 1972, pp. 229-239

- Zey-Ferrell, M., K.M. Weaver and O.C. Ferrell, "Predicting unethical behavior among marketing practitioners," *Human Relations*, 32, 1979, pp. 557-569
- Zey-Ferrell, M. and O.C. Ferrell, "Role-set configuration and opportunity as predictors of unethical behavior in organizations," *Human Relations*, vol. 35 no. 7, 1982, pp. 587-604
- Zier, J., *The Expert Accountant in Civil Litigation*, Butterworths, 1993
- Zucker, L.G., "Production of trust: institutional sources of economic structure," in M. Staw and L.L. Cummings (eds.), *Research in Organizational Behavior*, 8, JAI Press, Greenwich, 1986, pp. 53-111

APPENDICES

Appendix 1

Agenda for
follow-up research

The following, statistical research questions can be posed, using a database consisting of a large number of organizations which have been reviewed with the Ethics Thermometer.

1. *Should the presented model of the ethical content of corporations be modified based on advanced statistical techniques such as a factor analysis?*

   The presented model is arrived at by clustering the various context factors into 21 qualities on the grounds of logic and plausibility. It is, however, possible to join and split these qualities based on factor analysis of the information of a large number of organizations (and in calculating the interrelation and scale reliabilities). An important criterion for whether to change or maintain the current Ethical Qualities Model is the extent to which the detected differences between units of analysis become visible in the ethics profile so that the various scores to questions/aspects will not be lost during the processing of the data. At the same time, the model should be such that the organizations under review can understand it and that the auditors can make proper use of it.

2. *Can organizations be classified or typified according to the degree to which the qualities are embedded within the organization? Furthermore, in relation to the ethical content of organizations, are there significant differences that can be made between organizations of different sizes, organizational structures, market*

structures, business sectors, and countries and between for-profit and not-for-profit organizations?

Robin and Reidenbach's model (1991) consists of five consecutive levels of moral development (amoral, legalistic, responsive, emerging ethical, and ethical). The question, however, is whether the organizations can be typified with respect to their level of moral development. In the current model, development takes place according to one or more of the 21 qualities. In connection with a factor analysis, it may be determined whether organizations develop according to a certain pattern. Moreover, a discriminate or cluster analysis can be performed to determine the extent to which the ethical content is influenced by the type of organization, size of the staff, market structure, sector, and national culture.

3. *Are there general key qualities that can be indicated per moral dimension?*

For organizations that have already been reviewed with the Ethics Thermometer, the spearheads are always determined anew on the basis of a correlation analysis. A comparison of spearheads traced for each organization can indicate to what extent certain correlations are always present or whether the correlation of qualities differs per organization. For example, the presence of the quality of discussability of dilemmas could thereby constitute a prerequisite for the clarity of the moral expectations.

4. *Is there a correlation between different forms of unethical conduct?*

To lessen unethical conduct, one must ask to what extent the various forms of unethical conduct can be tackled separately and to what extent they should always be approached collectively. Does a policy aimed at limiting the acceptance of gifts only have a good chance of success when a similar policy is initiated to limit the giving of gifts? Is there a correlation between the degree of careless use of corporate assets and the frequency of sexual harassment? And, is there a correlation between the degree to which people cheat on their expense accounts and the degree to which the corporation circumvents tax law, for instance? The related research question is "how much does the improvement of the co-ordination of one dimension depend on improvements in the other dimensions?"

5. *To what degree can the described basic assumptions, the process phases and measures be considered effective?*

The purpose of this study was not to show that the ethics of a corporation can be improved within a single period of time. By performing a multi-case longitudinal study with the assistance of the Ethics Thermometer, it is possible to determine the effectiveness of the assumptions which are applied during the interim period, the activities which have been developed, and the measures which have been taken.

Appendix 2

The Ethics Thermometer

The Ethics Thermometer can be executed in the form of a written survey. The advantage of a survey over face-to-face interviews is that a survey requires relatively little time from both the auditor and the organization under review. The thermometer can, then, be completed within two months after it is received by the personnel. The respondents are asked to give their opinions on a number of propositions on a Likert scale from one (completely disagree) to five (completely agree). The use of multiple-choice questions makes it possible to quantify the perceived ethical content, which makes statistical analyses possible. A drawback in the use of surveys is that there is no face-to-face contact between the auditor and the respondent, which means that the auditor cannot immediately react to the respondent's answers. A survey is relatively mechanical and, in comparison with a (semi-structured) interview, not very flexible. It is also possible to combine a survey with interviews. The results of the survey can lead to the formulation of questions (on points that, for example, need to be clarified) which can then be put to the personnel in interviews or panel sessions.

The subject of ethics can constitute an emotionally charged term within an organization. Especially if internal criminality, fraud or corruption are the reasons for an audit, the process needs to be presented carefully to the employees. The auditor needs to make sure that the employees do not present their practice better or worse than it really is. An article in the organization's internal media can serve to announce the start of the study. The management can also make employees aware of the impending review by letter. The tone set at the introduction is important. The list of questions is not intended to track down ill-disposed employees. The survey must not be seen by the personnel as a threat, but as a chance to improve the organization. The results of the measurement are usually only intended for internal use. The organization will often work on its ethical development one its own. In addition, if the results are intended to be published at large, the respondents will be more inclined to give patent answers. Nor should the results be intended for use in ranking corporations or departments according to their ethical content. It is very important that the anonymity of the respondents be protected. Employees must not have the idea that their answers will be used against them later, for example, within the framework of a job evaluation. An auditor from outside the organization is better able to guarantee this anonymity that an auditor who is part of the organization (Wheeler and Sillanpää, 1997). A self-assessment undoubtedly comes at the cost of the trustworthiness of the results. The written material accompanying the survey and the verbal explanation by management to the personnel can ensure that the goal of the research is clearly presented: intentionally making things look better or worse than they are has little sense.

How the questions are formulated has an influence on the degree to which employees feel threatened by the survey. Employees must not be given the idea that they are turning in co-workers or that they are evaluating their own behavior (Victor and Cullen, 1987). In addition, questions involving any possible personal evaluation or condemnation must not be phrased in the first person. Rather than the proposition, "I can easily take company property home without anyone knowing," it is better to say "In our department, it is easy to take company property home without anyone knowing."

Sending the surveys to the employees' home addresses rather than to them at work has the advantage that the employees are not inhibited by the thought of co-workers looking over their shoulders. A disadvantage is that employees must fill the survey out on their own time which can lead to resentment. At some organizations where the survey has been used, employees have been given a free hour to fill it out.

Appendix 3

Ethics profiles of four organizations

This appendix shows the ethics profile of the context as well as the computed spearheads and the recommendations which were made for four organizations. The questionnaire was, with the exception of minor syntactical differences, identical for all four organizations. Brief notes to the twenty-one qualities are presented in Figure 4-4.

A police organization

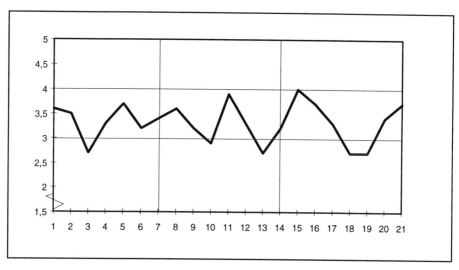

Based on a statistical analysis of the results of the Ethics Thermometer (September 1996) the computed spearheads were:

a. increasing the visibility of unethical behavior,
b. increasing feedback, and
c. increasing the external stakeholders' overview of the organization.

Several recommendations were:

1. Ad. a: supervisors' abilities to recognize indications or symptoms of unethical conduct (earlier) should be sharpened by means of training programs.
2. Ad a and b: supervisors should be more visible on the shop floor. To this end, other tasks should be carried out more efficiently, and the promotion process for supervisors should be improved.
3. Ad c: the management should better define the various duties within the organization. In that context, a clear prioritization should be indicated and clearly communicated to the personnel and external stakeholders.
4. Ad c: some rules and procedures should be changed and better communicated to outsiders. A Measures Scan is therefore recommended.

An international corporation

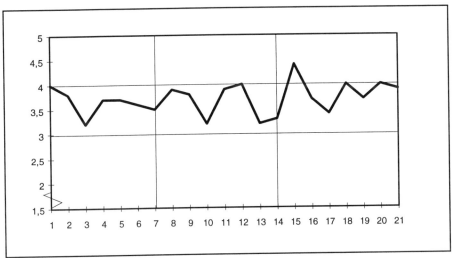

Based on a statistical analysis of the results of the thermometer (December 1996), and supplementary interviews, the spearheads were:
a. improving the communicative, corrective and stimulating role of the management,
b. increasing the visibility of unethical behavior,
c. stimulating an open attitude in regards to accepting criticism, and
d. improving the job evaluation procedure.

Several recommendations were:
1. Ad a: feedback from managers regarding the contributions of employees should be increased.
2. Ad a: supervisors should do a better job of communicating relevant decisions from higher levels to their employees.
3. Ad a: team meetings should be held in small groups of two to three employees.
4. Ad a: meetings should be held between departments (two at a time) to discuss mutually relevant issues.
5. Ad a: frequent job rotation should take place.
6. Ad a: new employees should be introduced to everyone in the department.
7. Ad a: the reception should be made aware of the duties and activities of everyone in the company.
8. Ad b: supervisors should be trained to recognize symptoms and indications of unethical conduct.
9. Ad b: there should be a systematic check and registration of client satisfaction.

10. Ad c: supervisors should be trained to encourage and handle criticism from their employees.
11. Ad d: periodic performance reviews should be made.
12. Ad d: during job evaluations, not only individual performance, but also departmental performance should be included.

A petrochemical corporation

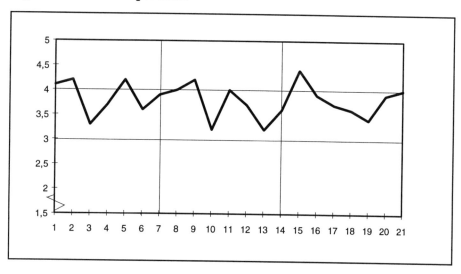

Based on a statistical analysis of the results of the thermometer (October 1996) and supplementary interviews, the spearheads were:
a. the role of supervisors should be strengthened, and
b. more support should be developed for current rules and procedures among external stakeholders.

Several recommendations were:
1. Ad a: the middle management should be coached more by the upper management.
2. Ad a: the management should occasionally (in the case of far-reaching decisions, once or twice a year) pay a visit to the departments.
3. Ad a: cooperation in teams should be stimulated.
4. Ad b: customers should be better informed regarding internal rules and procedures.
5. Ad b: a purchasing and sales codes should be developed.
6. As a consequence of the thermometer, a Measures Scan and Stakeholders Decoder should be carried out.

A Dutch governmental organization

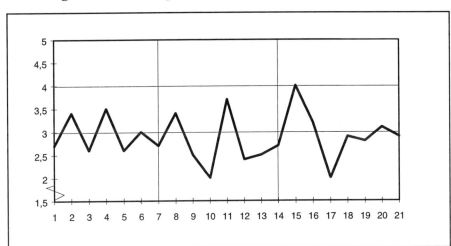

Based on a statistical analysis of the results of the thermometer (June 1996), several supplementary interviews, a panel meeting and various Dilemma Sessions, the main points for this organization were:

a.   The visibility within and of the organization should be increased. The lack of visibility appeared to be both horizontal (among co-workers and departments) and vertical (between management and subordinates) and concerned both direct and indirect visibility. Furthermore, it appeared that damage caused by employees to the interests of external stakeholders goes unnoticed within the organization.

b.   The discussability of conduct that deviates from the norm both in general and with someone in particular should be stimulated. Employees are virtually never addressed with respect to their behavior in cases of unethical conduct. In addition, it appears that there is a taboo on discussing a significant number of subjects in which the ethics of the organization is at risk. Criticism is generally not appreciated.

c.   The responsibility structure of the organization and the sanctionability of behavior that deviates from the desired norm should be improved.

d.   Attention to preventing and reducing undesirable conflicts of interest should be increased.

Several recommendations were:
1.   Ad a: creating a performance documentation system of a number of core details per activity and employee.
2.   Ad a: creating an ombudsman position.
3.   Ad a: creating a reporting center for external complaints.

4. Ad a and b: carrying out job reviews and evaluation discussions.
5. Ad b: activities in regards to increasing the acceptance of criticism.
6. Ad b: regular team meetings including periodic attention to ethics themes.
7. Ad c: determining how to deal with unethical behavior.
8. Ad c: reinforcing the coordinating functions of the management.
9. Ad c: cooperation in teams should be stimulated.
10. Ad d: making arrangements covering sideline activities and including a reporting requirement.
11. Ad d: developing an awareness development process regarding conflicts of interest.

Index

"See, here I am"
(1 Samuel, 3:4)